GAME FACE

GAME FACE

A LIFETIME OF HARD-EARNED LESSONS ON AND OFF THE BASKETBALL COURT

BERNARD KING

with JEROME PREISLER

TO Glenn

Bernard King

Da Capo Press

Da Capo Press
Hachette Book Group
1290 Avenue of the Americas, New York, NY 10104
www.dacapopress.com
@DaCapoPress

Printed in the United States of America

Originally published in hardcover and ebook by Da Capo Press in November 2017

First Edition: November 2017

Published by Da Capo Press, an imprint of Perseus Books, LLC, a subsidiary of Hachette Book Group, Inc.

Print book interior design and composition by Eclipse Publishing Services

ISBNs: 978-0-306-82570-5 (hardcover), 978-0-306-82571-2 (ebook)

LCCN: 2017953587
LSC-C

10 9 8 7 6 5 4 3 2 1

Dedicated to the loving memory of my mother,
Thelma King

Contents

B'BALL

I wouldn't be here if not for basketball.

Literally, I would not be alive.

The game taught me to believe in myself, and gave me love even when I didn't love myself. It gave me joy whenever I made a basket or grabbed a rebound because of the beautiful feelings it generated in my being—as would a sunny day after the rain.

Basketball gave me confidence and the freedom to weave a fabric of mind, body, and spirit so strongly constructed I was able to face all life's challenges.

As a young boy on the court, it was informative, providing no shortage of signals only I understood.

Basketball was my truth.

I seized the ball, spun it, shot it, and dribbled around and over any hurdles.

This is the uniqueness of what my basketball meant to me.

Oh, how I love you b'ball.

—Bernard King

Author's Note

This is my story, told from my own point of view. It is based primarily on my personal recollections of my experiences over time. While the events are all true, some names and identifying details have been changed, some timelines have been compressed, and some dialogue has been reconstructed.

Tip-off

At seven o'clock on the night of April 10, 1987, I was getting ready to step onto the hardwood for the first time in over two years. The first time since the injury that was supposed to end my NBA career. No one had come back from it before, and most of the experts said it couldn't be done.

Two years.

It felt like forever.

I'd worked tirelessly, relentlessly, to come back, pushed myself to defy all expectations. Throughout my rehab, I insisted it wasn't enough just to return to the game that I loved. I was determined to return as an elite player and compete at the *highest level*. Nothing less would satisfy me, despite all the questions about whether my goal was even achievable.

I couldn't begin to answer those questions until I plunged into the fast-paced action and physicality of a pro basketball game . . . a challenge that was now only minutes off.

The night my knee exploded, I was in my third year with the New York Knicks and playing the best basketball of my life. My All-Star appearance in 1984 was the springboard that elevated my confidence and my game, leading to what I call my Season of Ascension. That year I entered a zone, locked in, and never left, establishing my ability to match up against Larry Bird, Earvin "Magic" Johnson, or any of the top players in the world.

Representing the Eastern Conference alongside Bird, Julius Erving, and Isiah Thomas, and competing against the likes of Magic and George Gervin, I reached a new level of confidence. Whether I had one man guarding me, two, or three, I knew I could have my way offensively on the court.

That roll continued into the next year, becoming a new personal standard. In 1985, I was the league's leading scorer and could put the ball into the hoop almost at will.

I was twenty-eight years old. At the peak of my career.

I felt unstoppable, and I was.

Then one night in Kansas City, I jumped to block a layup after hustling down the court on a fast break, a situation I'd been in countless times, and a split-second later everything changed. Not just for my career, but for every facet of my life.

The opposing player's name was Reggie Theus. Only two of us were out on the break. No one was in front of him, and no one was parallel with me. He'd recovered possession of the ball on a turnover, and I was chasing him down hard toward our end of the court . . . trailing by more than I liked as he drove toward the hoop.

Going up to block his shot, I planted earlier and far more aggressively than usual and leaped into the air.

The crack of my knee blowing out was heard throughout the arena, but I didn't hear it. I didn't hear the horrified gasps from the crowd or really even know what had happened to me.

But I knew it was bad. As bad as it could be.

I screamed—"*Oh my God!*"—and landed in a heap, then curled into a semi-fetal position and couldn't get up. The pain was excruciating, more intense than any I'd ever felt. I repeatedly banged my fist on the floor, clutching my right knee with my left hand.

Imagine being in midair, soaring above the rim, and simultaneously knowing your career is over.

It was like I'd been struck down by a stray rifle shot.

Yet it would prove to be the best thing that ever happened to me.

Some might find that hard to believe, and it's understandable. I certainly didn't realize it while awaiting diagnostic surgery at Manhattan's Lenox Hill Hospital. All I knew was that my prospects looked grim.

I would soon learn I'd suffered a torn anterior cruciate ligament, torn knee cartilage, and a shattered bone in my right knee. The damage was so severe I was unable to lift my leg off my bed without a therapist's assistance, and I was bound to a wheelchair for months. But during my journey back, through all the obstacles I faced, I had evolved as a player and person.

Now, two years later, two *long* years, I sat at my locker in my New York Knicks uniform, my head lowered under a towel, even as my intensity, passion, and concentration rose inside me. I was gearing up for the most important game of my life.

At home the night before, I'd sat out on my terrace in northern New Jersey, enjoying the gentle spring breeze and listening to the great jazz trumpeter and bandleader Dizzy Gillespie on my stereo. I equated many aspects of my game and, in some ways, my life, to jazz. Its improvisational strains always relaxed me, and since Diz and I were friends, I found that especially true of his music. It gave us a profound connection.

Around 11:30 P.M., I went inside and dialed his number on the phone. He picked up after a just a couple of rings. I'd assumed he would be awake. Musicians, like athletes, are night owls.

"Diz . . . it's Bernard. I've been out here listening to your music," I said. "You probably know from the newspapers that I'm coming back tomorrow, and I'd like you to be at the game."

Dizzy lived in Teaneck, New Jersey, a relatively short distance from New York City. He didn't hesitate for a second.

"Of course. I'll be there," he said.

His answer gave me a sense of calm, of *balance*, for which I'll always be grateful.

Although I customarily drove myself to the Garden before my injury, I'd hired a limousine for my return appearance. For one thing, I knew my first wife and a couple of friends would be coming along to lend me their support and wanted a larger vehicle for their comfort. For another, I wanted to avoid having to drive through Friday night gridlock on the Jersey Turnpike and make the trip as stress-free as possible.

Our driver picked us up at 5 P.M. sharp, and we headed into Manhattan. It was a warm, clear evening, and there was still some light in the sky when we emerged from the Lincoln Tunnel. As we crept through congested Midtown traffic, I walled myself in silence, not conversing with anyone else in the car. Part of it was my habitual game preparation—I was going within myself. But I also wanted to fully soak in one of the biggest moments of my life.

I knew the game would be a challenge. We were facing the Milwaukee Bucks, a very good team that was headed for the playoffs. My likely matchup would be Paul Pressey, a tough, quick, lithe small forward. Along with Scottie Pippin, he'd always been one of my defensive nemeses. Pressey had excellent lateral movement, with a great deal of spacing between his legs and feet that enabled him to beat you to a spot.

Did I feel pressure?

Truthfully, I didn't. To succeed in New York, you can't feel pressure or even *think* about letting yourself feel pressure. Whatever the moment, regardless how big, you have to eliminate it from the equation. Too many players who came to the Big Apple couldn't do that, and the ball became a hot potato in their hands. But *in my hands* was precisely where I wanted it with the game on the line.

Arriving at the Garden, I broke my silence only to say hello to the security people, attendants, ushers, and other arena personnel. They had treated me well throughout my years in New York, and I always considered them to be very important to the organization. That night I especially wanted to let them know how I felt.

Everything was the same as the last time I'd played. Yet nothing was the same. Hubie Brown, my former head coach, was gone. He'd been replaced by Bob Hill, someone with a very different manner and style of play. I had new teammates, and a new, surgically rebuilt knee.

I'd been away from the game for quite a while.

One thing that hadn't changed since my days at Fort Hamilton High School was my preparation. It was practically a ritual. After Mike Saunders, our head trainer, taped my ankles, I went to my locker and got into uniform. Slowly putting on my left sock, my right sock, then my left Converse sneaker, my right. . . .

I was also wearing a knee brace at the insistence of my surgeon, the Knicks' team physician Dr. Norman Scott. Knowing it would inhibit my movement, I didn't want to use it and had *not* worn it in the gym during my practice sessions. But Scott was concerned about my knee sliding out of place, arguing that practice wasn't the same thing as bodying up against a muscular, two-hundred-pound-plus athlete in a real game situation.

I finally gave in. Doc had been with me all the way, and I felt obliged to take his advice. We were a team.

When I was finished dressing for the game, I did some stretches, then decided to go out onto the floor for pregame warm-ups, concentrating on the special drills I had learned from my physical therapist, Dania Sweitzer.

You'll hear much more about Dania later on, and with good reason. Throughout my rehabilitation, she worked with me five hours a day, six days a week, making countless personal sacrifices to bring me back. Again, not just to playing form, but All-Star form. I do not have the words to adequately express my debt to her.

The arena was filling up as I started my exercises, and although I normally blocked out the crowd noises, I could hear a murmur spreading through the stands. New York is a basketball town, and my return was being met with tremendous anticipation around the area. A legion of Knicks fans had left work early that day to find bars where they could watch the game on television. I was the team's captain and high scorer, and my presence on the floor had been greatly missed.

But there was another reason for excitement, and that reason had a name: *Patrick Ewing.*

The Knicks' 1984–1985 season was a struggle from the outset. My average of 32 points per game led the league, but I had no one to help shoulder the offensive load. After my injury in late March, the team went into a brutal twelve-game skid and would end the season with the Eastern Conference's worst record.

I never think losing has an upside, but that year we received some major consolation. The team's disqualification from the playoffs had led directly to our eligibility for the first NBA draft lottery, and to winning its number-one pick.

As Georgetown University's star player, Patrick was the grand prize. He was exactly the weapon we needed—a strong, intimidating, seven-foot-tall center. Somebody who could rebound and block shots from the post and outlet the ball to me on the open floor.

The Boston Celtics had the formidable duo of Larry Bird and Kevin McHale. The Chicago Bulls, Michael Jordan and Scottie Pippin. Now I could have a partner-in-force in Patrick Ewing. With the two of us sharing the court, I knew we had a real chance to bring New York its first championship in over a decade. But would that chance ever come? I was in a hospital bed with forty-one metal staples in my knee when NBA Commissioner David Stern drew Ewing's name from the barrel. Watching on television, I knew the Knicks had gained my dream teammate . . . and I couldn't even walk.

Instead, I cried.

I had a lot of restless nights. Nights when I couldn't sleep for more than a few minutes at a time without waking up soaked in sweat. On a couple of occasions, I dreamed my team was getting ready to go out to play a game, and we were all standing in the tunnel, waiting. Then I would hear my name called and prepare to take that first step onto the court . . . and the dream would end.

It was as if my subconscious was warning me not to look too far ahead into an uncertain future. To take things one day at a time. I wasn't ready to even think about getting on the court.

Now that moment was tantalizingly close. The fans were exhilarated, and I shared their feelings. As word of my return hit the newspapers and airwaves, they thought, *"All right! We have Patrick! Bernard's back! Championship!"* With only six games left in the season, and Ewing out with a severe knee sprain, I knew we wouldn't play together until the following year. But this was a start. We could be a potent, even unstoppable, tandem moving forward.

During my warm-ups, I noticed Don Nelson, the Bucks' head coach, quietly observing me from courtside. Nelly was a shrewd tactician, and I knew he was sniffing for an edge like a hound dog on the trail. He had a way of casting sidewise looks at players when sizing them up, so that you couldn't really catch him at it. But I felt his eyes on me and stayed clear of his side of the court. I didn't want to expose any vulnerabilities in my game.

About seven o'clock, I returned to the locker room for the pregame meeting. At those talks, you studied the scouting reports, discussed the opposition's strengths and weaknesses, and reviewed your overall game plan as a group. Then the coaches would toss questions around the room, asking each player about the man he was going to guard, and how he intended to go about it.

You couldn't get answers shorter than mine. A question about the player's tendencies? "He goes left." How was I going to stop him? "Block every damn shot."

I didn't give those clipped responses out of disrespect for my coaches or teammates. On the contrary, I wanted to be ready to do my best. For myself, the ballclub, and our fans.

So, minutes before game time, I hung a figurative *Do Not Disturb* sign from my locker, dropped my head to my chest, and went within, once again walling myself in silence. My expression twisted into a glowering, threatening scowl.

This was the face I'd worn as a kid growing up in Fort Greene, one of Brooklyn's toughest neighborhoods. The face I'd worn fighting off bullies and predators at school, standing up for myself and my siblings. The face I'd worn on the cracked asphalt courts near my housing development, where I played pickup basketball with kids much older than myself.

My Game Face.

I was more than focused. After years of playing the game, focus was natural for me. I could flip a switch and it was there. When my Game Face was on, I was tapping a deeper well of concentration.

I'd started visualizing as a form of meditation when I was a young boy, borrowing stacks of psychology books from the library, hoping I could learn to overcome my low self-esteem and painful shyness around other people. Visualization was something I picked up from those books, maybe the most important thing of all. In my bed at night, or riding the subway on weekends to read in solitude, *wherever* I was, I'd think about how I could use basketball to rise beyond the projects to become the best player in the world. Later, in my high school and college days, I applied it very deliberately to my game.

At my locker with my eyes shut, I pictured everything that was going to occur on the court, drawing a box around it, manipulating my opponents inside the box like chess pieces. Then I mentally executed my moves based on where I placed them, knowing that was where they'd be when they defended against me.

When my team finally gathered in the tunnel, it was like that dream I had in my hospital bed. Except now I was finally ready. At long last, ready. It was the moment I'd imagined for two grueling years.

As we went out onto the floor, I felt the charged atmosphere in the arena. The murmurs I'd heard before had become a loud, electric buzz. Normally I didn't hear it when I was locked in. But I couldn't block it out. Not that night. I was nervous, giddy with eagerness.

I stood there in the lights, trying to stay loose. *Heel and toe. Side to side.* My parents were in the crowd. Dania and her husband. My ex-wife and friends. And Diz, of course . . . all of them among the nineteen thousand fans in the arena.

"I think we've waited long enough! Here's the captain . . ."

It was incredible. John Condon, the renowned voice of Madison Square Garden, was announcing me. I wasn't even among the starters, and he was announcing me first. It gave me goose bumps.

". . . Bernard King!"

I'll never forget the noise from the rafters, the swelling roar of the crowd. The fans, my teammates, all were on their feet. People were cheering, applauding, and waving handmade signs.

I breathed once, twice, deep breaths to fill my lungs with oxygen. I started to clap my hands, wanting to let everyone around me know how I felt about their reception. But then I caught myself and awkwardly rubbed my palms together. I was fighting to control my emotions.

WELCOME BACK BERNARD.

The words flashed from the auxiliary scoreboard on the first promenade.

Suddenly a smile broke through my Game Face. That had never happened to me on the court. But I couldn't keep from letting the crowd in. I needed to honor them.

I looked around, glancing up at the seats, and brought my hands together in applause.

The crowd had taken me out of my comfort zone. I couldn't play like that. But I had to. I had to find a way.

I'd risen from the schoolyards to the legendary court at Madison Square Garden. I'd gone from a shy, lonely kid longing for my mother's embrace, to having thousands of people take me in, touching my heart with their raucous show of warmth and appreciation.

I owed it to them. . . owed it to *myself* . . . to take the ultimate test and see what I could do.

It was now or never.

Let's go, I thought, a flood of memories blurring through my mind. I can do this.

Let's go.

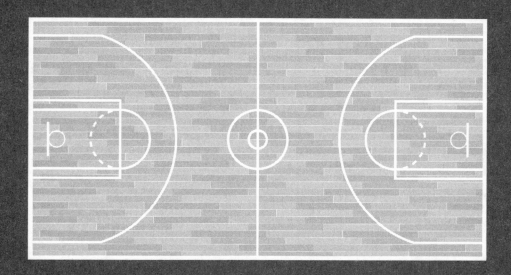

Fort Greene, Brooklyn

1 | The Birth of My Game Face

You never forget the first time you fall in love, the feeling of being swept up into a lofty realm you never knew existed. A world where paths merge in an unexpected journey, and you are made anew, soaring so high you can kiss the moonlight over the mountaintops.

No matter how many other loves you have as time goes on, that memory, that euphoric joy, occupies a special, untouchable place in your heart.

I was a third grader at P.S. 67 in Fort Greene, Brooklyn, when love struck me. The backboard and hoop were at one end of the cafeteria—a large space that doubled as a gym when they pushed the tables against the wall. Fixed on a stanchion, it rose ten feet above the floor . . . regulation height.

We had other baskets out in the schoolyard. But we could use this one winter or summer, rain or shine. I can see it clearly in my mind's eye. After eating my lunch, I would go over to it with some of the other kids and try to make shots.

I was eight years old but tall for my age. I was also awkward and swaybacked, with a high waist and backside.

Each day I went to school knowing I'd be mercilessly teased by the class bullies. Even the girls got into the act, calling me Blueberry Hill, after the Fats Domino song, because of my large, wide-browed head. It didn't help that my mother cut my hair, but with six children, five of us boys, and barely enough money to pay the bills, she couldn't afford to send us to the barbershop. And it showed.

As shy and nervous as I was at school, those feelings weren't caused by my young tormentors. I carried a hidden darkness, a secret pain that was both emotional *and* physical. And it originated at home.

But I didn't think about those things when I stood beneath the cafeteria's backboard. Didn't think about the teasing and feelings of shame.

When the ball was in my hands, I just wanted to make a basket. Nothing else mattered.

Early in my childhood, I'd seen the older boys on the basketball courts at the front and rear of my building. Those teenagers controlled the courts, and there was no room for younger kids unless one of them was empty.

That was hardly ever the case. Basketball was an inner-city game, the one athletic outlet that kids could afford. You didn't need expensive football or baseball gear to play. You just needed a ball, a blacktop court, and a hoop.

I wanted to compete. But before I could do it, I realized I needed to figure out how to put the ball inside the rim.

It wasn't easy. I was a big kid, sure. But eight's still eight. The hoop was a good five feet above me, the ball large and heavy for someone my age. I would heave it up underhanded, mustering all my strength.

I was drawn to that rim, and kept returning with my classmates. One by one, they took turns trying to make a shot. And one by one, they became exasperated. They either couldn't throw the ball up as high as the hoop or couldn't get it to go in. After a few tries, they all walked away in discouragement.

I didn't walk away. Something inside me refused to quit. I was single-mindedly focused on my goal.

How do I shoot the ball into that basket?

How?

I'd always been proficient at math, and I started to approach my objective almost as I would my homework assignments.

Do I aim for the backboard? Or for the center of the rim? Do I need to throw it high?

I finally realized the begin-point was touch. That meant getting a feel for the ball in my hands, then figuring how much upward thrust I needed to cover the height and distance between me and the basket.

This wasn't conscious, not at first. But on some level, I was developing a studied, analytical approach to the game. It would evolve into a methodology that carried me through high school, college, and my entire professional career.

Driven to make a basket, I kept trying each day after lunch, learning through trial and error, processing it all.

One day, *finally*, it dropped in.

I jumped with exhilaration. A quiet, reserved kid who was used to keeping his emotions in check, I couldn't restrain myself.

And that was it. The moment I fell in love with basketball. From that point on, I'd use every chance I got to practice and perfect my shooting. Under the basket, I felt liberated, like a bird freed from its cage.

As I mentioned, it was a different story at home.

EVERYTHING I AM, the good and the bad, traces back to my roots in Brooklyn, and the Walt Whitman Housing Projects where I grew up.

My parents had Southern origins. Thelma Brown King, my mother, was born and raised on Johns Island, a small farming community in Charleston County, South Carolina. My dad, Thomas, was from Rocky Mount on the coast of North Carolina.

Both left their home states during the Great Migration that began with World War One. This was a shift of over six million African Americans from the rural South to the industrialized North, where they resettled in hopes of finding better job opportunities and relief from oppressive segregationist laws.

Mom's life had been one of simple responsibility to her parents and siblings. After walking home from school, she would cook dinner for her whole family. Not only did she not mind the task, she found it a source of happiness and gratification.

Her upbringing on the farm was very strict, and that didn't change after the family's relocation to New York City. As a teenager, she didn't smoke or drink, and wasn't allowed to attend dances. Though it was not something I knew as a child, she'd been subjected to harsh physical discipline from her parents. It was an era that was far less enlightened than the present day, a time when corporal punishment was all too common among black Southern families.

One summer evening in 1949, a few of her school friends urged her to join them at the Savoy Ballroom up on Lenox Avenue. The Savoy was the largest and most popular nightclub in Harlem, with a glittering marquee, a marble stairway, and a sprung mahogany dance floor that would bounce with the rhythms of thousands of dancing feet. There were two bandstands where groups like the Savoy Bearcats and Cab Calloway's Missourians would hold wild battles of the bands every weekend.

As I heard it from Mom, she was reluctant to accept her girlfriends' invitation, but finally let herself be convinced. It was a Thursday night—Ladies' Night at the club—and young women could enter without paying for admission. One of her girlfriends knew an unattached young man named Thomas and wanted to introduce them.

Their first dance was to the jump blues of the Cootie Williams Orchestra. You didn't see much emotion in my father, but he had a glint in his eyes whenever he remembered that. I can only guess how much he must have enjoyed impressing her with his steps.

I suppose you could say he was Thelma's opposite number. He loved the night life, loved dancing . . . and loved to drink. Loved it too much for his own good. But she either did not see his flaws early on or saw enough goodness in him to look past them. Dad was a complex man. In those days, he was outgoing and gregarious, but had an awkward shyness around women. He was respectful and polite while courting Thelma—a perfect gentleman. Seven years her senior, he was more adult than the boys she knew at school. She also admired the fact that he was a hard worker, though he never held a dollar that couldn't slip through his fingers.

Two years after they met, Thomas and Thelma were married and moved to Brooklyn.

Unfortunately, Dad continued to enjoy his nightlife, and alcohol was a big part of it. His paychecks evaporated before the rent and bills were paid. It must have put tremendous strain on my mother.

In our family, we never discussed anything. Whatever the problem, my father's way of handling it was always the same:

"Take it to the back room," he'd say. "Take it to the back room and forget about it."

As the years went on, that back room became more than a physical space for all of us. It was a dark vault in our minds and hearts. I never gave voice to my fears, my anxieties, or my anguish. I never discussed my troubles with anyone. My coping mechanism was to push them out of sight, seal them off in the vault deep inside me, and forget about them.

Or tell myself I could forget.

When I was born in 1956, the second of six children, we were living in a walk-up row house on Carlton Avenue. My arrival marked a complete transformation for Dad. He stopped drinking and going to clubs, and started diligently attending church. He would even turn his paychecks over to Mom at the end of the week. For that reason, she called me her "Miracle Baby."

What changed him? Maybe the added responsibility of having another mouth to feed. Because of the total lack of communication at home, I can only guess. But he credited Mom with teaching him to save money and live within his means.

For her part, Mom never attributed his transformation to anything she might have done. I think she was just glad that it happened.

My memories of our first apartment are vague, but I do recall the move to Fort Greene. Dad had put in for a job with the Housing Department and was hired as a superintendent at the Walt Whitman Houses, a cluster of city-owned, low-income developments opposite the north end of Fort Greene Park, and not far from the Brooklyn docks. He said he owed that to Mom, too.

"My First Lady told me, you'd better sign your name on that paper and bring it in," he said of filling out the employment application. I suppose that if I was my mother's Miracle Baby, then she was his First Lady.

The new job required him to live at Whitman, so he took a two-bedroom apartment on the twelfth floor of one of the buildings. Our monthly rent was comparable to the other tenants', and his salary was barely adequate for our growing family. But the apartments were newly renovated, and the position offered my father stability and guaranteed union benefits.

Dad's work ethic made an indelible impression on me. Watching him go about his daily business taught me respect for consistency and routine, and helped me see the importance of putting in the hours. But it was like observing him through glass. A stoic, reclusive, tightly regimented man, he seemed bound up within himself, as though he dreaded what might happen if he lowered his guard against his old, reckless ways.

His schedule never varied. He would leave for work early, return home at dinnertime, carry his plate into the back bedroom, and eat with the door closed. *Alone.* While eating, he read his Bible. When he was finished, he changed into a suit and went to church. He attended church seven days a week.

Absorbed in religion, he rarely interacted with the family and seemed incapable of showing us any warmth. We didn't have company more than once a year, didn't go on family outings, didn't laugh or smile together. On the rare occasions there *was* laughter in the apartment, it stopped the moment he walked through the door.

Dad never spoke of his family in North Carolina. We never met any relatives on his side. This made me feel confused and isolated in a way I couldn't process.

It was only in adulthood that I asked him why he'd severed his relationship with them. All he would say was that he'd grown estranged from them because they were Jehovah's Witnesses. And that the Devil made him do it.

Was he blaming the Devil for his actions or their beliefs?

I'm still not sure. But my view of religion owes much to my dad.

I believe religion is very important. I consider myself a deeply spiritual person. But I also understand that religious views can destroy families as well as bring families together, divide nations or bring nations together. We need to remember that acceptance and understanding are part of all faiths. We need to be tolerant and flexible to accommodate each others' beliefs.

Dad was *in*flexible. He had his rules, and everyone obeyed. Every Sunday morning, we would all get into our dress clothes and take the bus over to the Evergreen Baptist Church on Carlton Avenue, near our old walk-up. Once we were home, the kids couldn't go back outside. We were forbidden from going to the movies or listening to the radio. We weren't allowed to see our friends. Often, we would gather at a window facing the Brooklyn-Queens Expressway and play "Colored Cars."

"Which color you have?"

"Which color *you* got?"

We'd each pick a color and count the matching cars on the elevated span. The first to count a hundred won the game. It was a way to pass the afternoon and ease our monotony.

Sometimes, I'd wander over to a window on the other side of the apartment and gaze down at the basketball court below. The best players in the neighborhood would gather there. Watching them, I knew that was where I wanted to be.

The only time I heard music in our house was when my father was out at work or church. Then Mom would put her gospel records on the turntable. She loved Mahalia Jackson, Shirley Caesar, and the Blind Boys of Alabama, but James Cleveland was her favorite singer. His deep foghorn voice would boom above the chorus.

Possibly because of Dad's physical and emotional isolation, Mom seemed to shut down her own feelings—or at least wall them off inside her. She never said she loved me. Not once during my childhood did I receive a hug. It left a void inside me, a desperate, unsatisfied hunger.

I'm convinced she did her best with the emotional and psychological tools available to her. She was a product of her generation and had her hands full just scraping by. Feeding six kids on what little Dad earned as a super was a year-round struggle. In the summer, she toiled over a hot kitchen stove without benefit of an air conditioner. She prepared our meals every day of the week, and her down-home cooking was delicious.

Breakfast on weekends was ham and eggs, with waffles, pancakes, or biscuits whipped up from scratch. Dinner might be fried chicken, or a pot roast served with string beans, collard greens, potato salad, and homemade muffins. I remember hearing the sounds of her cooking from my room—a wooden spoon beating against the side of the mixing bowls, the sizzle of chicken in a greased skillet. The aromas wafting through our apartment intoxicated me.

Mom was always finding ways to stretch the budget. She made her own clothes, ordering the patterns, cutting the fabric, and then sitting for hours at her sewing machine. She purchased the kids' clothes at secondhand shops, and our sneakers were bargain store irregulars. No shirt or pair of pants was ever thrown away. When one of us outgrew something, it was handed down to a younger sibling. Since there were no funds to spare for a washing machine or the coin laundry, Mom cleaned our clothes by hand on a scrub board and then hung them to dry in our cramped apartment, running a clothesline from room to room. The cold droplets of water would drip on my head at night. *Plop, plop.*

I doubt Mom ever missed a PTA meeting or parent-teacher conference. She would walk me to school each morning when I attended P.S. 67, stopping a block from its door so I could go the rest of the way by myself. She wanted to teach me independence, but *I* didn't want the neighborhood bullies to see her with me. If those predators had thought I was scared of them, I would have become a bigger target.

Weakness didn't last long in Fort Greene. I would have to learn to fight my own battles. Eventually, I would also fight my brothers' fights. I was always tougher than the other boys in the family. If somebody messed with one of them, he'd answer to me.

Though my brother Thomas Jr. was the first of us, I felt like the oldest. My mother must have noticed my maturity, because she gave me a lion's share of household responsibilities. I would accompany her to the butcher shop or supermarket to help push the shopping cart and carry home the groceries. I would sit in the kitchen tearing up the greens as she fixed dinner. She often sent me out to pick up items from the corner store, a white handkerchief pinned inside my pocket, folded carefully around a shopping list and some bills. I never knew what was on the list, or how much money she gave me. I would just pass my little bundle to the shopkeeper, and he'd fill her order from his shelves.

I have many memories of Mom's labor and sacrifice. She ran the household and was present for us while my father shuttled between his job, his solitary Bible reading, and church.

But there was another side to her, a side few people ever saw.

I've already mentioned that my mother's parents inflicted physical punishment on her. And I have mentioned a secret I carried for much of my life, a hidden pain that went to the innermost part of my soul.

Abusive behavior is part of a terrible cycle, a legacy of victimization perpetuated from generation to generation. Those who are abused have a threefold increased risk of becoming abusers. Before that intergenerational cycle can be broken, its secrets must be pulled from the darkness into the light.

My mother beat me. It's as simple and difficult to say as that. Throughout my childhood, she would beat me with a strap and kitchen broom.

Sometimes she made me strip out of my clothes and then hit me with the broomstick until my skin was red, swollen, and bruised. I would wonder what provoked her rage. Was it that I'd gotten into a fight defending myself against the bullies? I didn't know. I wasn't sure what I did to deserve such vicious punishment, or whether her beatings were even connected to anything I'd done.

But I got them. Time after time. I got them.

Standing there confused and vulnerable, just a skinny kid . . . words can hardly describe my shame and growing resentment toward my mother. I didn't understand. I *couldn't* understand.

I told myself I hated her. For a great many years, I believed I did.

The beatings hurt like hell. But I didn't cry. I refused to cry, knowing it would only make her beat me longer and harder.

I didn't care.

I would not cry.

That's where my Game Face came from. That's where the expression I carried onto the court for every game of my life was born. It was a mask, a shield. It allowed me to shut out the hurt, protect myself from the outside world.

I didn't tell anyone about the beatings. They were my secret. I felt disconnected from everything around me and even in some ways from myself.

As children, we learn a great deal from watching the adults around us. But I saw no significant communication between my parents. No outward displays of affection. No sharing of thoughts and dreams, of pain or happiness.

I didn't feel love in our household. I had no frame of reference, no outside points of comparison, no way of knowing if my existence was different from that of other kids. I *sensed* something was missing in my life, but I couldn't identify what it was. I tried, with the limited understanding of a young boy. But it was akin to looking through a window and finding it too smudged and dirty to see through with any clarity.

In those days, I rarely smiled or laughed. I had no outlet for my emotions or creativity, and no way to channel them. *Nowhere.*

Except for the basketball court.

IN MY NEIGHBORHOOD, we were surrounded by basketball courts. By the time I reached the fifth and sixth grades, I was on them whenever possible.

We had two courts at the Whitman Houses, right outside my building. Go out the front doors, go out the back doors . . . different courts, different styles of play. It was amazing. The best players were in the front of the building. Fort Greene had one of the city's highest juvenile delinquency rates, and the neighborhood gang members loved to play on that court. They were mostly teenagers and some of the toughest kids in Brooklyn. But I gravitated toward watching their games and wanting to measure myself against them. The younger kids on the back court weren't a fraction as good.

If the older kids were more talented, that's where I wanted to play. You played against the best, you were going to improve.

I remember a guy named Mike, the leader of the Avenue Kings (the gang name always bothered me), who was one of the top players on the front court. After his games, he went back to his gang fights and turf wars. But that court was like a watering hole. Nobody showed up there looking for trouble. They came to ball.

There was another court right across the street from my building, at Sands Junior High's schoolyard. Then you had the park on Tillary Street another block away in the shadow of the Manhattan Bridge. Across from the park, you could play on the three courts at Westinghouse High School. And a mile beyond that was the Boys Club of America.

Then you had the night centers, several of them in walking distance. One was at Sands, where I also learned karate. Another was at P.S. 46, my elementary school when I lived on Carlton Avenue. And if you walked a block to the Farragut Houses, over by the Brooklyn Navy Yard, you had a night center *there*.

Farragut Center was the most competitive because we played full court games. Armond and Wilburn Hill played on its courts. Armond was about the same age and height as my oldest brother, Thomas Jr. He was an All City high school player and received a basketball scholarship to West Virginia University.

A standout athlete who went on to play varsity with the Princeton Tigers, Armond later played in the NBA for eight seasons. He then coached at the collegiate level, was hired as an assistant coach for the Atlanta Hawks, and eventually became Doc Rivers's right-hand man with the Boston Celtics and Los Angeles Clippers.

So you could always find a game. And if you didn't find a game, you could shoot by yourself.

Every day after class was dismissed, I would follow the same routine: Go home, do my homework, eat dinner, and hurry over to the P.S. 67 night center. I was diligent about it. Absolutely nothing would deter me. Homework, dinner, practice at the center.

If I wasn't at the center, I shot baskets on the courts outside my building. The front courts had half-moon shaped backboards. The rear courts, out the back door, had rectangular backboards. There were no nets, and no lights for playing at night. At Sands and the other school centers, they had standardized rectangular backboards and chain nets.

When you practiced with a half-moon backboard, no net, you became a better shooter and scorer. You didn't have the board's wide surface to shoot the ball off. You couldn't rely on its borders framing your shot or the net as a centerpiece to help with your aim. You needed to concentrate harder to hit the shot, developing a sense of space.

At night, I shot in the moonlight on the outdoor courts. I wouldn't see anyone out there. I wouldn't hear anything other than my dribble. I was alone with my ball and the basket, in my own hoops world, moving to the rhythm of an inner music. It was like the words to that old song by the Blackbyrds: *"Walking in rhythm, moving in sound."* I didn't need to see the rim. Whether I was five feet away from it, ten feet, fifteen . . . after a while, it didn't matter. I *knew* where I was, and where it was. I made the ball drop into the rim. And I felt like a scoring king.

In the winter, when nobody was using the courts, I'd find one and scrape the snow off the blacktop with my sneaker, knowing the basket was mine for as long as I wanted. I hardly noticed the bitter cold, the steam puffing from my mouth, or the numbness of my cheeks and fingertips. The ball felt like a rock. But I focused on making my shots amid the knee-high snowdrifts.

I was head over heels in love with the game, burning with the desire to excel. Those courts lured me with their magic. They spoke to me unlike any adult ever did, with a clear, enticing voice, and a message that was unmistakable.

This is where you belong. Between the lines.

When I was on the court, the mental and emotional pain I felt over my home life went away. It was the only place I felt free. A place where my mind, my feelings, my body, and the ball would merge to create something all my own. Something special that couldn't be touched by the outside world.

Where you belong.

I didn't need to compete against other kids. Not in the beginning. When you play by yourself, you're challenging yourself, competing against *yourself*.

Basketball is a game of experimentation. You channel your personality and creativity into developing an individual style of play, and I was always trying to add new elements to mine. Being analytical even at a young age—I loved math—I *thought* the game, piecing it together like a puzzle.

The first element of the puzzle was understanding space, distance, and height to make a shot. That part of my development had started under the hoop in P.S. 67's cafeteria.

But I realized that was only one component of basketball. Rhythm and movement came next for me. It was a logical progression. I'd begun to accurately make my shots. So I asked myself some new questions. *How do I move my body, with this ball, from one space to another? As I spin this way, like the great Earl "The Pearl" Monroe, where's the basket going to be when I come out of the spin?*

Experimentation. Creativity. Repetition. They would give me the next puzzle piece.

I practiced spinning and then shooting the ball. I practiced shooting one-handed and shooting off balance. I practiced picking the ball off the ground, turning in one motion, and releasing it without a second's delay. I practiced shooting with my eyes closed. In the gym, I even practiced shooting while falling down.

I also practiced passing the ball to myself. I couldn't afford a passing apparatus or other gear, so I made do without it. I'd begun to imagine other players on the court with me. Defenders and teammates. I was establishing set places on the court from which I could shoot with confidence. I began to think of them as King spots, and could see them in my mind. If I could reach those places and execute my shot the way I practiced, nothing the defense did could stop me.

Month by month, my abilities grew. I was physically growing as well, growing faster than most boys my age; my body was getting bigger and stronger. At every stage, I built upon my skills. I was finding more missing pieces of the puzzle, continuing to analyze the game.

I've done this. I've figured it out. Okay, what's next?

My goal was to play the boys on the front court. I would learn from them. I would find a way to compete.

I didn't care that they were older than I was. I didn't care that they were better.

I would become the best.

2 | "Little Spal"

I was eleven years old and in the sixth grade when I tried out for my first organized basketball competition. At the time I didn't know it would lead to a major turning point in my youth, an experience that would change me forever.

The tournament wasn't held at my elementary school, but at Sands Junior High, the school I would attend the following year. Sands was less than a block north of P.S. 67 and a short walk from the Whitman Houses. You crossed the street under the elevated highway, swung left onto North Portland Avenue, and you were there.

No other kids my age went to the tryout. It was all older players at the school's night center. But I wanted to take a crack at it. I'll never forget getting on line in the gymnasium. The lines were at least ten deep and ten across, and each one had a coach-captain up front, usually a teacher or parent volunteer.

I don't know how they worked out their pecking order. But a captain would choose a player from the front of the line, and then the next captain would take his turn picking from among the kids that were left. And so on, like a draft, until they filled their team rosters.

Anyway, I made the cut. Maybe it was my height—I'd shot up like a beanstalk over the last year of elementary school and stood around six feet two inches, towering over many of the teachers and coaches. Also, my brother Thomas was already a student at Sands and had a reputation for being an excellent player. His nickname was Spalding, like the basketball manufacturer, and the neighborhood kids had started calling me "Little Spal." Maybe the captains were hoping I'd take after him on the court.

Believe it or not, our team was called the Knicks, and we were given orange T-shirts with that name emblazoned across the chest. I guess you could say that was the first time I wore a Knicks uniform, though it was *slightly* different than the one I'd wear at Madison Square Garden. Since I didn't own a pair of sweat socks, I sported black dress socks with my shorts, tee, and sneakers. Quite a look . . . although, looking back today at the Michigan Fab Five and *their* black socks, I might have been ahead of my time.

Anyway, I was not very good compared to the seventh, eighth, and ninth graders. I won't blame it on the socks.

In the NBA, the twelfth player on the team is kind of an extra man on the bench, the guy who comes in at the end of a blowout win—or loss—to let the regulars rest on the sidelines. The fans always cheer the guy because they're excited for him. In college, it's the same thing. In youth basketball, in the neighborhood, it's also the same.

The night of the tournament, I was that player.

I'll never forget being inserted into the game with something like ninety seconds left on the clock. My team had rolled over the competition, and our win was almost clinched.

As I set up for my shot, a tingling bundle of nerves, the crowd was cheering me on from the bleachers, chanting my name.

"Shoot the ball, Little Spal! Shoot the ball, Little Spal!"

Little Spal.

I wasn't Blueberry Hill. Wasn't a confused, naked boy under the broomstick and strap. Not that night, on that court. Never mind the dress socks.

"Shoot the ball, Little Spal, shoot, shoot, shoot . . ."

I took the shot. My *first* shot in organized competition. The basketball left my fingers, arced in the air, and sank in.

We won the tournament. There I was, the only elementary school player in the league and a member of a championship team. The Knicks!

I was proud and ecstatic. A *champ*. What a feeling. To top it off, each member of the team was given a trophy—a shiny gold-colored statue of a basketball player on a metal base.

A trophy.

It made my eyes light up. I could hardly wait to show it to my parents.

Carrying it from the schoolhouse, I hurried down the street toward Sarjay's Candy Store on the corner of North Portland Avenue and Myrtle, right across from Fort Greene Park. Straight ahead, I saw the Prison Ship Martyrs' Monument rising a hundred-fifty feet into the air. The entrance to the Whitman Houses was about a block to my right. I'd taken that route home a thousand times.

No sooner did I make the turn than I was punched in the eye. Hard. Stars exploded in my vision as I rocked back on my heels. Before I could recover, the trophy was torn from my hands. I didn't know what hit me. I never saw the blow coming. But I realized at once that my trophy was gone. Stolen.

I was only a minute or two from home. Walking through the front entryway and taking the elevator up to my apartment was a blur. My heart was filled with sadness. By the time I reached the twelfth floor, my eye was swollen and pulsing, its white stained blood red at the corners.

My father was home when I walked in. As I came through the door, he took one look at me and asked what happened. His tone of voice was something new. Dad was always so apart from us, so uninvolved; the urgency of his question shocked me.

I told him without tears. The pain didn't bother me. But someone had taken my trophy. That did.

"Show me where it happened, Bernard," Dad said. "You take me there right now."

I walked him to the corner where the trophy was stolen from me. There was no sign of it, of course. But Dad must have known the thief would be long gone. It struck me that his insistence in coming out there was his way of making me understand the seriousness of the attack. That it was an unspoken message: *Don't ever allow anyone to do this to you again.*

I took his message seriously. No one would ever steal what was mine again. From that point on, if somebody messed with me, he was going to get his ass kicked. I didn't care who he was. Gang member, bully, it didn't make a difference.

I wasn't trying to be a tough guy. I wasn't bothering anyone or looking for trouble. All I wanted to do was mind my business and play basketball. But if you came at me, I wouldn't run. If you got tough with me, I'd show you I was tougher.

The Bernard that kids had taunted because of his haircut and awkward build was no more. Blueberry Hill was gone. Things had changed for good. *I'd* changed.

And that was it.

Period.

I HAD ANOTHER TRANSFORMATIVE EXPERIENCE later that year, one that was different but no less important than the theft of my basketball trophy. It hurt too, and in its own big way, though I suppose you could say *this* pain was self-inflicted.

The Prison Ship Martyrs' Monument in Fort Greene Park—the one that was in sight when I was punched in my eye—is a high Doric column atop a hill, built to memorialize thousands of men and boys who died aboard British prison ships during the Revolutionary War. Ninety-nine large, broad granite stairs lead up to its base, and most people don't realize they rise from a crypt housing the remains of some of those prisoners. No one knows exactly how many are entombed in the vault, but there's a giant urn atop the column. Back when the monument was erected, the urn would light up at night.

That light was out all through my childhood. I hear it's been restored to working order, and that's good. People exercise around the monument nowadays, jogging up and down the steps, and skateboarding around the base. But it's important that we be reminded why it was built. I always knew about the bodies entombed in the vault. Even when I played near the stairs, my awareness of them was sobering.

On summer afternoons, my mother would take me and my brothers on occasional outings in the park. It was right across the street from our housing complex, with plenty of shade trees to keep us cool. We couldn't afford family trips outside the neighborhood, but Fort Greene Park was a nice place to go for inner-city kids; it exposed us to a natural setting and removed us from the sweltering apartment as we played under Mom's watchful eye.

One day, after I'd graduated from P.S. 67, I fell while horsing around with my brothers and running rings around the monument. I landed awkwardly on my right arm, and though it hurt the rest of the afternoon, I thought it was just bruised and sore from hitting the monument's concrete base.

Then came dinnertime. I'd said my prayers and was lifting my fork to my mouth when my arm locked up. I sat there unable to move it, not having taken a single bite of food. The arm was bent like a wishbone, stuck in an upraised position.

A puzzled look on her face, my mother got up and came around the table to look it over. Remember, she was from the Jim Crow South. Hospitals were a long distance from the farm, and if you could reach one and were black, you were segregated from white patients and treated under conditions that left much to be desired . . . assuming you were treated at all. Southern blacks understandably didn't rush to the hospital back then, but instead remedied most of their illnesses and injuries themselves.

Having hung onto those memories, Mom had also retained many of her old ways.

The arm was up? She decided to try to push it down.

Not a good idea. I saw flashes of white light in front of my eyes.

My agonized expression quickly convinced Mom to hurry me across the street to Cumberland Hospital, where a round of X-rays revealed my arm was broken. The doctors told me it would be in a heavy plaster cast for a month.

It was the worst thing I could have heard. All I could think was, *I'm not gonna be able to play basketball.*

I'd finally played in a school tournament. I was competing with the older kids. And now . . . I couldn't believe it. A whole month!

I went home feeling unhappy and dejected. I couldn't imagine not going to the courts. But what else was I going to do? Stay in my room? I didn't want that. It wasn't my personality to hang around the apartment and sulk.

Before long, I had enough of it. *Okay, fine*, I told myself. *I have a broken arm. I'm still able to shoot. I'll just use my other hand. That arm works.*

So I went out on the court and shot left-handed. I wasn't very proficient at it. I couldn't play in games. But I *was* able to shoot, and that's what I did, every day, until my right arm finally healed.

I learned a lot about myself that summer. It was my first time dealing with an injury, my first real physical challenge. And any challenge that you face helps to fortify you for the next one in your life. It's subconscious. It becomes part of the fabric of your being.

Years later, when I was unable to lift my leg off a hospital bed without help and had been told even walking normally again might be unattainable, some part of me would reference how I coped with the broken arm and motivate me not to give up.

But that perspective would only come in hindsight. On the courts, practicing lefty, I was just looking forward to my cast coming off.

Elementary school was behind me. In the fall, I would start my first year at Sands Junior High. The school had a basketball team, and my mind was set on joining it.

3 | Walking in Rhythm

Sands Junior High was an awfully tough school, tougher than I could have imagined.

In my last year at P.S. 67, I'd been appointed hallway monitor. I'm not sure if I received the position because I was tall, or because I had high marks for conduct on my report cards. Probably it was a little of both. I felt honored to be chosen and was proud to buckle the white Sam Browne crossbelt over my waist and shoulder.

My job was to stand near the exits and make sure kids didn't go yelling or running down the corridors at the morning bell, during lunch breaks, and then again when school let out at three o'clock. Sometimes I'd help the younger kids tie their shoes, find their classrooms when they got lost, or escort them to the main office or nurse's office at a teacher's request. Those kids listened to me. I was seen as an authority figure. I don't think I ever had a problem keeping order in the halls.

Sands was like another planet. There was no classroom discipline. The students were unruly and scornful of their teachers. They would throw chairs out the windows, desks out the windows, start fires in the closet, start fires in the trash can while the teacher's back was turned. It was a hard thing to deal with, but I had no choice.

I'd never gotten into a fight in elementary school. Now I was defending myself every day. If you didn't stand up to the predators and bullies, they would take everything that belonged to you. I never looked for trouble with them, but wouldn't run either.

Basketball was my refuge, my one constant, an outlet for everything I felt inside, and that included a tremendous amount of anger. I was angry at my mother for beating me. I was angry over my father's detachment from the family, angry over my low self-esteem and lack of social skills. And I was angry about having to put up with the bullies.

That pent-up anger fueled my passion and competitive intensity. I didn't just want to beat my opponents. I wanted to dominate them through sheer force of will. Rage became an asset, my secret weapon on the court.

During my first year of junior high school, I began playing a lot of organized ball. After making the basketball team, I competed against other junior highs throughout the borough. For road games, we wore royal blue satin warm-up jackets with the word SANDS emblazoned in white across the back. On travel days, we would pick them up from a storage room. I took pride in putting mine on before we climbed aboard the school bus for our trips.

Once when I was carrying my jacket downstairs on its hanger, someone sneaked up behind me, split it across the letters with a butcher knife, and took off running. If I'd been wearing the jacket, my back would have been sliced open too.

My neighborhood was in free fall, and I could see it everywhere around me. When I was very young, the street gangs fought with clackers—a toy that was banned because the hard plastic balls could be used to break teeth, noses, and cheekbones. That was dangerous enough. But the gang members were now carrying switchblades and battling over drugs along with their turf . . . and that was more dangerous.

The plague of heroin addiction had infiltrated my community. In Vietnam, our soldiers faced a conflict they didn't understand, and an enemy that used bloody guerrilla tactics they were unprepared for. Southeast Asia was where most of the world's heroin was produced, and the boys that used the drug found it gave them a cheap, easily available means of escape. It also turned them into addicts. When they returned to the poverty of their inner-city communities, they brought along their heroin addictions. And it took those communities down.

You witnessed the impact all around Fort Greene. Once heroin was introduced into the neighborhood, you couldn't walk near the park at night. It was full of dope fiends. They would approach you from just off the paths and rob you to support their habits.

I was constantly on guard. The basketball courts became more of a safe haven than ever, and I tried to be on them as much as possible.

This still didn't include Sundays. Dad had not relaxed his edict that the family stay indoors after church. I couldn't figure out why; it wasn't as if he would discuss what we'd heard at the sermon so we could better understand its relevance to our lives, or engage in meaningful conversations with us at all. Once we got home, he simply retreated into his bedroom. Yet he was intimidating in his silent remove, making it clear his wishes weren't open to negotiation. We were forbidden to leave the apartment.

I wanted desperately to play. The courts were jumping on Sundays, and I yearned to participate in weekend tournaments. But none of the kids in my family ever disobeyed or questioned my father. We hardly had the nerve to *talk* around him. We just sat staring out the windows, counting cars on the highway, or somberly watching the basketball games twelve stories below.

How could I stand up to Dad? With my mother as the disciplinarian, I knew defying him might mean more stinging humiliation under her strap and broom.

I didn't have any answers. I only knew that sooner or later, I'd have to learn them.

I'm sure that's what drew me to psychology books. I felt a need to investigate and understand my feelings . . . to find my place in life . . . and they seemed a good place to start. I checked them out of the library in stacks and read them under my blankets after bedtime, shining a flashlight on their pages. Those books were my secret, and I didn't want my brother to know about them. I believed they might tell me why I felt such a bottomless void within myself.

Reading the books, I realized that the basis of psychology, at least the type I was reading about, was analytical thought. In my mind, that was a thread connecting it to basketball. The game, to me, wasn't about walking on the court and grabbing a ball. It was about the *thought* that went into the game. Although I couldn't have articulated it, I came to believe that understanding basketball and understanding psychology were one and the same.

I first read about visualization techniques in the pages of my library books. They said the subconscious mind was unable to distinguish between what was real or imaginary. If you pictured something you wanted to achieve, concentrated on that goal until you could see yourself attaining it—see it as clearly as anything around you—then the subconscious would *register* it as real. In other words, you could trick your subconscious into thinking you'd already succeeded at the goal.

The concept resonated with me at once—and, again, it was through a link to basketball. I'd used that approach since third grade without naming it. If I imagined myself sinking the ball, actually saw how I would accomplish it, I could do it in reality. In the deepest part of my mind, I'd already done it, and that gave me confidence. There was no fear of failure, no anxiety, nothing to hold me back.

Maybe, I thought, I could apply that same technique to other things. Other goals.

My blanket pulled up over my head, flashlight in hand, I devoured the psychology books, one after another.

I believe it was right around this time that I became friendly with a kid named Arthur, who lived at the Wycoff projects. Arthur always made sure he had a job, and we would often look for work together. I learned a lot from him, including how to go about finding gainful employment. If he was hired, I'd get hired.

Arthur was the best hustle dancer in Brooklyn. He carried a little black book around, and had the best rap conversation for girls. He also studied the dictionary, and consequently built up a large vocabulary. It was one of the things I really admired about him, reminding me of my favorite actor.

You see, other than basketball, the greatest influence of my youth was Sidney Poitier. There weren't many black movie stars to rank with him back then, and he stood alone and unequaled as a leading man. I saw Poitier as the epitome of success—articulate, dignified, impeccably dressed, and supremely confident. I would sneak out and watch his films despite Dad's orders, mesmerized by his gait, speech, and poise.

Whenever I watched Sidney Poitier on-screen, I wanted to be like him. He communicated his thoughts and feelings with quiet grace, and emulating him gave me a measure of self-esteem I lacked. He was someone to model myself after.

For me, Poitier exuded power—power in his eloquence; power in his graceful, confident bearing; and power in his respected stature. In an era when Hollywood regularly reinforced and exploited negative stereotypes of African Americans, I'd watch him dominate the screen in one meaningful, nuanced role after another. In Norman Jewison's *In the Heat of the Night*, he was Detective Virgil Tibbs, fighting Southern racism to find a killer. As John Prentice in *Guess Who's Coming to Dinner*, he played a black physician planning to marry a white woman—and did it at a time when interracial marriage was still illegal in many states.

To Sir, with Love; *The Bedford Incident*; *They Call Me Mr. Tibbs!* . . . I caught all of Poitier's movies, whether in the theater or at home on our black-and-white television. I observed his posture, his style of dress, and especially his diction—listening to how he spoke, looking up the words he used, and then trying to use them myself.

I don't know that I always applied those words in their proper context. But I did grow more comfortable interacting with adults, and that, in turn, gave me confidence at the job interviews I went in for with Arthur.

My first job was Saturdays at a light bulb and fixture factory that was going out of business. Because of my height, and perhaps my ability to express myself, the owners didn't know or care that I was underage. They needed help packing away the fixtures, bulbs, and other lamp parts, saw a kid who could handle the heavy lifting, and hired me on the spot.

It was hard, grueling work, and the hourly wage was low, but it put a little money in my pocket and gave me some independence. I would keep half my pay and give the rest to my mother, contributing to our household finances and steering clear of bad elements on the street.

But despite gaining some independence, I was barely in my teens and hadn't yet challenged my father's dictates. I knew what the church meant to him. I understood it was his refuge from life's hardships. I only wish he'd been capable of understanding, or caring enough to understand, that basketball meant the same to me.

Still, I played whenever possible, usually at the after-school centers.

One kid I remember from that time was named Stanley. He lived at Whitman Houses and was a pretty good ballplayer. But as far as I was concerned, the best thing about Stanley was his mother's record collection. She had forty-fives and LPs by all the great black recording artists of that era, records I wasn't allowed to play at home. It was a fertile period for soul music, with one great after another coming onto the scene. The O'Jays. Diana Ross and the Supremes. James Brown, Wilson Pickett, and Marvin Gaye. The Manhattans. The Delfonics. The Chi-Lites . . .

Stanley and I would sit in his room playing records for hours. It was music heaven. Or would have been if not for the smell of the chitlins his mom was always fixing in the kitchen. If you've never had chitlins—fried pig's intestines—I'll only say they smell exactly like you'd expect. I guess you either love them or hate them.

Let's just say I never touched the chitlins at Stanley's apartment. But I didn't go there to eat. I went to listen to the music on the turntable and have fun.

As the days got longer in the spring and summer, I would spend more time in the playgrounds adjacent to my building. Everyone on the courts played three-on-three, half-court ball. That was different from the school tournaments, where you played full-court, five-on-five games. With five men on the squad, utilizing the open court, you ran transition, fast-break basketball, a game of speed and finesse.

Three-on-three was grittier. You operated in a limited space and got up close to your opponents. You played man defense, battled for rebounds, and gave and took hard fouls. You had to be mentally and physically tough.

Three-on-three was tougher than NBA games, because you didn't have officials stepping in when tempers flared. You couldn't just hit somebody without repercussions. You either understood your boundaries or learned them the hard way. It took a fortitude some guys didn't possess.

But the beauty of three-on-three pickup games, if you had that fortitude, was that it raised you to a higher level of competitiveness. In Brooklyn's playgrounds, the best players stayed on the court. You stayed on if your team won, and stepped aside if they lost. It was survival of the fittest. When you were sidelined, you hoped the next guys coming up would choose you for their team. There was always an open slot for a good player, so if you'd already played and lost, and you were better than somebody *else* waiting to get into a game, you still had a chance for more basketball that day.

It was no fun standing on the sidelines. I didn't want to watch other kids play the game I loved. All my self-esteem was tied up in staying on the court as long as possible.

That was where stamina entered the equation. Someone could possess all the qualities of a tremendous player—strength, coordination, timing, shooting ability, passing ability, the ability to rebound in traffic—but without stamina, he would be unable to utilize those attributes to their fullest. On the other hand, if he had more stamina than the other guy, he could outplay him no matter how talented and powerful that guy was. Eventually the guy would tire. His legs became fatigued. He'd be unable to outrun the better-conditioned player and would fall behind when he was chasing him around the court.

Early in my basketball life, I realized that stamina was the great equalizer. Though I didn't consider myself the most talented player on the court, I made sure I was the most highly conditioned.

I never lifted weights. Not once. To me, you could lift all the weights you wanted, but strength and size didn't matter unless conditioning was the foundation of your play.

Stamina and endurance can be developed in many ways. The goal for an athlete is to build up your wind and be able to get a second or third wind when you need it. A lot of guys would jog, but I felt jogging didn't have the right pace for basketball.

You run on the court. You sprint on the court. You don't jog.

By the seventh and eighth grades, I'd started running circuits around playgrounds, schoolyards, Fort Greene Park, and the streets of my neighborhood. But I was always dodging people and traffic, and that made it hard to run at a fast, uninterrupted clip.

One day I passed a guy on the sidewalk who looked like he'd stepped right out of a weight-lifting magazine. He must have been a boxer or competitive bodybuilder. As he talked about his training with his friend, I overheard him say he ran on the Brooklyn Bridge.

A light bulb blinked on over my head.

Oh wow, I told myself. *That's an idea!*

The Brooklyn Bridge was about a ten-minute walk from Whitman. It was even closer to the Farragut Houses where I played ball once in a while. I also played three-on-three in a park opposite the community college a few blocks away from the bridge. Any of those places would be a good starting point, I thought.

But running the Brooklyn Bridge would not be as easy as getting there. With its enormous granite towers and steel cables, the bridge is pure architectural majesty, connecting the boroughs of Brooklyn and Manhattan across the East River. Its main span is 486 meters, which once made it the world's longest suspension bridge, but its wood-plank pedestrian walkway is even longer. Raised high above traffic in the middle of the bridge, it is slightly over a mile from end to end.

I intended to run it in both directions—a total of two miles—at a full sprint.

To put this in perspective, the two-mile run is an Olympic-level track and field event. I was barely thirteen and knew handling that span would be a challenge. But I felt the secret to accomplishing my goal was in the books I'd been reading under my blanket at night. In visualization, the same technique I used to mentally rehearse my moves on the basketball court.

On my first run, I imagined myself to be a lone African warrior delivering an urgent message to my tribal leader. Surrounded by enemies, running over arid, sunbaked plains. Running with unstoppable persistence through risk of capture or death.

I could not fail. The fate of my tribe hung on my success.

And I succeeded. I ran the Brooklyn Bridge. It quickly became a regular part of my workout routine. Spring, summer, winter, fall, the weather made no difference. I was a warrior on a mission, and nothing would prevent me from accomplishing it.

Whether I started out from Farragut or the community college, I'd take Prospect Street straight under the Brooklyn-Queens Expressway to the entrance ramp, running at a moderate but steady pace. There was a busy thoroughfare just off the ramp, with traffic leaving the expressway to turn onto the bridge or bear farther north, toward the Manhattan Bridge, the cars going one way or another as they moved across the river.

I would keep up my medium speed until I reached the thoroughfare, then jog in place, waiting for a break in traffic so I could cross the street to the ramp. The first few yards of the walk were paved with concrete, a metal rail separating me from the cars. But once I felt the bounce of wood underfoot, I accelerated, not jogging anymore, no longer feeling the shock of my feet pounding on hard concrete.

As the walkway rose above the tops of the vehicles, I was no longer concerned with traffic. I didn't have to worry about safety. I ran with speed over the planks, thumbs up, a warrior on a mission of great importance. I could not allow myself to tire. I *refused* to tire or weaken.

Sprinting, one foot after the other, my legs stretched, I paid no attention to the people strolling around me. I hardly noticed anyone else on the planks. Somehow the air always seemed fresh and clean despite the traffic. I could run in a summer heat wave and still feel a breeze. On those days, the baked asphalt sidewalks of Fort Greene seemed very far away.

It was beautiful. The bridge's sweeping magnificence, the beauty of its long, uninterrupted span extending over the water, the barges heading out past the Statue of Liberty toward the open sea, and the skyscrapers of Manhattan across the river . . . I ran, taking everything in. When I reached the end of the walkway, I'd turn back toward Brooklyn without pause and start my run all over again.

Thumbs up, always thumbs up.

The bridge was an incredible place to train. Running it gave me a special sense of freedom. But going home was the opposite. Life there continued to be stifling and joyless. I needed something more, needed to expand my horizons, but what I wanted most was still frustratingly out of reach.

My situation had to change. I had to *make* it change.

That meant rebelling against my father.

4 | The Restoration Eagles

New York City summer basketball was like cotton candy to me. I couldn't resist it. I craved it for my soul, for my spirit, for my insatiable love of the game.

Back when I was growing up, there were youth leagues in all five boroughs, but the top teams were always from the Bronx, Manhattan, and Brooklyn. In my neighborhood, the team coaches were legends, and we knew their names the way some kids knew the names of the astronauts. These men were mostly African American males who cared about young kids and their development. They had a positive outlook about the necessity of community service and the difference it could make on young people's lives. For many of the boys, they were father figures; I was one of the few players who didn't come from a single-parent home.

They were our heroes, and we spoke their names on the courts with a respect bordering on reverence. There was Billy Townsend, a professional photographer who volunteered his time at the Wyckoff Houses in Red Hook. Buddy Keaton was a coach at the St. John's Recreational Center in Bedford-Stuyvesant, where a lot of the tournaments were held. Lester Roberts, who owned a sporting goods shop in Brownsville called Sports Unlimited, also coached a team at St. John's Rec. Lester was a gentle, cheerful man who couldn't do enough for his boys.

And then there was Gil Reynolds. Gil was a legendary figure to us, a hard-nosed former Marine sergeant who coached like he was still at boot camp. His Restoration Eagles had flowed out of the Bedford-

Stuyvesant Restoration Corporation, an urban renewal group that Senator Robert F. Kennedy, Mayor John Lindsay, and Senator Jacob Javits kicked off in the late sixties.

The Eagles were the best team in New York. They never seemed to lose to anybody. But most guys were terrified of playing for Gil. His mildest tone of voice was a snarl. He'd yell at you, he'd punch you in your chest, whatever it took to get you motivated. He was a teaching coach who not only hammered home the game's fundamentals, but understood that the lessons you learned on the court were the same ones that could help you during challenging times. There were always going to be obstacles when you tried to make a team, become a better player, beat another team, just as there were obstacles to overcome in life.

But I'm getting ahead of my story. Before I could play on weekends, I would have to challenge my father about his Sunday prohibition. Until then, I would be stuck sitting in the window all day after services, watching other kids play the game.

I wanted to go across the street, to Sands Park, behind my school, and practice. If there were games outside my building, I wanted to compete in them. And I wanted to participate in the tournaments at Soul in the Hole. The Hole was officially the P.S. 44 playground in Bedford-Stuyvesant, near the Marcy Houses. But it got its name, the one we all used, because the court was sunken below street level, with low cement walls separating it from the sidewalk outside.

There are moments in life when you don't have to think everything through before you act. I knew I'd reached one of them, knew what I needed to do. In my mind, I had no choice.

It was either church or basketball.

I didn't dress for services on the morning I declared my independence. I assumed Dad would not react well. I knew my siblings wouldn't take my side—none of them had ever said no to him about anything. I could not, however, predict what my mother would say.

Mom was a very religious woman. She prayed every day, listened to her gospel music every day. She also ran the household and made every major decision for the family. If she aligned with my father and insisted I go to church, things would get very difficult for me.

I was still a young teenager in the ninth grade. I lived under my parents' roof. But I suppose I had tunnel vision when it came to basketball and didn't really consider the consequences I'd face if I was denied. It never entered my thoughts.

Standing outside my room in my house clothes, I could see Dad's surprised expression. He'd noticed I wasn't in my Sunday finest.

"You're supposed to be getting ready for church," he said, staring. "Am I right?"

I looked back at him, not budging while everyone else got ready.

"Am I right?"

My father always asked that question when he dealt with a possible conflict. Its purpose wasn't to draw an honest answer or get someone's opinion, but to intimidate. The only response he expected was yes.

"No," I said. "I'm not getting ready. I'm not going to church anymore."

Neither of us budged an inch. No one else in the apartment spoke. I don't know how long the silence lasted, but it was thick as jelly.

Dad kept staring at me.

"It's Sunday," he said finally. He did not raise his voice. "You're going."

More silence. My father was a tall man, but we were almost the same height, and I kept my eyes leveled on his.

"You go seven days a week," I said. "You come home. Eat your dinner. Read the Bible. Put on your suit. And then you leave and go back to church." I took a deep breath. "That brings you joy, but it's not what I want to do. Basketball is *my* joy."

Dad stayed very still. This was something new; no one in the family had ever stood up to him. He couldn't grasp what was happening, and it upset him. Though it didn't give me happiness to see him that way, I'd felt liberated just getting those words out of my mouth.

Then I heard my mother's voice from over my shoulder.

"Leave him alone," she said.

Dad's eyes went from my face to hers.

"He's not getting in trouble, and he's bringing money into the household," she added. "If Bernard wants to go play . . . leave him alone."

Dad didn't utter a sound. He seemed mystified and unsure how to respond.

I don't remember him saying anything to my mother—or to me. He might have, but it wouldn't have mattered at that point. Mom had made the decision.

I turned into my room and put on my jeans, T-shirt, and dress socks—sweat socks were still an expense neither my family nor I could afford. Then I laced up my Converse sneakers, picked up my basketball, went back into the hall, and walked out the front door.

Riding the elevator downstairs, I realized nothing would be the same for me again. I presumed what little relationship I had with my father was irreparably fractured. I didn't know the impact it would have on my home life, or whether I might still wind up getting beaten for it. But I didn't doubt myself for an instant.

I felt free. Liberated. Summer basketball lay ahead, and I knew it would be something special.

Cotton candy.

I could hardly wait for my first sweet mouthful.

THE YOUTH BASKETBALL LEAGUES fell into a loose framework of tournaments. Every borough had separate league organizers, and coaches would pay small entry fees to register their teams. You had tourneys sponsored by different community groups—Police Athletic League games, New York City Housing Authority ball, and the Amateur Athletic Union competitions, to name a few. No one ran a youth basketball league intending to make a buck, and the fees they collected went toward covering expenses and charitable fundraising.

Citywide championship tournaments brought together the best teams from each borough with divisional semifinals and finals. Because the AAU was a nationwide organization, it would hold regional round-robin tournaments culminating in matchups between champs from different cities.

I played in as many of those competitions as I could. When I wasn't playing the game, I was practicing alone on the court. And when I wasn't practicing, I was thinking about it.

It was right around this time that my mother stopped beating me. She didn't give a reason. The beatings had always been a secret, kept out of the light, and nothing was ever said about them. But it didn't seem coincidental that they ended soon after the Sunday I refused to go to church. When I declared my independence to my father, something must have changed for Mom, too. Possibly she equated the beatings with discipline, and I'd ceased to be a child in her eyes. Not quite an adult, but someone moving out from under her control.

I'll never be entirely sure. But I'm now aware that they were about her demons, not mine. That it all traumatized me and left open wounds where my own demons could enter and grow. And that I would have to face them and the reality of what happened to me before I could exorcise them.

But I really didn't think about it back then, or want to think about it. Instead, I threw my entire being into basketball. Nothing else mattered to me. When I wasn't in a pickup game, I'd be on the court alone, experimenting, working on my moves. Practice was the game, and the game was practice.

The game taught me lessons I couldn't get anywhere else. If you join a team and want to fit into the team *concept*, you have to adapt your individual game to being part of a unit. And when you're part of a unit, your personal objectives become one with its goals. You never want to let your teammates down. Without consciously realizing it, you're developing new social skills. You're *growing*, not just as a player, but as a human being. I've always said basketball mirrors life. Now more than ever, I believe it to be true.

On the basketball court, I wasn't shy and introverted. The court was the one place I carried myself with complete assurance. The one place I belonged.

Still, drugs, street gangs, and other negative influences were everywhere. There were some great streetballers in the playgrounds around Whitman, kids with unbelievable talent who should have made it to the NBA. But too many slipped through the cracks. The best was a guy named Gordy. He was like a young George Gervin: fast, gliding, and athletic, with a silky shooting touch. I don't know what happened to him. Or to another kid, a tough competitor named Jose. He also should've made it. And Mike, the gang leader with the Avenue Kings. He was terrific and should've made it.

I remember a kid at the Hanson Place center whose game would be comparable to Steph Curry's in today's NBA. This guy would drop shots from deep on the court like they were layups. Then one day after we played, I went up to the lockers to change and he was shooting up heroin. I can still see him nodding out, a needle in his arm.

These were all guys who should have made it. They were that good. But too many were lost to drugs and other temptations on the street.

What kept me from falling victim to them? I give a lot of credit to my father, ironically the same person who'd opposed my playing on weekends. I don't think Dad ever realized the example of consistency he'd set by never missing a day of work. He knew my family counted on him to provide for us, and that taught me about responsibility and what it meant to have my team count on *me*.

But most kids I knew were raised without father figures at home, and it had an adverse impact on them. Fatherlessness was epidemic in the inner cities, and that led to greater poverty and a lack of structure and supervision. It was not an atmosphere that prepared children to succeed.

My coaches also anchored me. I can't overstate what a difference someone like Lester Roberts, the Sports Unlimited coach, made for the kids on his teams. Lester was a special man, warm, lighthearted, and quick with a smile. He would provide the entrance fees for our tournaments out of pocket, supply our uniforms for free, and then pay to have them cleaned. The only thing he asked in return was that we play our hearts out for the team.

Lester would haul us to our games in a passenger van that was like a tugboat on wheels. Whether they were in Brooklyn, other boroughs, or other cities, he was always happy to drive us. Highway tolls, gasoline, meals . . . he'd cover those expenses without asking for a dime.

One particular tournament in Baltimore was a major championship event, the New York All-Stars versus the Baltimore All-Stars. The players on my team were the best in our division. Lester booked and paid for hotel rooms in advance and drove us there the night before the tourney.

I remember bringing my little transistor radio along for the trip. An inexpensive pocket radio, with a leather case and earplugs, it was one of the first things I'd bought with the money I earned working part-time at the lamp factory. I would bring it everywhere with me, listening to stations like WBLS-FM and WLIB-AM play the latest soul and R&B music. With a turn of the dial, I could hear all the artists I'd grown to love at my friend Stanley's apartment, but without the smell of chitlins.

During our ride to Baltimore, I heard "Love Don't Love Nobody" by The Spinners for the first time. I was swept up by the group's passionate delivery, their soulful expression of longing, of reaching for absent love. The song's poetic lyrics pierced my heart and were permanently embedded there.

But that isn't all I remember about that night. Just as we were arriving at the hotel, my team faced an unexpected development. One of the boys realized he'd left his identification at home in Brooklyn.

The kid was distraught. Youth leagues were organized by age to ensure a team didn't gain an unfair advantage by running a lot of older, taller, more experienced young men onto the floor. Anytime there's competition, you'll find participants who try to skirt the rules, and in the past, teams had been suspected of playing ringers too old for their category. For that reason, tournament officials were strict about requiring kids to bring proof of age and identity.

On a good night, Baltimore was a four-hour trip south on the I-95, and Lester must have been pretty wrung out after driving almost two hundred miles through heavy weekend traffic. But the kid was ineligible to play without his ID, and everybody could feel his dejection. Basketball was our lifeblood. None of us could imagine sitting out the tournament.

Lester took one look at the kid's face and made up his mind. He would drive back to Brooklyn by himself and pick up his ID. There was no time for him to rest up. The tourney was the very next day, and he had to formally register and prepare us for our game. Dropping us off at the hotel, Lester drove all the way to the kid's home for his birth certif-icate, then turned around, and returned to Baltimore without a break.

Three trips, six hundred miles, a dozen hours behind the steering wheel . . . that was Coach Lester Roberts. He'd have done anything for his boys, and then some.

If he was tired in the morning, none of us ever knew it. But I'll admit we were about to have other things on our minds.

In college and the NBA, you received scouting reports on the oppos-ing team. Typically you were able to watch film of their performances.

It wasn't so in the youth leagues. You had your first look at your opponents on the day of the game. In a sense, it was a purer form of competition. Not that we would have complained if we'd received some advance scouting on them.

That hot, steamy summer day in Baltimore, we arrived at the gym, changed into uniform, jogged out of the locker room . . . and were stunned by the size of the players doing their drills at the opposite end of the floor.

There were some big men playing in the NBA when I was young. Wilt Chamberlain was six feet eleven entering high school, and he would shoot up to a height of seven feet before turning professional. But there weren't many like him. Even Kareem Abdul-Jabbar, who was one of the tallest men ever to play the game and still a dominant All-Star during my era, was only six feet eight in ninth grade.

Every center and small forward on the other team looked to be a seven-footer, or close to it. I'd never before played against a squad that huge.

We might be in a little trouble here, I thought. Watching them take practice layups, I felt trepidation for the first time in my basketball life. Then my competitive instincts kicked in. I reached deep down into my well of intensity and recalled something I'd always told myself. *Height can't play basketball. But talent can.*

I dominated the boards that day, leading our team's charge by pull-ing down rebound after rebound against my bigger opponents. Height and jumping ability are great advantages under the basket, but nothing can beat heart, will, and desire.

That game was the hardest fought I'd ever been part of. Baltimore was a great defensive team, with a guard named Skip Wise who would become a high school legend in that city. I remember him raining in one thirty-foot shot after another to loud cheers from the home crowd. But we were ferocious offensively. And we silenced them, pulling out a narrow win against a formidable opponent.

We showered and left the building in an animated mood, cracking jokes, bubbling with excitement and laughter. Beyond our well-deserved celebration, that game taught me an unforgettable lesson: You grow as a player when you're challenged. Without accepting and conquering challenges, you have no shot at achieving greatness.

As we left Baltimore for home, my new favorite Spinners song came on the radio. What more could I have wanted? It was a perfect capper to the trip.

Listening through my earplug, I realized I knew the words and quietly sang along.

THE ONE TEAM NOBODY COULD DEFEAT was Gil Reynolds's Restoration Eagles. They steamrolled over the competition, including the teams I played on under Lester Roberts.

As an opposing player, I could see Gil took coaching to another level. Lester was a special, generous man. He loved basketball and was always present for us. But Gil's approach was marked by discipline, discipline, and more discipline. His teams didn't play in a fancy way. Most of the young men in the New York City playgrounds played a street style of basketball. They wanted to be flashy. Gil scowled at that. He had a conservative coaching style that appealed to me. Since I was a conservative player to begin with, it suited my existing game.

"Son, you don't get two points for the way it looks."

I would hear Gil say it whenever he caught the slightest hint of showboating. This was later on, of course. While playing for Lester's Sports Unlimited teams, I only knew Gil's players were all highly conditioned and fundamentally sound. Their game was about strategy and focus. About execution in the half-court set. Pushing the ball, no turnovers.

Tough, in-your-face defense. Setting screens. That was Gil Reynolds's brand of coaching.

The Restoration Eagles always had a confident swagger about them. They assumed they were going to beat you. And they did. As I said, they seemed to win *everything*.

Gil's young players carried green uniform bags with white lettering and an eagle emblem. For me, the bag was a symbol of success. If you had one, you were a member of the best team in New York. And that made you one of the best players in New York.

The winning aside, most guys didn't want to play for Gil. He ran his gym like a boot camp, and you either accepted it or else. He'd yell at you, he'd punch you in the chest, and then he'd yell even louder, whatever it took to motivate you. *"Go get your mother and your father if you don't like it. I'll punch them too. You either play or get the hell out of here."*

I was familiar with Gil's reputation, but wouldn't have cared if he spit rusty nails and broken glass. I'd had enough of losing to the Eagles. I was tired of watching them collect trophies. I wanted that green bag. And that meant moving on from Lester Roberts's Sports Unlimited team.

I realized Lester would feel disappointed and hoped he wouldn't see me as a defector. I respected him tremendously and loved playing for his team. But I needed to take the next step in my growth.

I needed a coach like Gil.

One day I rode the bus down to his facility and confidently walked in. Gil was holding a practice, and there was no missing him. A stout, solidly built man in his mid-thirties, with dark, close-cropped hair, he was wearing his usual sweatpants and sneakers.

I'm sure he noticed me right away. I waited till he was ready to let me know it.

"WHAT D'YOU WANT?" he barked.

"I want to try out for your team."

"GO GET YOUR ASS DRESSED!"

That was Gil's personality. But I'd competed against him before, and he knew me as one of the best young players in the city.

I remember Gil inserting me into some scrimmages and having me participate in his team drills. I left the gym a member of his team. With the coveted green bag.

Wow. I was on Cloud Nine.

Gil and I mirrored each other in many ways. He understood my work ethic. He understood my studied, scientific approach to the game. And he recognized my burning desire to be great. I knew playing for him was exactly what I needed to raise my game to a higher level. He made the mental, physical, and emotional aspects of basketball click into place. In hindsight, Gil developed me into someone who could play NBA ball.

Like me, Gil always had a chip on his shoulder. Maybe he felt he should have gone further than the youth leagues in his coaching career. But his hard-nosed, no-bullshit style didn't mesh with too many college programs at the time.

One thing I noticed about Gil—despite his intensity, he did not let emotions change his approach. He had structured plays we were going to run, and we practiced them daily as a full team. Defensively, we had schemes we wanted to implement in every game, and positioning ourselves on the court within those defensive schemes was important. Gil would not react to external circumstances, always sticking to his plan.

I quickly adopted the same attitude. I'd played with anger since I was young. Anger had fueled my performances. After a loss, I wouldn't speak to anyone. Instead I'd sulk and become furiously unapproachable. While playing for Gil, I learned to convert my anger into intensity, and it made me a more consistent, well-rounded player.

We had many common traits before I joined the Eagles. But as coach and player, we complemented each other perfectly. I'd no longer get too up or down over games, but would keep my emotions in balance.

I think Gil saw that type of lesson as less a basketball fundamental and more a fundamental of life, although he never really separated the two. That was what Gil was about. For him, basketball was a means to an end. Yes, he wanted to see us improve as players. But his chief interest was molding us as human beings. Gil had no sons of his own and seemed to relish being a father figure to all the young men on his teams.

Once Gil actually took us to the Rikers Island penitentiary in the East River, a prison for hardcore inmates. We put on a basketball clinic there, but really the point of the trip was to give us a glimpse of life behind bars, and let us know it was not a place any of us wanted to wind up.

We were demonstrating some skills in the gym when a couple of inmates shouted a familiar nickname at me: *"Hey, Little Spal!"*

No one had called me that in years. I turned to the bleachers and recognized the faces of guys who'd known my older brother. I probably shouldn't have been surprised. Far too many kids growing up in Fort Greene eventually found themselves incarcerated.

I never forgot the clang of the cellblock door as we left for home.

GIL DRILLED US CONSTANTLY AND RELENTLESSLY. If anyone griped, he'd remind him who was the leader of the team, and he wouldn't be polite. I suppose it was the hard-ass leatherneck in him.

I was already in good shape when I joined the Eagles. I'd developed my own workout routine that included running the Brooklyn Bridge. But adding his drills, his *regimentation*, as another layer to what I was doing helped me tremendously.

Conditioning was always Gil's priority. He would push us through a series of rigorous workouts every day, sometimes after we'd had a full basketball practice. At the sound of his whistle we'd run "suicides," line drills for cardio conditioning. Players would start at one baseline, run to the free throw line, touch the line, and then return to the baseline. Repeating the process, they would run to the half court line, the opposite free throw line, and the far court baseline. The last player to finish would go again.

Next we would go sideline to sideline in shorter sprints—seventeens, they're called. You ran them against the clock and, occasionally, against your teammates. The objective was to cross the court seventeen times in under two minutes.

We jumped rope to increase our endurance, and we did defensive slide drills to improve our lateral movement. During a slide, Gil would face us and shout a command: *"Right! Left! Backward! Forward!"*

Imagine the guy with the flashlights on an airport runway, the one who instructs the pilot to go in one or another direction. That was like Gil on the court. He would bark his command and you'd have to react immediately, taking a low, squatting stance, your hands up at shoulder level to deflect a pass upward, downward, or to the side.

These were the sort of workouts you'd typically see in NBA training camps and practices, not youth league basketball. The sudden changes of direction were hard for young players, testing our wits, reflexes, coordination, and leg strength. But Gil was uncompromising. He prided himself on making sure we were an outstanding defensive team, and the drills were crucial to our preparation.

At the offensive end, Gil preached aggressive, unselfish play. We practiced bounce passes, chest passes, no-looks . . . the skills it took to move and distribute the basketball down the floor. He had us play three-on-three half-court games—the trademark of New York City playground ball—but we wouldn't have to take the ball back to the foul line after a miss. That kept us in position to attack the ball relentlessly and put up rebounds for baskets. We didn't wait for opportunities to score. We *created* them.

Gil insisted that we know the strategy behind why we did things. He wanted us to understand the purpose of any given play and have insight into the situation that called for it. And he taught us to respect the game and our teammates. You didn't drift off when you played, and you didn't drift off when he was talking to you.

These were the reasons I went to Gil. He was a farmer watering the soil. I soaked up what he taught, incorporated it into my existing game, and then implemented it on the court.

As a young man, I found it invaluable to be a member of his team. It was a perfect marriage between player and coach. He was analytical, I was analytical. He wanted to teach, I wanted to learn. And we both wanted to *win*.

The Eagles won every tournament we were in. We were going up against some of the best young players in the city. But we had the best team. And I was the best player on the best team. So no one was going to beat us.

Some of our biggest matches were at Soul in the Hole. Nothing compared to the action on that blacktop. You had great streetball players coming up in that neighborhood. That's why Boys High School there was ranked first in the country. The talent level in the park was sky high, and the school actively invited players into its program. A generation before my time, the Hall of Famers Lenny Wilkens and Connie Hawkins came out of Boys High. In my day, we had guys like Ernie Douse, John Rushmore, and others.

Summer tournaments at the Hole were noisy, festive events. The bleachers filled up fast, and it would be standing-room only. They were almost like street fairs, with ice cream trucks pulling up outside the park to sell cones, Popsicles, and soda.

When people talk about street basketball, they always mention the park at West Fourth Street in Greenwich Village—the Cage. Along with Rucker Park, where the venerable Dr. J took his game to New York's playgrounds, it's the most famous setting for amateur hoops in the city, and I take nothing away from the talent it's showcased. But I personally didn't like playing there. The court wasn't regulation length. It was too small. I wanted to get up and down the court and felt constrained playing on West Fourth. To me, Soul in the Hole was second to none for the caliber of players it attracted and the sheer action you'd find on the court. I'd take the bus there, looking to join in really good pickup games.

The Restoration Eagles participated in a lot of tournaments at Soul in the Hole. Gil wanted us to play against the toughest competition around, and that was where we found it. And we won. Time and again, we won. Once you get a taste of victory, it only makes you hungrier. You just keep after it. With the Eagles, I feasted on success.

I was too young to realize it wouldn't always be that way, and that part of being the best was learning how to get back up after you were knocked to the ground.

Gil Reynolds was such a profound influence, it's hard to adequately express my debt to him. He cultivated my analytical approach to basketball and gave me the knowledge I needed to completely dissect the game, breaking it down to its most fundamental elements. During my years with Gil, I formulated the scoring method I used throughout my playing career—and that's always been my closely guarded secret.

But I'll get around to that later on.

I will always carry my memories of summer hoops and the lessons learned from it. As I entered my mid-teens, though, I would start to gather momentum along a separate path into the future.

High school, and high school basketball, lay ahead.

5 | Brooklyn to Tennessee

In the late sixties and early seventies, several landmark U.S. Supreme Court rulings favored public school busing as a tool for integration. Though segregation had been illegal for almost twenty years, the reality was that blacks and whites lived in different neighborhoods, and that their schools had racially separate student bodies. Also, since inner-city neighborhoods had poorer tax bases, their school districts invariably received less funding for their classrooms than white areas. The result was an inferior education.

Busing was an attempt to bring greater racial balance to the educational system and to break down the pockets of school segregation that, in practice, still existed in some states. In New York City, the program went into full force a few years before my graduation from Sands Junior High. When the time came for me to choose a high school, I had the option of attending Fort Hamilton in Bay Ridge, New Utrecht farther south in Bensonhurst, or the George Westinghouse Technical High School in Flatbush. The first two were in white, working-class enclaves and offered comprehensive academic degrees. Westinghouse, a trade school, was closer to home.

I was hoping to attend college someday. I also wanted to get out of the neighborhood. At Sands, there was always a fight going on, and I'd had enough of it. That scratched Westinghouse off my list.

During the first few years of integration, my older brother had gone to Fort Hamilton and played on its basketball team, the Tigers, under Coach Ken Kern, whose old-school game was known to have several things in common with Gil Reynolds's style of play. Thomas excelled and had won a college athletic scholarship, so I decided to follow his lead.

I expected to face some racial issues at Fort Hamilton, but wasn't sure how serious they would be. In 1974 Bay Ridge was not what you would call a melting pot. The ethnic mix was mainly Italian, Irish, and Scandinavian, with many first- and second-generation Americans who did very little mingling with blacks or other people of color. Some residents—adults *and* kids—reacted to the efforts to integrate their school with suspicion, hostility, and occasional flare-ups of violence.

None of that concerned me early on. Sands was bad, and I didn't see how my new school could be any worse. I was just excited by the change of atmosphere.

In my first year at Fort Hamilton, I tried out for the basketball team and made it. But I didn't tell Coach Kern I was Thomas's younger brother. He'd graduated in June, and I came along as a freshman in September, so we never spent a day of school together.

I can't recall how the coach found out about Thomas and me. We had the same last name, of course, so it wasn't exactly the world's biggest secret. But one day right before practice, Kern came up to me with a curious look on his face.

"Why didn't you tell me about Thomas?"

I just kind of shrugged. "I wanted to make the team on my own merit," I explained.

He didn't comment. But I think he understood. Kern knew what made his kids tick. With his straight, longish hair, heavy sideburns, and narrow face, he looked like the quiet man in a jazz or rock band in those days—the bass player who'd stand outside of the spotlight and provide a steady bottom to the music.

That could have described his coaching style. Solid and dependable. Laying out guidelines for us, then holding things together so we could "play the changes," as musicians call improvising over, around, and between a song's basic chords. He was a steady presence that allowed us to stay loose on the court, free our talent, and play with imagination and creativity.

Being on the Tigers, my curriculum had to be adjusted to fit the team schedule. Fort Hamilton had such a large student population that it held morning and afternoon sessions to reduce overcrowding. Sophomores, juniors, and seniors attended morning sessions, and freshmen usually came in at one in the afternoon. But I had to be at 8 A.M. home room so I could finish classes at one o'clock and then go on to basketball practice or travel to a game.

It wasn't easy. I would wake up at 5:30 A.M. or so, eat a bowl of Kellogg's Corn Flakes, dress, and leave the apartment by 6:30. Then I'd take a ten-minute walk to the BMT subway line, which left me off a couple of miles from school. Though I could have transferred to a bus near the station, they always seemed to be running late, so I'd walk the rest of the way down 86th Street, the neighborhood's main strip.

That hike to school seemed longest in the dead of winter, with bitter cold gusts lashing in off the Narrows and, sometimes, the blinding, wind-driven snow in my eyes. But that time of year, when it got dark early, leaving practice made me uncomfortable in an altogether different way.

As a black kid, I didn't feel safe. Walking back to the train station at night, I would see people watching me, their eyes following me up the street like I was a criminal. Only after I'd hurried aboard the train would I breathe a sigh of relief.

I won't claim I ever got used to the racial tensions. But I lived with them.

We had three white players on the Tigers. The rest of us were African American. Before we went to play against certain schools in Brooklyn, the black kids on the team would plot out the fastest and most direct routes home, knowing we might have trouble afterward. One school was in Gravesend. Another in Bensonhurst.

Few black people lived in those areas. After games—especially if we won—we'd grab our clothes, rush out of the gym, and hustle down the street toward the train station or bus stop as bottles started flying behind us.

That's just how it was. I'm sure the same would have occurred to white kids in Fort Greene, Brownsville, or Bed-Stuy. Suspicion and mistrust are rooted in unfamiliarity. Things only change for the better when different groups interact.

At Fort Hamilton, there really wasn't much interaction at all. Blacks and whites had a mostly peaceful coexistence, but they didn't mix. That led to misunderstandings that I've come to realize were often more cultural than racial.

Here's an example. I loved math. In fact, I was good enough at algebra to tutor my classmates. Once, while the teacher was explaining something in class, one of the kids seated near me became disruptive. I didn't think he intended to start anything. He was just horsing around. But I was trying to concentrate on the lesson. I loved working with numbers.

When I asked the kid to settle down, he only got louder.

"What if I don't?" he said.

I looked around at him from my desk. He happened to be a white kid of Italian descent. Though his background didn't matter to me, it would become important soon enough.

"Squash it," I said. Among black kids in the projects that meant *forget it, let it go*. I didn't want a fight.

But the kid just seemed to get more agitated. He puffed out his chest and swore.

When I saw how worked up he was, I decided to take my own advice and let it go. I turned back toward my books, positive that would be the end of it.

I was mistaken.

A few periods later, I was called from my classroom to the principal's office. The kid was sitting there too. I could see he was still fuming, and I couldn't understand why. The incident in class hadn't seemed like a big deal.

Then the principal began explaining why we'd been summoned. He'd heard that there would be a showdown between the black and Italian students after school and that the threat I'd made in class was causing the uproar.

I cocked my head to one side. "Sir . . . what threat?"

The principal faced the other kid. "Would you please repeat what you told me a minute ago?"

"King said he'd squash me."

"*What?*" I said.

"Squash me," the kid repeated. "Like in, 'You wanna squash me, I'll squash you first.'"

I sat there in astonishment.

"Wait," I said. "I told you to squash *it*."

"*It?*"

"Right. What happened in class. I meant, *forget it*."

The principal stared at us from behind his desk. The office had gotten so quiet you could have heard dust fall.

I broke into a grin and saw the kid was grinning too.

"'Forget it'?" he asked.

"Uh-huh," I said.

We both cracked up. I didn't want the principal to think I was disrespecting him, but I couldn't help myself.

Luckily, he didn't take exception. I think he was glad to have averted a race riot at his school. The kid had his crew ready for a showdown. There's no telling how far it would have escalated if the principal hadn't called us in.

The whole thing was a crazy mix-up. But it illustrates the racial realities in that period. Our coexistence was fragile, a bubble that could have burst under the slightest of social pressures.

The incident in math class was the closest I came to a fight at Fort Hamilton. There really weren't any problems of that nature. But I felt I was living in two worlds. The world where I was cheered as one of the top varsity players in the city, and the solitary world I inhabited after leaving the gym. I didn't feel fully accepted by the student body or the surrounding community. After practices or games, I never lingered with my classmates, but would get right on a bus or train and ride back to Fort Greene. On the court, there was no room for shyness. But off the court, I was an introvert—nervous around people, lacking social skills, and unable to form meaningful connections with others.

Looking back, I realize I didn't truly live in either of those worlds, but in the world behind my Game Face . . . the world inside me. It was a world apart, and no one could penetrate its thick outer walls.

On Friday nights, I enjoyed riding the subway alone. There weren't any basketball games, and basketball was my only real interest. Some guys would get together or go on dates. But I viewed riding the train as a break from everything around me and never told anybody about it. My parents certainly didn't know.

I'd always been drawn to trains, a youthful fascination many boys of my generation shared. I grew up in an era before video games, when we played with miniature railroad sets, watched Western heroes tangle with villains in the cabs of moving locomotives, saw Choo Choo Charlie in Good & Plenty television commercials, and then made whistle noises by blowing in the empty box of candy. Trains were the best.

As a tenth grader, I still hadn't outgrown that attraction. Besides, a token only cost thirty-five cents in those days. The subway was cheaper than Coney Island.

I knew my way around the city. I rode the trains and buses to tournaments and was familiar with their different routes. So, on Fridays, I would get on the J train at Flatbush and Fulton, take the long ride out past John F. Kennedy Airport in Queens to the last stop, then turn around and head back into Brooklyn. As the train swayed rhythmically along the tracks, I would sit and think, read my psychology books, or just stare out the windows at the passing stations. I also remember writing some of my earliest poems, a hobby that would become a lifelong means of self-expression.

Mostly, riding the subway gave me time to relax. I liked the plaques with the station names, the tile walls along the platforms, and the way the stripes above the plain white tiles changed color from station to station. I liked going up into the train's front car and watching its headlights spill over the tracks as it rumbled from the station's brightness into the pitch-black tunnel. I liked the feeling of acceleration in my stomach and the metal-on-metal sound of the wheels picking up speed

on the rails. *Clank-clank . . . clank-clank . . . clankclankclankclank . . .*
Then the squeal of the brakes as it pulled into the next stop on
the line.

Riding the subway on Fridays was better than sitting around the
cheerless apartment. I didn't want to share that with anyone. It was
mine. The rest of the week, I lived for basketball.

Memory is like a collage made by pasting together snapshots, or
even cut-up pieces of snapshots . . . hundreds upon hundreds of them,
more than we can ever count. The standout moments can be scattered
or in clusters, at least for me. That's how it is when I recall my teenage
playing years.

I competed in tournament after tournament. With the high school
league, the Restoration Eagles, the Police Athletic League, and later
under my old coach Lester Roberts, who'd changed the name of his
team to Brooklyn USA ahead of the nation's bicentennial, issuing them
uniform T-shirts with American flags on the front.

As a member of the Tigers, I averaged 26 points and 28 rebounds
a game, was named to the All New York first team, and was also named
Most Valuable Player in eleven of the sixteen high school All-Star tournaments in which I participated.

During my senior year, we were in a conference with New Utrecht
High School in the heart of Bensonhurst—the school that the comedian and actor Gabe Kaplan, a fellow Brooklyn kid, went to in real life
and the one you'd see over the El train in the opening and closing shots
of his TV show *Welcome Back, Kotter.*

A kid named George Johnson played for Utrecht. We were almost
exactly the same age and height, and had matched up in the playground
since we were younger, so I knew him pretty well.

Johnson had a big reputation; the scouts who reported to college
recruiters around the country were buzzing about him, saying he was
the best high school forward in New York City. The only one who'd
formed a different opinion was a talent evaluator from Queens named
Tom Konchalski.

Though I didn't know it, Konchalski had been keeping tabs on me
since my junior year, when Gil Reynolds entered the Eagles in a spring

tourney at Mosholu Montefiore Community Center in the Bronx. It was one of the better local competitions, mainly city teams, with a few from Westchester and possibly one from Connecticut.

Konchalski attended, taking notes in the legal yellow pad he carried everywhere. The Eagles won, and I was MVP, and I caught his eye. He kept it on me for the rest of my high school playing career.

He didn't have much company. During my senior year, Johnson was one of two New York high school players getting most of the attention from scouts. The other kid they were watching was Butch Lee, a guard with DeWitt Clinton High School in the Bronx—a top basketball school that had won the city championship the year before.

I knew of Lee's reputation, though we hadn't faced against one another on the hardwood. Since our schools were at opposite ends of the city, we didn't compete during the regular high school season. Also, we played different positions—I'd been converted to a center in my junior year, and he was a guard—so we wouldn't have gone head-to-head, even in the playoffs.

Lee had gone to the Five-Star Camp in Honesdale, Pennsylvania, run by another talent evaluator, Howie Garfinkle. Garfinkle put out a newsletter called *High School Basketball Illustrated* that was considered the bible of New York and New Jersey high school players. Almost every college basketball coach in the country subscribed to *HSBI*, and its success led Garfinkle to start his own scouting service. It was the first of its kind in the country.

Garfinkle was promoting Lee and had heavily showcased him at Five-Star. Some of the top young college coaches in America instructed at the camp—Chuck Daly and Bobby Knight were two originals—so kids who went there had an edge in getting noticed.

I would have loved to attend Five-Star, of course. But enrollment at the camp wasn't something I could realistically consider. My parents didn't have the money to pay for it, and Garfinkle never thought enough of my abilities to ask me to his summer-long, invitation-only program.

That only made the chip on my shoulder bigger and heavier. I had no problem with Lee catching the eyes of scouts. He was a great, tough-minded player, as I would see for myself when we eventually played together in a tournament.

But George Johnson?

He was the best forward in New York?

Really?

I'd faced Johnson many times in the playground and youth tournaments, and always outplayed—spell that *d-e-s-t-r-o-y-e-d*—him. A good enough finesse player, he was always put on his heels by my ferocity and determination. For me, winning meant everything, and Johnson could never match that.

The rivalry between our high schools was intense. Bay Ridge and Bensonhurst were bordering sections of Brooklyn with largely blue-collar, Italian American residents. The students came from similar backgrounds; a kid attending one school was likely to have friends and family in the other. All kinds of bragging rights were at stake.

I marked the dates of our two scheduled games with the Utrecht team ahead of time. The bleachers were always packed for our showdowns, and the teams came ready to play. They would be noisy, hard-fought contests.

I overpowered Johnson. Dominated him defensively and offensively. In the first game, I scored 36 points off him. In the second, I hit 29. He couldn't stop me.

Unfortunately, Utrecht was more cohesive. They had very good performances as a squad and won both games. The losses were hard for my team to shake off. Everyone was badly disappointed. But besting Johnson was a consolation for me. He walked off the floor demoralized in spite of Utrecht's victories.

I was in his head. I'd proven something. To him, myself, and to anyone else who had paid attention.

Tom Konchalski was one of those people.

AS MY SENIOR YEAR AT FORT HAMILTON WENT ALONG, Coach Kern occasionally gave me brochures and copies of recruiting letters from universities around the country. Even though I'd had a very good season with the

Tigers, I didn't make it onto the radar of the top-tier basketball colleges. But a few candidates grabbed my attention.

Arizona State University was one of the first to invite me. The Sun Devils had reached the NCAA several times under head coach Ned Wulk, and his winning reputation was a lure. I decided to check out the program there.

I also heard from the University of Dayton, a private Catholic school in Ohio. A special education teacher at Brooklyn's Westinghouse High named Artie Hirsh had seen me play in local tournaments, and his old friend Jack Butler was a coaching assistant at UD. He told Butler and head coach Don Donoher about me, and they wanted to arrange a visit.

Marquette University in Milwaukee, Wisconsin, was another school that expressed interest. The Warriors was a competitive team that had recently recruited one of the top forwards in the country, Maurice "Bo" Ellis, for what it was hoping would be a championship push. Although the school wasn't high on my list, it felt my talents would add to the team's chances, and I agreed to tour its campus and facilities in June after visiting the rest.

Then another opportunity came in an unexpected way.

Right around Easter break, I was asked to play in a tournament by talent scout Mike Tynberg, who coached a team called the New York Gems that brought together elite players from around the city. Tynberg's offer was a high mark of respect, and I was honored to be considered. But I'd already committed to a tourney in Baltimore—the Baltimore Shootout—with Lester Roberts's Brooklyn USA team and knew I might have to miss one or two of the games. When Tynberg said he'd be okay with that, I joined his squad.

The tourney was at the Hoboken YMCA and pitted us against New Jersey's best. The Gems had a big-name front court—Mike Pyatt, an All-City player at Bishop Dubois High; Bernard Toone, a junior at Gordon in Yonkers; and myself. Our guards were supposed to be Butch Lee and Jackie Gilloon, a kid from Memorial High School in Hudson County, but for one reason or another, both were no-shows.

Tynberg needed replacements fast and turned to Konchalski to plug the holes. Konchalski picked Paul Eibeler from Holy Trinity, and

Andy Sabo, who'd been on a Forest Hills, Queens, team with All-City player Ernie Grunfeld.

Just the year before, Konchalski had helped the University of Tennessee recruit Grunfeld for its basketball team, the Volunteers, based on his tight relationship with its assistant coach, Stu Aberdeen. Though I didn't know it at the time, Howie Garfinkle's nickname for Konchalski was "Tennessee Tom" because he attended so many high school and youth league games as a scout for Tennessee.

When it comes to basketball, it's a very small world.

A worn red-brick building that was over a century old, the Hoboken YMCA had a typically small gym with an overhead track so it could be partitioned for half-court games. Without Lee and Gilloon to help with the scoring, I knew I'd have to lead our offensive charge and had a great series opener that helped carry the team to a win.

Right afterward, I headed down to Baltimore with Lester Roberts and couldn't play in the tourney's second game—what turned out to be a tough loss for the Gems. But I came back with an MVP in time for the finals.

Our opponent in that round was a team from Jersey City. Its two best players were sophomores—Mike O'Koren, a small forward, and Luke Griffin, a guard. O'Koren was a sharpshooter and presented the biggest threat.

I had another hot game coming off the Shootout, holding O'Koren in check and scoring almost at will. Our team won the series two games to one. We were still celebrating our victory when a thin, gray-haired man in a cardigan sweater and loafers came straight over from the bleachers. I'd seen Konchalski and his legal pad before, and recognized him as a scout. But he'd never approached me.

"You were terrific, Bernard," he said, squeezing my hand. "I think you would've gotten the MVP if you'd played the second game."

I thanked him for the compliment. His hand was still locked around mine; Konchalski had some kind of grip.

"Feel like grabbing some dinner?" he asked. "My treat. I'd like to discuss an excellent college basketball program."

That was all I needed to hear.

After changing into my street clothes, I let Konchalski lead me over to a nearby diner, where I think I ordered a sandwich or burger. It was my first time eating out anywhere.

"Bernard," Konochlski said from his side of the booth. "You familiar with the University of Tennessee Volunteers?"

I shrugged. It barely rang a bell.

"Most people have heard of the football Vols," Konchalski went on. "But the *basketball* Vols are really coming on strong in their conference. I can vouch for its head coach, Ray Mears, being top notch. And his assistant, Stu Aberdeen, would very much like to discuss their plans with you."

Aberdeen was already in town, he explained. He'd been seeking a complementary player for Grunfeld, the Forest Hills kid, and Konchalski had told him all about me. In fact, he'd told him I was better than Grunfeld. But I wouldn't find that out till later on.

What I did know was Konchalski's reputation as a decent, trustworthy man. He loved the game of basketball and had flawless instincts for pairing up players and coaches. I was also impressed that Aberdeen had flown up to meet me in person. No other recruiter had gone that extra mile.

I told Konchalski I was interested, but wanted to discuss the offer with Ken Kern, my coach at Fort Hamilton, before setting up a meeting. Konchalski agreed that was a good idea and said he'd wait to hear back from me.

When I asked Kern's advice, he brought up Grunfeld right off.

"Sounds like a good fit for you," he said. "It would be fantastic having another player on the team with New York basketball acumen."

That was all the encouragement I needed. Soon afterward, I spoke to Aberdeen on the telephone. He suggested we have dinner at a place called Mama Leone's.

Wow.

The closest I'd ever come to eating at a restaurant was the diner in Hoboken. But Mama Leone's was a famous Italian restaurant in Manhattan's theater district. It had been around for almost a hundred years and was an unofficial landmark. I accepted the invite in a heartbeat.

Before we got off the phone, Aberdeen said he would make dinner reservations and pick me up that evening. I told him that would be great, gave him my address, and asked him to wait outside the main entrance. I was glad he didn't ask about coming upstairs to meet my parents. I wouldn't have known how to explain that we didn't have visitors.

A few hours later, I left the apartment in a dress shirt and my comfortable suede Playboy loafers—bunny logo, and all—and went to the twelfth-floor hallway window where I'd once spent Sunday afternoons gazing down at the players on the front basketball court.

Aberdeen was waiting near the big glass entry doors. Although we'd never met in person, and it was already getting dark out, I had no trouble recognizing him. A short, bald white man in an orange blazer, he definitely couldn't have been mistaken for anyone from the projects.

But I should give you the full, crystal-clear picture.

When I say short, I mean *extremely* short, as short a man as I'd ever seen—possibly five feet one or two in his shoes. When I say bald, I mean *shiny* bald, his head smooth and round as a cue ball. And when I say orange, I mean *bright* orange, the official color of the University of Tennessee. It was a tradition for UT coaches to wear orange blazers at games, but bringing that custom to the streets of Fort Greene, Brooklyn, was not something I'd have recommended. Not in a million years.

The jacket might as well have screamed VICTIM.

And I haven't even mentioned his trousers.

They were plaid.

Orange, yellow, and blue plaid.

I remember staring downstairs for about thirty seconds, frozen with disbelief. Then I snapped myself out of it, rushed to the elevator, hit the lobby button, and waited nervously for the car, hoping he wouldn't get jumped before I reached him.

I felt like slapping my forehead. *Does the man know where he's at?*

Stu had no more trouble recognizing me than I did him. At six feet seven, all arms and legs, I wasn't easily confused with anyone else, although, funny thing, it *would* happen later that night.

We took a car service into Manhattan; he'd had the driver wait for him outside my building. I had only ridden in a car once or twice before, and felt like I was going off on an adventure.

With its troops of busy waiters and red-and-white checkered tablecloths, Mama Leone's seemed like another world. I could hear murmurs of conversation, and the clicking of silverware against plates. It was a bright, lively place with diners laughing, smiling, and enjoying one another's company. I could not help but compare it to the inhibited silence around our table at home, my father eating alone and apart from us in the back room.

This was something new. Something I'd longed for without even knowing it existed.

People looked around as the long and short of us walked into the crowded dining room, Aberdeen in his neon orange blazer, his head barely reaching my chest. I sported an afro at the time, which made me look even taller alongside him.

Then I heard one of the guests blurt out, *"Oh! Hey! It's Moses Malone!"*

If anyone in the place wasn't staring at us yet, that clinched it.

That year, Moses Malone, a six-foot-eleven center from Virginia, had become the first basketball player in history to vault directly from high school to the pros, signing with the American Basketball Association's Utah Stars. His breakthrough made headlines around the country and would open the way for young phenoms like Kobe Bryant and LeBron James to do the same in the future.

Since we were both black, tall, and wore 'fros, I guessed the mix-up was understandable. I really didn't mind; I'd played against Moses in a tournament upstate called the Seamco Classic and thought he was a great athlete and nice guy. If people were going to mistake me for another player, I was okay with it being Moses Malone.

Curious eyes stuck to us like glue as we were led to our seats.

I'll never forget that meal. The baskets of bread and rolls, the giant platters of antipasto, the heaping portions of spaghetti in meat sauce . . . the tastes, the smells, and the cheerful professionalism of the wait staff as they served us.

At first, the place settings confounded me. I saw all the different utensils, the multiple forks and knives, and ate with trepidation, not knowing when to use them. But I watched the other diners out of the corners of my eyes and discerned the order. They were working inward toward the plates. Once I realized that, I could settle down to eat and enjoy myself.

Aberdeen was a smart, charismatic guy with a brain full of basketball knowledge. It made him a great salesman for the Volunteers and UT in general. He hardly mentioned finances, but explained the college's commitment to academic and athletic excellence. He discussed Konchalski's enthusiasm for me and underscored how much weight that carried with him and Head Coach Mears. The team wanted to build on the tough, lightning-quick style of basketball that Grunfeld had brought from New York, and they saw tremendous possibilities in our sharing the court. I would have a chance to grow as a player even as the Vols benefited from my talents.

When Aberdeen dropped me off at home, full of good feelings and incredible Italian food, I thanked him profusely for dinner and assured him I'd be continuing the evaluation process with his school.

He and his flashy getup had left quite an impression on me. I knew it wouldn't be long before my eyes burned from the orange-and-plaid again.

FIRST, THOUGH, I PLANNED TO FOLLOW THROUGH on my standing agreements. Arizona State had already purchased an airline ticket for me. I owed it to the school—and myself—to fly out and see the campus.

Back then, NCAA regulations prohibited official visits until the high school basketball playoffs concluded in late March. Since classes were still in session, the trips had to be scheduled for weekends, so the whole thing was whirlwind.

I left from LaGuardia Airport in Queens. It was my first time flying, and I recall feeling amazed that a large commercial plane could become airborne with hundreds of passengers and their stowed luggage aboard, and then have enough fuel in its tanks for the five-hour flight to Arizona. As we taxied onto the runway, I paid nervous attention to the flight attendant's safety instructions for buckling our seatbelts, putting on the oxygen mask in an emergency, and using the seat cushion as a life preserver.

None of it exactly settled me. I didn't enjoy takeoff. The loud whine of the turbines, my popping ears, the g-forces shoving me back against my seat. It was a far cry from how I felt riding the J train.

Once we were up, I grew calmer. It was a beautiful sunny day, and I had a window seat. Looking down at the city from the air took my breath away.

I slept for the bulk of the flight to combat my recurring anxieties. My seatmate was a professor from the university, and she must have picked up on my nervousness as a rookie flyer. When I wasn't dozing, she made pleasant small talk. It helped the trip go by faster.

The visit itself wasn't very memorable. A delegation of school coaches and officials met me at the airport in Phoenix and drove me out to the Tempe campus. Then we went somewhere for lunch.

They mostly talked finances. I was offered a full academic scholarship and various stipends and grants that could legitimately slip through NCAA loopholes. But there was hardly a word about academics or their long-term goals for the basketball program.

Scholarship packages are a big part of every college recruitment offer. I couldn't afford tuition. My family didn't have any money. So that was an important consideration. But their hard sell was a turnoff. I was interested in learning how they'd make me a better person and player. They only seemed interested in the player.

I remember a strange thought crossing my mind. *What if I went to the school and something happened to me? If I was injured on the court or had some other serious issue? Would I receive the proper help?*

My misgivings weren't strictly logical, but I trusted them.

I struck Arizona State off my list even before getting on my morning flight back to New York.

DAYTON WAS SCHEDULED for a week later. The school made an earnest offer and had a reputable basketball program, but nothing stood out about it or convinced me we'd be a good match. For one reason or another, I wasn't confident its system would aid in my development.

Back at Fort Hamilton, I asked Coach Kern to let Dayton know I wouldn't be signing there. I'd done the same right after my trip to Arizona. I respected the schools' interest in me too much to keep either one hanging.

That left two colleges on my list, Tennessee and Marquette.

Tennessee was up first. I would fly down to visit its campus the very next weekend.

KNOXVILLE SITS DEEP in the Tennessee Valley, and the countryside around it was awe-inspiring from the air. I'd played in tournaments in the Catskill Mountains, but had never seen anything as vast and green as the Smokies. The range sprawled on and on below as my plane banked toward the airport.

The mild Southern weather was no letdown. It had been chilly in New York and I'd worn a coat heading to LaGuardia. But I could sling it over my shoulder stepping off the plane.

I can still see my greeting party—city officials, representatives from the school's athletic department, Stu Aberdeen in his full orange-and-plaid glory, and a young woman who played for the Lady Vols, UT's female basketball team. Aberdeen had wanted me to have a student's perspective on the school and arranged for her to be my chaperone for the entire visit.

You wouldn't think anything could have made me feel more welcomed. But the biggest eye-opener by far was a banner held up by the group declaring it Bernard King Day in Knoxville. Before I could recover from my surprise, a town leader with the delegation read the official proclamation. Right there at the terminal.

Bernard King Day.

For a kid from Fort Greene, it was like being reborn from one life into another. But I didn't have a chance to soak everything up. No sooner was the proclamation read than I was loaded into a car and then driven straight to the university under police escort.

The ride was like being inside a kaleidoscope, with all kinds of sights and impressions rushing over me. I remember the clean, fresh air pouring through my window, the trees lining the road, the blue Tennessee River on my right, and those emerald-green Appalachian slopes in the background.

As we rode along, flanked by police cruisers, my hosts explained they'd booked a room for me at a downtown hotel. The Hyatt Regency. A hotel? The other two schools I'd visited had put me up overnight in dorm rooms.

But we weren't heading over there yet. There's a football game at the school this afternoon, and we want you to enjoy it, Bernard. Don't worry about your bags. We'll retain them for you till after the game, and then make sure they're brought right over to the Hyatt. If that's okay.

Oo-kay, I thought. *Got it.*

Neyland Stadium, where the Tennessee University Football Vols play their home games, holds over a hundred thousand spectators and is the sixth-largest outdoor sports arena in the world. When we arrived that afternoon, it was filled to the upper deck with fans from the area. Although it was spring break, Aberdeen's blazer had loads of company. I saw orange jerseys and T-shirts all around me.

Earlier that year, the New York *Daily News* had selected me as one of the city's top-five high school players. As part of the awards presentation, we'd walked onto the court at Madison Square Garden during halftime at a Knicks-Celtics game. We also were given tickets to the game. It was the final year of the legendary "Rolls-Royce Backcourt," with Walt Frazier and Earl Monroe, who'd won a championship with the team in 1973. Along with Dave DeBusschere, they were two of my favorite players while I was growing up. Although our seats were in the upper deck, I'd savored every minute of that experience.

When we arrived at Neyland Stadium, I was given a VIP seat near the field . . . no nosebleeds this time. Looking around, I was amazed by the bowl's enormity. It was hard to imagine a more imposing sports arena than Madison Square Garden; it had seemed huge to me. But Neyland dwarfed it by comparison. I could hardly believe a school could have a venue holding that many spectators. Not somewhere off campus, but *on campus*.

The game was deafeningly loud from start to finish. Led by black quarterback Condredge Holloway, the football Vols were on their way to a 7-2-3 season that would climax with a victory over the Maryland Terrapins in the Liberty Bowl, their second bowl appearance in two years. The fans expected a win and showed it by making an uproarious racket.

At the end of the second quarter, I was brought downstairs into the area beneath the stadium and then walked out onto the field at halftime to be introduced to the fans. It was the largest crowd I'd ever seen. Hearing my name on the public address system, followed by the cheers rolling down from the stands . . . cheers for *me* . . . I was blown away.

After the game, I received another introduction—this one to Holloway, who hadn't just gained fame as a star quarterback, but as one of the first African American quarterbacks to play college football. Back then, the Vols were one of the best teams in the nation, and that made Condredge not just a big deal, but the *Big Deal*, at Tennessee. Meeting him was an honor.

Next stop, the Hyatt so I could check into my room. I don't know if my hosts noticed me staring out my car window at the hotel. The last time I'd stayed at one was when I was fourteen or so—the night Lester Roberts and our whole Sports Unlimited team jammed into two rooms at a small, no-frills place in Baltimore.

This was something else. Modern and upscale, with rows and rows of windows. I craned my head to see how high they ascended, thinking the hotel's design resembled a manual typewriter with several tiers of keys.

I spent the next few hours touring UT's campus. I'd never seen anything like it. Classes were not yet in session, and with very few students around, the grounds seemed even more spacious than they were. Everything was clean and pristine. You didn't see a scrap of litter anywhere. Not on the grass, the footpaths, or the sidewalks. I was overwhelmed by the expansive majesty of the campus and charmed by everyone's friendliness and graciousness.

Another life.

I recall being brought to the basketball stadium, Stokely Athletic Center, all while school representatives talked about how well the Vols were doing and outlined their plans for making the team even better. They said they were intent on improving its national profile and guaranteed I would be a starter in the upcoming season. Then they went on to discuss the academic side of things.

The presentation was balanced and well rounded. I was skeptical of their promise of a starting role with the team—I didn't think any coach would, or could, make that decision till he saw me in an intra-squad scrimmage—but was convinced I would have the opportunity to contribute.

Last on the agenda was Knoxville's finest restaurant. I had a nice, easy time at dinner with Stu Aberdeen and the chaperone from the Lady Vols, both of whom shared their thoughts about the school and city.

When I finally returned to my room, I felt equal parts excitement and exhaustion. It had been a long, long day, and I dropped into bed like a rock.

My flight back to New York left early Sunday morning. By the time I boarded it, my mind was made up.

There would be no trip to Marquette. I knew my future was with the Tennessee Vols basketball team.

No one could have predicted that I was about to become half of the biggest show in its history.

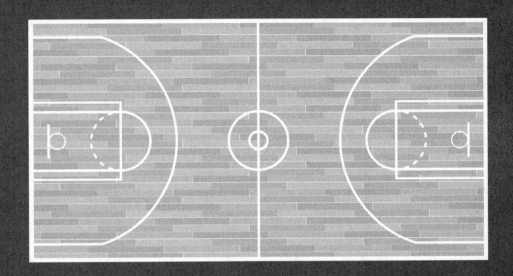

The Big Orange

6 | The Ernie and Bernie Show

A pair of king-size suitcases, basketball, and a solitary goodbye. That was my final six weeks in New York in a nutshell.

I'm going crack open the shell, though not all of it's easy.

I didn't discuss my trip to Tennessee with my parents after coming home. They'd been unmindful of the whole recruitment process, and nothing changed after I decided on UT. Other than to tell them where I was going, I didn't see any purpose in talking about it.

I remember catching a nationally televised Vols football game a week after my return, and feeling delighted that they represented my future academic institution.

"This football team's from my school," I said, gesturing at the screen. "They're famous. One of the best."

Mom and Dad seemed vaguely pleased. But they were disinterested more than anything, and I left it at that. I now believe they were as happy as they could be. Their capacity for happiness was limited, and I think distancing themselves from their emotions was part of how they got along.

I didn't let their indifference blunt my excitement. Soon I'd be going off to college. There was a lot to do before I left.

At Fort Hamilton, Coach Kern and my guidance counselors helped me with the form-filling procedures for entry to UT and securing the full four-year scholarship I'd been offered. Meanwhile, my high school basketball season was over. With several weeks to go before I left New York, it meant a busy slate of summer basketball.

I'm not sure whether or not Gil Reynolds's funding from the Restoration program had dried up—New York saw tough times in the early seventies, so it's possible—but he wasn't taking his team on the road much at that point. It left me available for Lester Roberts, who was assembling a team to play in three big youth tournaments—the Baltimore, Boston, and Philly shootouts.

Our squad was identical for the first two tourneys. Skip Wise, the sharpshooting guard I'd faced years before in Baltimore, was on it with me. Also Kenny Carr and Terry Tyler, two guys who went on to play in the NBA. Another top high school player, Bruce Campbell, rounded out the lineup. He never made the pros, but would have an outstanding college career.

I don't recall which of those tournaments originated first, or if any one of them directly inspired the others. But I do know the Boston Shootout came about in response to racial tensions over the city's school busing program. African American NBA referee Ken Hudson had convened a group of civic organizers to see if they could pull together the black and white communities, and that led to the Boston Shootout in 1972.

Within a couple of years, the Shootout became the premier high school tourney in the country. Over three weekends in June, Hudson's tournament would draw the best players from all over the East Coast.

At the Baltimore series, our All-Tournament team, as Lester christened us, was quick to build up a head of steam. We took that tourney, and I was awarded the MVP.

Boston followed in June, and it would be a more important tournament for me than I knew.

Although he never said a word about it—not before the Shootout, not during my time with the Vols, not once afterward—Coach Ray Mears flew up from Tennessee to watch me play. I only found out about it over forty years later, when Tom Konchalski revealed he had been there . . . and that my performance in the series would be deeply stamped into his mind.

As for me, I just wanted to compete. Our team would be going up against the best high school and playground players in the nation, at the hottest amateur basketball event in the nation. One of the squads would be the All-America Boys Basketball Team, which was made up of kids named as top players by *Parade* magazine. Though I'd averaged 25 points and 28 rebounds a game in high school, I was never chosen for the team.

Enter the chip on my shoulder.

The truth is, I don't remember many specifics about my individual performance in Boston. Odd as that must sound—I've just mentioned the series was very important for me—it often happened when I was playing at my highest level of ability. And I'd established a personal standard of dominance against All-Americans.

At the Boston Shootout, I was in the Zone.

This might a good time to explain what I mean by the term. It's probably somewhat different from how other athletes use it. In the Zone, your perception of time and space changes. You don't have to look for seams in the defense. You know where they are because you feel them. Not see, but feel. So when you make a move, you know where everything around you is coming from. It's in slow motion. And because it's in slow motion, your execution is refined. You can navigate wherever you want.

When I was in that space, the game was like abstract art. With figurative art, you see the objects being represented, and you can identify them. But abstract art is different. It's doesn't necessarily connect to a visual reality.

So for me being in the Zone was an abstract state. And the pieces around me, meaning the other players, were all part of the feeling. It was a knowingness of placement within every moment of the game . . . my placement, my teammates', and the opposition's.

In Boston, I was at peak performance. I'd arrived at that abstract place. It wasn't about separate moves or plays, but rather my knowingness of the game as it unfolded on the court.

One thing I *do* recall—and only because it briefly removed me from the action—was taking an unintentional elbow to the eye from Mike Mitchell, who went on to play at Auburn University and eventually became an NBA All-Star with the San Antonio Spurs. The open cut above my eye wouldn't stop bleeding, and I was forced to leave the floor and take care of it.

Mike had done nothing wrong. If you didn't play a tough, physical basketball in Fort Greene, you would find yourself watching from the sidelines. I got stitched up and reentered the game after the next time-out. It was no big deal to me.

But it was for Ray Mears. I think he realized right then what Brooklyn-bred toughness was all about. It showed him what kind of player I was and gave him a better sense of what I was bringing to his team.

As I said, I never knew Coach Mears was in the gym. Unlike Stu Aberdeen, he must have left his orange-and-plaid ensemble back in Tennessee. I wouldn't have missed him in the crowd if he'd worn it, not even if we'd been playing in the dark.

At any rate, our team won the tournament, and I was once again named MVP. We'd beaten the leading high school players in the country, so that trophy was pretty special.

In August, the All-Tournament games went to Philly. We won our third series in a row, and I picked up another MVP.

When I left for Tennessee later that month, I had a different mind-set than I'd had during my recruitment visit. I always felt I was an outstanding player. But that great run of championships and MVP awards was the sort of experience that cements confidence. It had validated me—validated my talent—in my own eyes.

I still didn't know if Coach Mears really envisioned me as a starter with his Vols. But I knew I could make it hard for him to see things any other way.

I DIDN'T HAVE MANY CLOTHES or other belongings, but used the money I earned from a part-time job to buy two king-size suitcases. I've always felt it was better to be overprepared than underprepared, and not just when it related to basketball.

I'll never forget getting ready to leave the familiar surroundings of Fort Greene to begin a new phase in life. I was going off to an institution of higher learning. Starting *college*.

I had never discussed it with my parents. For them, it was enough that you graduated high school and found a steady job. They did not look beyond those modest aspirations for their children.

I'd excitedly begun packing the night before my Friday departure. The next morning, I showered and dressed in a very quiet apartment. Dad had gone to work without saying a word about my future. My brothers and sister were either at summer school or out with friends.

It was just me and my mother at home.

Mom did not offer any advice or encouragement as I put some last-minute items into my suitcases. No conversation passed between us. Except for the bags, I could have been heading out for a typical day of classes at Fort Hamilton. Before leaving the apartment, I paused, looked over at her, and said goodbye.

I was waiting, I suppose. Still waiting for something more from her.

"Bye," she said. That was it.

I went out to the elevator and pressed the call button. When the door slid open, I entered the car without a backward glance. I didn't feel anxious about leaving home. There wasn't the slightest tinge of melancholy or sadness in me. I knew I'd never live there again, and wouldn't miss it.

Sadness? I was *ecstatic*.

Downstairs, I pushed through the glass lobby doors and turned past the spot where, a few short weeks before, Stu Aberdeen had stood waiting for me, all decked out in orange and plaid. Then I walked to Park Avenue, alongside the buildings where I'd grown up, and hailed a taxi.

It was nine o'clock in the morning. My plane would leave at one. *Four hours and counting.*

When a cab finally showed up, I lifted my bags into the trunk and took a final look at the basketball court where my dreams came to life and I developed the skills that opened the way for me to attend college.

Thank you, I said silently. *Thank you.*

Thirty minutes later, I was at LaGuardia Airport.

Fort Greene was in my past.

I never looked back.

MY STATE OF MIND aboard the plane was very different than it had been on my first recruitment trip. Not only was I not nervous, but I'd managed to buckle up without a hitch. Bernard, the jet-setter.

Okay, not exactly. But with five flights under my belt, I felt more comfortable in the air. My run of tournament wins and MVP awards had bolstered my confidence that I'd be able to fit in with the Volunteers basketball team. Finally, I knew what to expect in Knoxville. I wasn't going on a visit this time, but heading off to my new home for the next several years.

My first weekend on campus was a lot of fun. I was assigned a room in Gibbs Hall, the athletic dormitory that exclusively housed members of the football and basketball teams. My roommate hadn't yet arrived, and there wasn't much to do until Monday's freshman orientation, so I unpacked, got acquainted with some of the other students, and wound up being invited to a black fraternity party.

Boy, did I have myself a time. Back then, TV shows like *Soul Train* and *American Bandstand* would start new dance crazes faster than you could keep up. The big one that summer was the Bump, and we could get extremely creative with it. As to how creative, I'll leave it alone . . . other than to say that I met a pretty Southern girl with imagination to spare, and that it was quite the kickoff to my freshman year at the University of Tennessee. After that night, I never dreamed it would be anything but a great experience.

I spent the rest of the weekend relaxing and learning my way around campus. Then, on Monday, everything shifted into high gear. The coming days were taken up by meetings with academic advisors, the process of matriculation and choosing a study program, tours of the buildings, and filling out rafts of forms. I chose the College of Communications. Broadcasting had always interested me and I thought I could excel at it.

Gradually, my teammates started to arrive. My roomie, Mike Jackson, was a sophomore from Nashville. Besides being a nice guy, Mike was a solid, reliable guard, and we got along well from the start. Though his race didn't matter to me at all—I only cared about a guy's playing ability and will to win—he was the only other African American on our Vols squad.

Then there was Ernie Grunfeld. As big-city kids, we hit it off right away. Ernie was coming off an outstanding 1973–1974 season in which he'd averaged over 17 points a game. His performance had made him one of the best freshmen in the Southeastern Conference, and now he knew he'd have help at the offensive end going into 1974–1975.

We both expressed excitement about playing together, and I recall wondering aloud how it was that we'd never run across each other in New York.

"Hang on, B, you're wrong," Ernie said. This was one of our first conversations on campus. "Our high school teams scrimmaged."

"Scrimmaged?"

"Right. Against each other," Ernie said. "It was an exhibition game."

I shook my head. "Nope. Never happened."

"How're you so sure?"

"'Cause I'd remember if it happened," I said. "But I don't, so it didn't."

"But I do," Ernie insisted. "So it did."

I was getting lost.

"All right," I said. "We scrimmaged. Accepted. What'd you think of how I played?"

Ernie shrugged. "I don't remember," he said.

"But you just told me . . ."

"I remember our teams scrimmaging," he said. "Remembering how you played is something else. Though I can vaguely picture you being there that day."

I looked at him. *Vaguely?*

"Kinda, yeah." Ernie shrugged. "I mustn't have been too impressed."

I didn't say anything for a minute. Ernie shrugged again.

"So," he said. "Now I reminded you of that scrimmage. You remember me?"

I gave him a look.

"No," I said.

"No?"

"Not at all," I said coolly.

We cracked smiles. That's just how it was between us. Ernie and I clicked the way only two kids from the New York playgrounds could click. While we outwardly had very different backgrounds, we shared the heart and grit that comes from battling your way up through tough times and persistent obstacles. I was a black kid from one of the poorest and most dangerous sections of Brooklyn; the single white family there moved out when I was in elementary school. Ernie was a Jewish kid from Forest Hills, a solid middle-class neighborhood in the borough of Queens. But that doesn't tell his whole story.

Ernie was born in Satu Mare, Romania, to Holocaust survivors. In 1963, when he was nine and his older brother, Leslie, was seventeen, his parents immigrated to New York to escape anti-Semitism. They didn't have much money, but scraped enough together to open a fabric shop, where they worked long hours to feed their family.

Not long after the Grunfelds came to this country, Ernie's brother died of leukemia. It was major blow to Ernie, who idolized him. Ernie spoke almost no English and didn't fit in at school. The loss left him without his best friend.

Maybe being on the basketball court helped Ernie channel his emotions. Maybe it was an escape. And maybe feeling like an outsider gave him something to prove. It was all those things for me, and I think we've always had that in common. But what's unquestionable is that Ernie became a fierce competitor. He hated giving in. To injuries, to other players, to anything.

"I never get hurt and I never get tired," he'd say.

No wonder we were a good combo.

A writer, I believe from *Sports Illustrated*, once called us "Thick and Thin." It was a suitable description. Ernie and I stood at almost the same height—he was six feet six, an inch shorter than I am—but we were built differently and had very different games. I was long limbed and quick as a whip; he was thick around the chest and waist, with legs so strong they could have been made of concrete.

Good luck if you were an opposing player who wanted to outpace or outmaneuver me. Better luck if you tried using your weight against Ernie. Our skills and physical strengths were complementary. Neither of us was going to wear down. Neither of us could be blocked. We both had high basketball IQs, knew how to handle the ball, and could get around any defense you threw at us.

It would be a while before we played in a meaningful game together, though. One reason was because the collegiate basketball season started in November, and NCAA rules prohibited official practices until October. That left us with a month before we could work out at Stokely with our team coaches.

Those first weeks at school were a happy time. I focused on settling into my classes and went out with Ernie and his best friend, Jerry Finestone, on weekends. We'd go to parties on campus or hit the student hangouts on Cumberland Avenue—the Strip as we called it. Running straight along the north end of the campus, it was lined with bars and restaurants.

For me, the environment was new, fresh, and exciting. I felt a freedom, a *lightness*, that I had never before experienced in my life.

But I've mentioned obstacles. Late that month, I suddenly ran into one that became a defining moment for me at school. It was like pulling to a short stop on the open highway.

My freshman English professor had assigned the class its first paper. I don't recall the topic now, but I felt I had done a decent job. When it was returned, I was stunned to see it all marked up in red. No, stunned doesn't describe my reaction. There isn't a single word that could.

How had it happened? I'd believed all along that I was getting a good education in Brooklyn's public schools. But I was not. I was *not*. That unsettled me.

Attending Fort Hamilton in Bay Ridge helped prepare me for being a minority among Tennessee's larger white population—of its thirty-five thousand students, only a thousand were African American. But my inner-city grade school education had not given me the educational tools I needed to thrive in a higher-learning institution. Additionally, as an introvert, I was socially unprepared to move out into the larger college culture. Coupled with the reality that I'd been educated to get a blue-collar job, the transition was devastating to me.

For the first time since my arrival at Tennessee, I felt out of place. The person who'd arrived in June to have a day named in his honor was someone else. Bernard King, the basketball player. He looked like me and sounded like me. But he was an outer shell. Tough, strong, but still a shell. The wearer of my Game Face.

Underneath, I was Bernard, the Fort Greene kid with low self-esteem. Alone in a strange place, I felt unequipped for the challenges ahead.

I kept those thoughts to myself. Didn't share them with anybody. When Ernie went into town that weekend, I told him to go on without me. I didn't give him a reason.

As I'd always done, as everyone in my family was conditioned to do, I took it to the back room.

This is a problem, I thought. *This is a serious problem.*

How would I rectify things? It wasn't like a foul call in basketball. I couldn't review the tape and hope it would be reversed. Nor could I improve my writing skills overnight. But my basketball scholarship meant nothing if I failed my courses. I could either maintain the required grade-point average, or flunk out and go back to Fort Greene. And I'd promised myself I would never do that. I would not allow it.

Needing a plan, I met with my counselors in the athletic department to work one out. Since I wasn't required to declare a major until midway through my sophomore year, I reluctantly dropped the core communications curriculum, acknowledging I wasn't ready for it. Instead, I concentrated on electives that would allow me to maintain my GPA, while working with a tutor to improve my academic skills.

That eased my anxieties. But abandoning my major was painful. The reality that I had not been properly schooled as a young person bothered me. I never forgot that rude awakening.

In September, the Vols started basketball practices, and my excitement about it swept aside any lingering stress. Collegiate rules prohibited official practices at the arena, so we would go to a recreational gymnasium on campus.

I was elated to finally get on the floor with my teammates. Though the school's general student population shared the gym, we arranged to meet there when we could control one of the courts and hold scrimmages against each other.

Then, it was on to our workouts at Stokely, where I first met Coach Ray Mears. He was a tight-schedule sort of man who would block out our practices to the minute—precisely fifteen minutes for this drill, ten for that, five for something else. Once a drill was in progress, he'd stand with his hands behind his back like a general watching his troops on parade. His idol was George S. Patton, and I think he deliberately mimicked his stance.

I remember Coach Mears and his assistants leading us through a series of stretches and warm-up exercises to start our practice. They were easy but different from those I'd done in high school—or with Gil Reynolds. Thinking they would elevate the team's conditioning, I was happy to learn them.

Not so for the basketball drills. From the onset, I knew they would do nothing to enhance my skills. In fact, I worried they'd cause me to backslide.

We had six baskets in the gym. Coach Mears had the guards and forwards line up at one basket, the centers at a second. That left four baskets unused while most of us stood around and watched.

"Okay," he barked at the centers, a basketball against his hip. "I want to show you some big man drills!"

Big man drills? Big . . . man . . . drills?

What on earth were big man drills?

I would find out soon enough. Slowly, mechanically, the players positioned themselves under the rim and put up the ball. It was like watching basketball robots. Robots programmed to execute moves from a basketball instructional book. One written for grade schoolers.

An eye on the clock, I crossed my arms and waited.

Then waited some more.

Ten minutes later, I was still waiting.

The basketball robots seemed to be taking their time.

It was a jolt to my sensibilities. I was accustomed to working swiftly. To executing drills at game speed. Whether practicing by myself in the playground, at Fort Hamilton, or with Gil, it was always *movemovemove* . . .

On my very first day at Stokely, I was growing roots. I remember thinking, *Is this what I'm going to do for four years?*

I just couldn't see it.

At last, I peeled off from the group and went over to Coach Mears, who was standing with his back to me. When I tapped him on the shoulder, he spun around and looked straight up into my face.

"What d'you want, King?" His voice was brusque.

I gestured around the gym.

"Coach, we have six baskets here, and we're only using two of them," I said. "How about I go over there to that third basket, and I work by myself?"

He screwed up his features. I'd find out later on that he was shocked anyone would approach him in the middle of practice. For him, everything was strictly regimented. We weren't supposed to stop.

After a few seconds, he nodded and tossed me the ball. I had the sense he'd been wondering what this new kid from New York was all about.

"Okay, King!" he snapped, pointing across the floor. "Go on over to that basket!"

I worked out at a fast clip, shooting, rebounding, moving . . . doing more under the basket in twenty minutes than the other guys had done in that entire practice.

Mears watched me work on the court, his shoulders square, hands folded behind him. I think he saw I wasn't like any other player he'd coached before, and didn't know exactly what to do about it. Change doesn't come easily to someone who's had success doing things a certain way, and he'd been a winning basketball coach for over a quarter century.

I should perhaps mention here that I was only the third African American ever to play for the Vols. It wasn't coincidental that the numbers were so small; for a while, major universities shied away from recruiting inner-city players, labeling them as streetballers who couldn't incorporate their games into organized systems. No one voiced this in public, but word had traveled around. Like most generalities, it wasn't entirely fair or accurate.

I didn't play that way. My style wasn't freelance or showy. I was a conservative player when I walked into Gil Reynolds's gym, and he'd only reinforced that type of game. Gil had a system he'd developed over many years. You played within it or were out the door.

I want to distinguish between conforming to a system and converting to a new style of play. My style of play was all about speed, aggressive physicality, and explosiveness. It was about finding ways to score, whether by attacking the basket or drawing fouls so I could get to the free-throw line. But I could adjust that style of play to fit any system. It was the essence of being coachable. Of being a team player. For me, those qualities were one and the same.

Coach Mears got a close look at my style of play at our initial practice. But that was just half the equation. The other half was how I would adjust that style for the team. In his mind, it was still an open question.

He got his answer at our first intra-squad scrimmage. When I made 23 of 24 shots, it dawned on him that he'd have to change.

At a coaches' meeting afterward, an assistant named Gerald Oliver gave him an extra push.

"Bernard knows what he's doing," he said. "When it comes to what's best for his game, we don't need to teach him anything."

Mears didn't argue. Oliver had confirmed what he already knew. And to his great credit, Mears quickly altered our practices and his system.

I didn't realize the effect I had on him until many years after. It truly never entered my mind. My focus was on helping the Vols win, not changing the culture or the system. I thought: *This is how I play. This is how I work out. This is what got me here. And ultimately it makes me a better asset to the team.*

From that point on, our practices were faster paced. The elementary moves under the basket were removed from our set. The University of Tennessee Vols were playing a different game.

"We changed our brand of basketball," Mears said later on.

And that brand was very exciting to me, our coaching staff, and eventually our fan base. Ernie and I were a perfect tandem. With him on the left wing and me on the high post, we could split team defenses and score almost 50 points a game. As we entered the preseason exhibition season, word about us got out. Tennessee was historically a football school. We understood that. But we were entertaining, we were good, and we were selling out every game in advance.

That gave us instant swagger. We could hardly wait to get the season underway with Ernie and me leading the charge.

But things wouldn't go as planned. Just six days before the start of our season, Ernie went down in an exhibition game.

Hard.

IT WAS SUNDAY, NOVEMBER 24. We were having a final tune-up against the Western Kentucky Hilltoppers, one of our main conference rivals, on our home court. As Ernie was driving to the basket for a layup, he lost his footing and hit the floor.

CRASH.

Every man on our squad held his breath. It wasn't like Ernie to show pain. But you could see it all over his face as the coaches and medical staff clustered around him.

The court at Stokely had a Tartan rubberized surface with extreme traction. No basketball player likes playing on that kind of floor. Wood is far more forgiving. You slide on wood. It has bounce. But when you make a move on rubber, it can trip you up. If you fall, it has no spring, no give. It can cause injuries.

I didn't think about Ernie being hurt as he was brought to the University of Tennessee Hospital. When you're in the thick of battle, you have to stay focused, do whatever you can to win.

I scored 22 of 25 shots that game. It gave my teammates and coaches a boost—one we'd all need after we got the news about Ernie's injury. The X-rays revealed a simple fracture of his shooting arm, and there was no telling how much time he would miss. It depended on how quickly he healed.

Ernie frowned glumly when we saw each other. He'd never been injured before. Now his season was in jeopardy.

"It's broken right here," he said, tapping his cast. "Just above the wrist."

I shook my head. "What bad luck," I said.

We couldn't hide our disappointment. As his friend, I felt for him and understood how tough it would be watching from the sidelines. And from a team perspective, I knew we faced a challenge. Ernie was an All-SEC player. There was no replacing his production or court presence. And we had stiff competition in the Southeastern Conference. Alabama, Kentucky, and Auburn had been great the year before, and were improved teams going into the season. The rest of the conference was also more competitive.

After the game, Coach Mears told reporters that my roommate, Mike Jackson, would man the left-wing position until Ernie's return. A junior named Austin Clark took over right-wing job, and Rodney Woods, a senior, would be our point. Bob Brykalski, a seven-footer, had the low post, but he was nursing an ankle sprain that made his ability to stay on the court a big concern.

At the same press conference, Mears officially named me a starter. I'd had a dominant preseason, so that was no surprise.

"He has everything it takes to become a big star in this game," the coach said about me.

I appreciated his comments, but stardom wasn't on my mind. Ernie was our leading scorer. Now I knew that responsibility was mine to start the season. I'd have to shoulder the offensive workload.

Our season opener was at home against the Wisconsin Badgers. I went into it wanting to make it clear we'd be okay in Ernie's absence. Though I didn't need added motivation, I wound up getting some anyway.

As our teams gathered around the jump ball circle to shake hands before tip-off, one of the opposing players—I guessed he would be responsible for guarding me—leaned in close and whispered something I will never forget.

"If you let me get mine, I'll let you get yours."

I couldn't believe it. I'd been in more youth tournaments than I could count, and never heard anything like that from a player's lips. How could he think so little of himself and debase the game in that way?

How could he want to trade off in points?

All those thoughts raced through my head in under a second. I was shocked and disgusted. But I didn't show it.

My voice flat, I said, "I'm gonna get mine anyway."

And I kept my word. At the age of seventeen, and in my first collegiate game, I totaled 42 points and grabbed 15 rebounds . . . and that was before fouling out after thirty minutes of play. It remains the highest-scoring debut in Tennessee history and stands as the ninth-highest scoring performance by any Vol player.

That Saturday night we won 85–65, and I got mine.

THAT FIRST VICTORY CAME at a considerable price.

After the game, I felt some soreness in my knee and then noticed it swelling up. A medical exam later that week revealed that I'd torn knee cartilage.

The Stokely Tartan had struck again. At one point in the game, the bottom of my sneaker had caught on the rubber floor and led to the injury.

The doctors told me I'd need open knee surgery to remove the damaged tissue, but said I could wait to take care of it in the offseason. Since the tear probably wouldn't worsen if I played with it, my staying on the court depended on my ability to handle the pain.

That left me with an easy decision.

With Ernie out for the foreseeable future, I wasn't going anywhere.

IN BASKETBALL, the competition is always feeling you out, putting your toughness to the test.

Once, when I was playing some older guys at the Farragut Houses, the neighborhood bully shoved his elbow into my stomach so hard I doubled over, gasping for air.

I can see it as if it was yesterday. I was on the far side of the court, in the center of the lane. The court was fenced in, and when he hit me, that fence blurred in my vision. I'll never forget that.

I used the same hit once, when I was in the NBA, to send a dirty player a message.

You close your right hand, making a fist. You take your left hand, open palm, and you place it against that fist. And you take your right elbow—now you've got leverage—and BAM! Right in the stomach.

The kid at Farragut was a lot older and bigger than I was. The neighborhood bully.

I did nothing.

He got the better of me that day. He knew it. I knew it. I can still see his face.

I promised myself afterward that I'd never let it happen again.

The Vols' second matchup of the 1974 season was a nonconference road game against the Michigan State Wolverines.

I was tested that Saturday night.

Michigan's two top players were its co-captains, Joe Johnson, a guard, and C. J. Kupec, a center, who'd also played tight end on the varsity football team. The year before they beat Bobby Knight's Hoosiers to become Big Ten champions, so they were entering the new season with attitude and a head of steam.

With the Vols coming to face them on their home floor, Michigan's head coach, Johnny Orr, would have shared several things with his team. He knew Ernie was out of commission. He knew that left me as our top scorer. He knew I'd dropped 42 points against Milwaukee, and he'd have gotten scouting reports on my excellent preseason. It's also likely his team had read Ray Mears's positive comments about me, as well as a magazine article ranking me as one of the nation's fifteen best college prospects. And they all knew I was a freshman.

It only made sense that they'd key their defense on me. Any team would've done the same.

I was ready.

It was a punishing battle. Kupec outweighed me by thirty pounds, and he and Johnson were all over me on defense, swinging their elbows into my chest and sides.

But I didn't forget the lessons I learned in Brooklyn. Guys wouldn't mess with me. I wouldn't allow it. I didn't back down and gave as I received. If an illegal elbow was thrown at me, I'd give one back. Otherwise you developed a reputation. Before you knew it, the scouting reports on you would say, "Hit him and he'll disappear." That's exactly the kind wording you'd see. "Hit him and he'll disappear for the night."

Early in the second half, Johnson got called for a foul against me under the boards and took an angry step in my direction. I didn't back off. The next thing I knew we were shoving and bumping chests.

The referees broke it up before things got out of hand, and Orr and his assistant coach had to be restrained from stepping onto the court. But things calmed down.

The Vols played a solid game that night, and we were ahead for most of it, holding a 7-point lead with fifteen minutes left in the game. But Michigan got hot down the stretch, and we made some mental mistakes. Also, I missed some opportunities to score from the line because I'd gotten into foul trouble.

In the end, Michigan defeated us 78–74.

I didn't like it. I hated to lose. But I'd hauled down 13 rebounds and led both teams in scoring with 34 points. The Wolverines would remember that. Word would spread that I couldn't be intimidated.

I'd passed a test.

There were more to come.

OUR NEXT FOUR GAMES were one-sided victories for the Vols. During that run, I was the highest-scoring college player in the nation, averaging over 30 points a game.

The team's confidence grew. We were a very cohesive unit, and we were holding our own without Ernie.

In the short time since I'd landed in Tennessee, my life had changed tremendously. There were stories about me in the papers. Everyone on campus recognized me, and the same was true in Knoxville. Up in his radio broadcast booth, John Ward, the Vols' legendary play-by-play announcer, took to calling me "King of the Volunteers." I got a kick out of that.

What I was doing as a seventeen-year-old freshman had caught people by surprise, but it honestly didn't surprise me. I'd played against older kids my whole life, so competing against upperclassmen was nothing exceptional. I just cared about winning and enjoyed seeing our fans charged up. I'd gone from playing in front of a few hundred people in high school gyms to performing before sellout crowds of almost thirteen thousand at our home arena, with students camping out at the box office to buy tickets before they disappeared.

The excitement was fantastic.

Then, around the middle of December, we got some great news. Ernie's arm had healed faster than the doctors originally expected, and his cast was about to be removed. Coach Mears penciled him in to rejoin us before the end of the year, providing he came through a team scrimmage without setbacks.

Though he'd picked up some rust during his layoff, Ernie was cleared to play and returned to our active roster for a December 31 home game against the University of Vermont. It was our first nationally televised game of the season—ABC was broadcasting it on time-delay—and the crowd was in wild New Year's Eve form. With all the anticipation around Ernie's return, Stokely Athletic Center was jumping that night.

We pounced on Vermont from the start and won 115–66. I scored 40 points, but Ernie was the main attraction. When he stepped onto the court, taped wrist and all, the ovation around us was unbelievable. Our fans brought every kind of noisemaker you could imagine and let loose as if they were in Times Square to see the ball drop.

In fifteen minutes of play, Ernie went 6 for 9 from the floor, hit 4 of 6 from the free-throw line, and scored 16. But the main thing was that he got out there and didn't feel any pain.

Ernie was back. We were finally going to play meaningful games together. And the timing couldn't have been better.

In two weeks, we were playing the Kentucky Wildcats on their home floor—our first meeting of the season. Kentucky was one of the storied basketball colleges in the conference and the Vols' longtime rival. Our records within the SEC were tied at 2–2. It was going to be our biggest game so far.

The Vols were ready to make a statement.

AS AN INCOMING FRESHMAN PLAYER, I had heard a lot about the Tennessee-Kentucky rivalry. But hearing about it and experiencing it were two different things.

A solid bunch from top to bottom, the Wildcats had a bruising front court with six-foot-ten freshman Rick Robey in the low post, and Mike Phillips and their star performer, Jack Givens, as forwards.

I knew going up against that front line was another test. This time, though, I'd be taking it under a spotlight. And not alone.

The Ernie and Bernie Show. That's what they'd dubbed us in Tennessee. We didn't make it up. Mears loved catchy slogans, and he'd worked on it with the Vols's public relations department.

It caught on fast with everyone but my mother. "I named you Bernard," she said when she heard it.

I didn't argue with her.

As we arrived at Rupp Arena, I was glad Ernie was finally with us. With some added games on the schedule for the holiday break, he'd had three games to strengthen his arm and get back his rhythm and stamina. He was close to a hundred percent.

I wasn't at all nervous that cold January night. Going back to my childhood tournaments, I'd never felt nervous before a game. In the visitor's locker room, I lowered my head and mentally prepared for what was sure to be a very physical contest. I visualized success against that formidable Kentucky front line, saw myself ferociously driving down the lane for layups and dominating the boards for rebounds.

I was intense as I entered the tunnel, my Game Face on. Around me, my teammates were pumped up, bouncing on their knees like they had springs in them. We knew Kentucky's reputation. They were a powerhouse, one of the country's top teams. But Ernie and I could combine for 50 points on a nightly basis. When you have a pair of scorers like us, you're in every single game. Nobody's going to blow you out. We could compete against anyone and win.

Then it was game time. Boos and curses rained over us as we stepped onto the floor. They were louder than any crowd noises I'd ever heard. Until that moment, I hadn't understood the full depth of hostility between the Vols and the Wildcats. The bitter contempt didn't stop at the student bodies of our respective schools. It seeped through to our athletic departments.

Both teams were well coached. Ray Mears and the Wildcats's Joe B. Hall were legendary. As you might expect, the game was close, with the advantage swinging back and forth. We fell behind by 7 points early in the first quarter, cut the deficit to one, then fell behind by a dozen. By halftime, we came to within 7, but then the Wildcats pulled ahead again, taking a 14-point lead.

We kept up the pressure. I had a very good second half, Ernie got red hot, and we tied the score at 65–65. Then, with just under eight minutes left in the third quarter, Ernie nailed a couple of free throws to put us on top by a point.

Then the momentum turned. Kevin Grevey, a guard who later played for the Washington Bullets and Milwaukee Bucks, was Kentucky's high scorer. But their bench made the difference. It was deep, and one of their strongest assets. Late in the game, a player named Dan Hall came off it to make two big shots and a couple of rebounds that helped push the Wildcats to a 6-point win.

The loss was upsetting, but that wasn't the worst of it. As I exited the floor, jeering Wildcats fans started pelting me with oranges. It took a moment before I realized what was going on. Then it struck me. Orange was our school color.

I was the best scorer in the SEC. King of the Volunteers. This was Kentucky's version of a freshman initiation.

If someone hadn't tossed a lit cigarette into my hair, I would have ignored them. At first, I was too shocked to believe it. But then my afro started to burn. I could feel it and smell it. I pulled the cigarette from my hair, turned toward the spectator in what seemed like slow motion. Even the fans around him looked stunned.

The guy stood there staring back at me.

It is one thing to be passionate about your team. But what he'd done was dangerous and belligerent, and what I saw in his eyes was pure malice. I tried to go after him, but felt several restraining hands on my arms, guiding me to the locker room.

By the time the press entered, I'd calmed down about the incident. I wasn't about to forget it, though. Our team hadn't made the statement we'd desired. Not that night. But there would be others.

As the reporters assembled at my locker, I spoke to them in slow, measured words.

"The Wildcats outplayed us," I said. "They were the better team today." Then I paused and made a vow. "As long as I am playing for the University of Tennessee, Kentucky will never beat us again."

I don't know if the people in that room took me seriously. I'm sure some thought my words were emotional, resulting from my disappointment over a tough loss. But what they thought didn't concern me.

I knew. I *knew*.

Eventually, so would everyone.

HIS NAME WAS JACKY DORSEY. He was a freshman forward with the University of Georgia Bulldogs, and a *Parade magazine* All-American.

Georgia fans, and certain members of the press, were calling Dorsey the best rookie in the Southeastern Conference. Some Georgians were magnanimous enough to say I was almost as good.

Coach Mears made sure I knew. He posted his stats and the articles in the shower room. He also put our stats on the wall, side by side. I'm first in scoring. Dorsey's first in rebounding. Like that.

Mears understood the competitive drive. He gave us material to read as we prepared to scrub clean. He believed in getting his guys fired up.

Let's just say it worked. I grew tired of looking at the comparisons.

When I checked the schedule, I saw that February 1 was the date of our first game against Georgia. We'd be on the road. The Georgia arena would be packed with thousands of fans. The game would be locally televised. As one newspaper said, everyone watching in their living rooms would zero in on the matchup between Dorsey and me.

Sometimes I'd decide to be dominant, take my game up a level. Georgia was one of those times.

Jacky Dorsey, the best freshman in the conference? I intended to end the debate once and for all.

That night, a group of Georgia fans were waving a banner at tip-off. A very large banner. It said Jacky Dorsey was number one. They needed several pairs of hands to hold that banner up over their heads.

I scored 31 points by halftime, and that banner sank like the *Titanic*.

I finished that game scoring 42 points and pulling down 18 rebounds. Ernie also had a terrific night and canned 29. Together we combined for 71 points, 2 more than the whole Georgia team.

The final score was a 105–69 blowout, Vols over Bulldogs. Dorsey only scored two in the first half until Coach Mears emptied the bench to rest our regulars. Though the game's outcome was decided by then, Bulldogs coach John Guthrie left him in to play our second line, possibly because he'd started the night edging me out for the SEC's high-scoring average. If he could hit enough buckets against our backups, Dorsey would hold onto his top position.

The added 2 points he scored before the final buzzer weren't enough. It left me averaging 27.9 points to Dorsey's 27.7 for the SEC lead.

One newspaper story the next day read:

VOL DUO DESTROYS BULLDOGS

Not since General William Tecumseh Sherman in 1865 have Yankees wreaked as much devastation on Georgia as Bernard King and Ernie Grunfeld did here yesterday . . .

You could almost say we did it in a New York minute.

Then something very unfortunate happened.

UT had a brief intercession in early February, so the Volunteers traveled straight from Georgia to Alabama for our next game against the Auburn University Tigers. It was February 3, just two days after our victory over the Bulldogs.

I was in my hotel room a few hours before the game when the phone rang. Coach Mears was at the other end of the line.

"I need to see you," he said in a heavy voice. "Right away."

I held the receiver to my ear. *This can't be good*, I thought. Mears usually spoke in a growl or a snarl. I'd never heard him sound that subdued.

After a second, I said, "Okay. I'll be right over."

I hung up, wondering what was wrong. The team was playing exceptionally well. I'd come off a great game. I couldn't figure it out.

When I got to his room, I saw that Mears wasn't alone. Stu Aberdeen was with him, and he looked as grim as the coach had sounded. It was the only time I ever saw Stu when his gaudy orange blazer seemed a bad fit for his mood. There was nothing bright about his expression.

Mears waved me into a seat and got right to it.

"Your junior high school transcript's been called into question," he said. "Someone wrote a letter to the NCAA suggesting it was revised."

I couldn't believe my ears. His words seemed unreal.

"Revised?"

"Altered to raise your GPA," the coach explained. "The junior high record counts toward your overall average. And based on what they've been informed, the NCAA's begun an investigation into whether you had the grades to be accepted to the university."

Stu leaned forward in his chair.

"They're sending people to New York," he said, "so they can look at the original transcripts."

I was quiet a minute. I felt like I'd walked into a bad dream.

"You said somebody wrote a letter," I asked Mears. "Do you know who?"

He shook his head. "That hasn't been disclosed," he said. "But you have to ask yourself who'd stand to benefit."

I understood what he meant. If a college team has interest in recruiting you, it can ask your high school to send along your transcripts. Once it reviews them, the team knows whether or not you meet the academic requirements for a Division One college—in other words, a school with a major basketball program.

There wasn't any way I could know how many schools saw my transcripts. You usually weren't informed unless they followed through. If there was a question about my grades, it would have explained why so few Division One basketball colleges tried to recruit me.

I'd thought all along that my high school GPA was acceptable. In the first half of my senior year, Coach Kern told me I needed to buckle down in my studies, and I'd attended night school at Erasmus High.

Every single night, besides practice and playing, I took the bus there and worked hard to raise my grades. Before the end of the year, I'd pulled up my average.

But now it hit me that a lot of universities must have passed on me early because my GPA wasn't right. I got it right by graduation, but some of those schools didn't circle back. They didn't know.

I could see how somebody in an athletic department would think: Here's a seventeen-year-old kid, putting up these mega numbers. Playing at a much higher level than everyone else. He wasn't an All-American in high school, and he's playing better than the All-Americans the blue-chip colleges recruited. How does he land at the University of Tennessee?

The truth was it happened because of Tom Konchalski. If it hadn't been for him, Tennessee might not have been interested in me. But he only brought me to Stu Aberdeen's attention late in the school year. By then, my GPA was okay.

Someone on the outside wouldn't have known the timeline. It might have appeared as if my grades were manipulated.

"I'm going to New York with the NCAA officials," Stu said. "Hopefully I can get things straightened out."

I sat there looking at their faces, speechless. I knew what was coming before Coach Mears spoke the words.

"Bernard, we can't play you in the meantime. I'm sorry."

It was still hard to believe. Two days before, I'd left Georgia on a high. But I'd suddenly crashed to earth. The thought of not being able to play, that I might lose my scholarship . . . the sense of inadequacy I'd felt since receiving that marked-up English paper in my first weeks at Tennessee . . .

I hadn't cried since I was a child. Now I dug my knuckles into my eyes to stop the tears, but couldn't do it. My Game Face cracked, and I tasted salt on my lips.

My suspension started with that night's game; the decree had come down from somewhere above Coach Mears's head. I sat out as my team lost 51–62, and I remember the coach stewing afterward. Though Auburn was physically larger than we were, the Vols were ranked the better team. In his eyes, they got a lucky break.

"We played a superior ball game! When you're outweighed by twenty pounds and out-heighted by three inches . . . we just couldn't play any better!" he barked to the press.

The next morning Aberdeen flew to New York, where he and the NCAA representatives went to Fort Hamilton and Sands to reexamine the original transcripts. They checked out okay. Two days after my suspension, I was cleared and reinstated.

I was relieved beyond my ability to express, but my benching at Auburn hurt us. We'd entered the season's home stretch right behind Kentucky and Alabama for the SEC title. With an easier schedule than either team, and face-to-face matchups against both of them, a win against the Tigers would have pulled us closer to the top of our conference and made us the odds-on favorite to win the championship.

Instead, we lost to them and then took another two defeats after I returned to the roster—including our showdown with Alabama. My suspension had knocked me off stride, but there was another issue.

The right knee injury I'd suffered early in the year was giving me trouble. I had a very high pain threshold, so that part was manageable. But as our season wore on, my knee would repeatedly fill with fluid. The swelling made it hard to bend.

Our head trainer had started draining it before and after every game. Occasionally, it would balloon during a game, and he'd have to drain it in the locker room at halftime. I'd wince as his needle went deep into my knee joint, then wait as a mix of blood, pus, and water flowed out through the transparent tube. When all the fluid was drawn, he would tightly wind adhesive tape around my knee to compress it.

Over the past few games, the inflammation had been hampering my ability to jump, run, and move laterally on the court. It had become so bad that Coach Mears was thinking I might have to be sidelined.

In my own mind, there was no chance I'd sit. Our losing streak left us facing the most important game of our season. On February 15, Kentucky was coming to Big Orange Country for our first game since they'd beaten us on their home court. If we were going to overtake them and stay in the SEC Championship hunt, I had to keep my promise.

The Wildcats couldn't be allowed to defeat us again.

THE VOLS' REMATCH AGAINST KENTUCKY was played on a Saturday afternoon in front of a loud, passionate, sellout Tennessee crowd.

It was surprisingly mild for February, the fifty-one-degree weather making life easier for the students who'd slept out, waiting in line for available tickets. The Ernie and Bernie Show had instilled pride and excitement in our fans. We didn't intend to let them down.

Our preparations for the game started the previous day, Friday, with Coach Mears and his staff going over how we'd defend Kentucky's schemes, then running us through offensive sets in the gym so we could fine-tune our timing and positioning.

Mears had been responsible for some controversy after our road loss in Lexington, claiming the Wildcats used a "karate defense" against us and hinting that the officials had turned a blind eye.

"They won't get away with it in Knoxville!" he barked.

Kentucky's head coach, Joe Hall, disagreed with him. Angrily.

"Our defense is aggressive . . . not dirty!" he said. "Ray Mears is just trying to create a psychological situation favorable to his Vols!"

Hall's opinion hadn't come out of nowhere. With Coach Mears, you could always count on some creative motivational gimmicks.

I've mentioned that the coach admired General Patton to the point that he adopted his physical bearing and mannerisms. What I haven't said is that he had the soundtrack from the 1970 film *Patton* looped into our locker room before practices and games.

As a proud American, I've always loved our country. I happen to think the movie was pretty good. But listening to that soundtrack every single day rattled my brain!

Finally, I decided to quiz my teammates about it, asking if the crashing cymbals and snare drums were making them as nuts as they made me. They all said yes. Then I polled them on whether they'd prefer a mix of more popular music.

Everyone chimed in at once. Resoundingly.

"Anything!"

"Seriously, B . . ."

"We'll take anything!"

Armed with that unanimous agreement, I passed the message along to Coach Mears in his office.

He seemed bewildered. "Wait," he said. "Are you telling me the boys don't like the movie *Patton*?"

"They think it's great, coach," I said. "George C. Scott . . . *wow*!"

"Then what's wrong with the soundtrack?"

"Nothing, coach," I said. "The soundtrack is also great."

"So what's the problem?"

"Well, I wouldn't call it a problem," I said. "It's just that they'd like some . . . musical variety."

"Variety?"

"Respectfully, yes. Contemporary music. To get them going before games."

Mears squinted at me for a long minute. Then he shrugged. "Okay, King. I'll see what I can do."

Within a couple of days, we found a jukebox installed in the locker room. It was loaded with the most up-to-date forty-fives.

I guess the coach saw it as a way to keep his troops happy.

Mears had another interesting team mandate involving our sneakers. I'm not sure where he picked it up. He'd served in the army in the 1950s, so maybe it was a carryover from boot camp.

After every practice and game, we had to stow our sneakers side by side on the second shelves of our lockers, toes pointing outward. The tongue of each sneaker had to be folded back, on top of the laces, and the outer laces had to drape down over the left and right sides of the shoe. I'm not sure what to say about that requirement, except that none of us really minded. We just saw it as keeping our leader happy.

For the upcoming game against Kentucky, Coach Mears pulled out all the stops. In the entrance to our locker room, and between the lockers and shower, we found Kentucky blue mats with the name WILDCATS printed across them in large white block letters. The mats covered the floor where they were placed, so you couldn't step around them as you entered or left the shower, but had to walk straight across the lettering.

I had no need for extra motivation, especially for that game, although my pregame routine was always the same. The Friday before a home game would be a long one after classes and practice, and I never ventured into town to relax. Instead, I would eat dinner in the cafeteria, then retreat to my dorm to rest and study the written scouting report.

Before going to bed that night, I'd filed all the Wildcats' plays into my memory. I woke up the next day in game mode, joining my teammates and coaches for an early-morning film session, followed by our traditional milkshakes, oatmeal cookies, and green Jell-o.

The athletic dormitory is connected to Stokely via a short, glass-walled skywalk. I always chose to go down to the lower level and walk into the arena through the parking lot. The locker room was on that level, and I could reach my cubicle unnoticed. I didn't want fanfare from the students who would line up below the skywalk to cheer us on. I preferred not to speak to anyone before a game. I was already in a different mental space.

At my locker, I suited up, putting on my left sock, then my right sock. I wore three pairs of socks because of Stokely's unforgiving Tartan floor; since I was flat-footed, they helped cushion me when I jumped for a ball.

When I was fully dressed to play, I closed my eyes, folded my hands on my lap, bowed my head, and visualized. My knee had been drained but was throbbing with pain, and I had to go deeper into my mental reserves of toughness and intensity.

I silently told myself there was no way a team led by Ernie and me would let Kentucky walk into our house and beat us. It didn't matter that the Wildcats were ranked fourth in the nation and held the top berth in our conference. All our home games were televised. We had classes to attend Monday. We weren't losing to them in front of UT's fans and student body.

Elsewhere in the room, Ernie was kidding around with the guys, being his usual gregarious and funny self. But he was no less determined than I to win the game.

Ernie was a great basketball player, friend, and teammate. We never had conversations about Kentucky. We didn't need to. We counted on each other to play our best. We were winners, unaccustomed to losing.

The team reflected our combined attitudes, Ernie relentlessly battling away while I led the charge across the floor, pumping my fists, exhorting my teammates to push harder. We would back down from no one on the court.

Now I suddenly heard our coaches gathering us together and knew my preparations were over. Opening my eyes, I got up and joined my teammates.

We headed into the tunnel, Coach Mears yelling out his encouragement.

It was just minutes before game time.

THE ENTRANCE TO THE COURT was shaped like the letter "T" and covered with a huge sheet of orange paper. As we waited in the tunnel, I moved to the front of the squad and said aloud, with fire in my voice, the words I'd been silently repeating at my locker.

"We don't lose to Kentucky!"

Then I heard John Ward introduce me and went busting through the paper onto the floor. I was always first, my teammates following me through the big T as their names were called over the PA system.

Stokely blared with sound and light. The brass band was marching around the arena, going up and down the aisles, playing our school fight song, "Rocky Top," while the fans cheerfully sang along at the top of their lungs:

Oh Rocky Top, you'll always be,
Home sweet home to me,
Good ole Rocky Top,
WHOA!

On the floor, the cheerleaders waved their orange-and-white pom-poms as we went through our warm-ups. We put on a show like the Harlem Globetrotters—no-look passes, over-the-head reverse dunks, trick shots, a display of basketball wizardry that brought the crowd to its feet.

Good ole Rocky Top,
WHOA!

The Kentucky players were introduced next, the cheers from the stands turning to lusty boos as they emerged from the tunnel.

Ernie and I traded glances. We understood the game's significance. And we knew what we had to do.

Our team was pumped, and we showed it right from the tip-off, shooting at over 63 percent in the first half. But Kentucky also came to play, and the Wildcats' big three, Kevin Grevey, Jack Givens, and Rick Robey, had outstanding games.

We made sure we were better.

All five of our starters hit the double digits in points. Ernie poured in 29; and Mike Jackson, 24; with our center Doug Ashworth and guard Rodney Woods combining for 26. I bucketed 24 of my own and dominated the backboards, grabbing 20 rebounds.

At halftime, we led 56–44. Then we pulled ahead 74–60.

But in the third quarter, Givens scored 10 and the score became 74–70. Robey also got hot.

They inched closer in the fourth, making a comeback push.

80–78.

88–86.

We didn't fold. The game was very physical, and I was in foul trouble for most of the fourth. But I stayed inside and wrestled down rebound after rebound, repeatedly hurling the ball off to Ernie, who'd go 11 for 12 from the free-throw line.

In the last few minutes, we moved ahead 98–92.

But it was Grevey's turn. Among the game's best shooters, he made a pair of jumpers, one from deep in the court. The Wildcats were coming on again.

The score was 98–94. Then 99–96.

With the clock down to about three minutes, Jackson got to the line and gave us a little space.

101–96.

Then Givens. A jumper. 101–98. They were breathing down our necks again . . .

In the last few seconds, Ernie drew a foul. Positioned himself on the line. Eyed the basket. Bounced the ball.

Shot.

It went in. *Swish*. All net.

I felt the crowd's roar in my belly. In my bones. Felt the floor trembling under my feet.

The score was 102–98.

Ernie shot again, made the basket, and the horn sounded. Game over.

Final score, Volunteers 103, Wildcats 98.

The roof blew off the arena.

We'd knocked Kentucky out of a tie for first place in the SEC, leaving them a game behind Alabama. And we'd done it scoring in the triple digits, something no Vols team had ever managed against them.

Oh, did we celebrate. The Vols were for real, and our fans had helped bring it home.

"Coming off a three-game losing streak, and having Rodney Woods and Bernard King injured . . . this has to stand with our biggest wins in my thirteen years here," Coach Mears told the press.

He was happy.

The same couldn't be said for Joe Hall, though you had to give him credit for composure and decorum. Sometime during the second half, he'd gotten hit in the head by an orange lobbed from the stands.

"I'm all right," Hall told a newspaperman before hurrying into the locker room.

If it hurt, he didn't let on.

WRITING ABOUT THE RIVALRY, I get pumped and feel like suiting up to play. Even after all these years, it comes back to me like it was yesterday. But when I get up for a glass of water, reality sets in. My body reminds me that playing is in my memories.

I'm also reminded that all my memories of Tennessee aren't happy ones. Some are deeply painful. It would be easy to ignore them, but they're part of my story. If I'm to tell it fully and honestly, they mustn't be pushed aside.

I'd turned to basketball to channel my energies. That was why I'd been recruited by the university. But off the court, away from the cheers, I was still in an academic environment I no longer felt altogether part of. Still an introvert. And still barely eighteen years old.

After a winning ball game, it was customary for our team to go upstairs and walk across the windowed walkway leading from Stokely to Gibbs Hall, where the lobby would be filled with individuals who came to congratulate us for our performance. There were students, members of the athletic department, Knoxville VIPs . . . all kinds of people.

I wasn't at ease with that. For me, it was an awkward situation. I did it once, early in our season, and realized I didn't like it. I needed time to decompress after the intensity of a game.

My routine leaving the arena became the reverse of what I did when I entered. I would always go out the back exit, walk around the corner, get to the dormitory, walk in its back door, and head straight upstairs to my room.

Bernard, the shy, socially awkward loner from Fort Greene, was still inside Bernard King, the basketball player. I couldn't balance the two personas. Couldn't make myself feel whole.

It wasn't going to get any easier.

7 | Outside the Lines

When I look back on my freshman season at Tennessee, I'm proud to say it was successful in many aspects. I earned first-team All-SEC and SEC Player of the Year honors. I led the Southeastern Conference with 26.4 points per game—setting a single-season Tennessee record—and led the nation in field goal percentage, making 62 percent of my shots. Possibly best of all, I'd totaled 24 points and 20 rebounds in our upset of Kentucky after missing our final workout because of my injured knee.

As a team, we were disappointed. Though we finished 18–8 overall and 12–6 within the SEC—not a bad record—a tie for third place wasn't our ultimate goal. We'd proven we were for real in the SEC, but couldn't wait to go after a championship again the following season.

Overall, it was a good start to my collegiate basketball career. I was proud of being a Volunteer. I loved our coaches, loved sharing the floor with Ernie and my other teammates, loved the enthusiasm our crowds brought to every home game.

But the euphoria I felt on the court was shaded by some very difficult off-the-court realities. Over the years, I've come to realize our inner and outer worlds are in constant interplay, each tugging at the other in ways both subtle and powerful. What happens around us shapes what's going on in our minds and hearts, and our thoughts, emotions, and attitudes will affect how we relate to everything around us.

I talked about balance at the end of the last chapter. When you're in mental and emotional pain, when you're not *right* within yourself, the weight of external situations can throw off your judgment and tip the scales so you make unwise decisions. And when you're young and in that sort of pain, the danger is even greater. By definition, youth is a time of life when one's mind, heart, thoughts, emotions, and attitudes are still unformed. They haven't reached full maturity.

I'd experienced some tough situations since starting college. There was the emotional upheaval of learning I was academically unprepared for Tennessee, and all the ramifications of dropping my communications major. Then realizing the basketball program wasn't initially suited to my skill level under Gil Reynolds's measuring stick. Tearing my knee cartilage. Going through the NCAA investigation and being sidelined at a critical part of the season. Wondering if I'd lose my scholarship and be forced to leave the university . . .

It was a heavy load for a seventeen-year-old to endure in just a few short months. But I couldn't go to my parents for advice and guidance. We'd never had that sort of communication.

Then I had to face the hardest reality of all.

Sometime toward the end of the season, Coach Mears called to ask me into his office. His tone reminded me of how he'd sounded in Alabama after finding out about my junior high school transcripts. But this time, it was even more serious. I didn't know what to make of it. Could the problem have somehow cropped up again? I'd thought it had been settled for good. But I was positive something was wrong.

When I faced him across his desk, I knew I wasn't mistaken. I'd never seen him so agitated.

"Bernard," the coach said. He looked straight into my eyes. "I just had a visit from the police chief."

I sat there, confused. What did that have to do with me?

Before I could say anything, he went on, "The chief told me he has officers on his staff that 'don't like that uppity nigger.' His exact words. Then he says, 'They're out to get him. And there's nothing he can do about it.'"

I felt my stomach turn to ice. Earlier in the season, Coach Mears had pulled me from the middle of a road game after receiving information about a threat on my life—someone had claimed he was going to shoot me on the court.

I'd been too stunned to ask questions. But the Vols were winning games in the conference, and I'd been getting a lot of attention in the press. I was a black man in a part of the country where old prejudices died hard.

That incident was my introduction to racial hatred in the South, and it stung.

This was worse, though. Much worse. This was the police.

"Do you know what they've got against me?" I asked. "Did the chief tell you anything?"

Coach Mears slowly shook his head.

"No," he said. "That was all." He took a deep breath. "I just wanted you to be aware of it."

The office was quiet. Mears had always offered suggestions when problems arose. Solutions. Now he was offering neither. I didn't understand.

I went back to my dorm room, devastated. It was one thing to be threatened by a deranged individual. Some fanatic in another state. But the local police? They were supposed to protect people from harm. How would I protect myself from *them*?

I had no idea what to do. I had a recognizable face in Knoxville. Everyone knew who I was. Where could I hide?

And there were other lingering questions. Why wasn't Stu Aberdeen with the coach in his office? He'd been with him the day I was called in about the transcripts, and was at virtually every other meeting of comparable gravity. He should have been present for that conversation. And not only Stu. We'd been warned of a threat to my safety by members of the police force. Someone from the district attorney's office should have attended. The university president. We all should have sat in front of the police chief and addressed the problem.

To this day, I wonder if Coach Mears told anyone but me about the police chief's visit. He was very focused on public relations. A racially charged clash between the school and police force could have had highly negative consequences for the Vols in 1970s Tennessee. And the team was his whole world.

I have no doubt the coach cared deeply about my welfare. This was the same person who slept in the hospital when I had knee surgery. But he was a man of his time and place, facing a problem of a sort he'd never encountered before. Maybe he hoped it would somehow go away on its own. That he could warn me and everything would be fine.

I don't know. I'll never have a definitive answer.

I didn't tell anyone about that meeting with Coach Mears—not Ernie, not my other teammates, no one. Instead, I retreated another step socially. The pain inside was too much to handle, yet I told myself I could do it alone. From the day I picked up my first psychology book, I'd always handled it alone.

But now I couldn't cope.

I tried numbing the hurt with alcohol and pot. Half the students I knew got high—we just called it "partying" in those days—and I told myself I was doing pretty much what everyone else did.

It didn't seem to be a big deal. This was the 1970s and there was a feeling of freedom and openness on America's college campuses. People streaked, inhibitions were loose, and pot was everywhere. Also, I only drank or smoked on weekends after Saturday games, and always made sure I was ready to play. I saw it as a way to de-stress and wouldn't let it affect my performance on the court or attendance of classes.

Of course, that didn't make my decision any wiser. In hindsight, I realize it was another way to disguise my unresolved problems . . . hiding them, not from the world, but from myself. It was a temporary remedy that didn't address the roots of my pain.

In the long run, nothing good would come of it.

I STAYED ON CAMPUS the summer following my freshman year. Most students went home on vacation, but after visiting my parents for Christmas, I realized that my life had changed, and that Fort Greene was not where I wanted to be. The crime and street gangs of Brooklyn were behind me. Despite what Coach Mears had told me about the police chief's visit, I was better off in Knoxville.

There were a couple of other reasons to stick around. One was that I knew I could improve my GPA with summer classes. Also, I'd undergone knee surgery immediately after the end of the NCAA basketball season, and needed to rehab my knee and prepare for the Vols sophomore campaign. The campus and its open, green surroundings were an ideal setting for it.

In 1975, the medical community had not yet developed the refined arthroscopic techniques that allow doctors to trim small, torn pieces of damaged knee cartilage—called the meniscus—using a fiber optic scope. The entire meniscus was usually removed by total meniscectomy, a much more invasive type of open knee surgery. But the meniscus is a natural cushion that helps the knee absorb shock and keep it stable. When you remove all of it, or even a large portion, from an athlete's knee, there are no guarantees he will come back to his previous form.

I had open knee surgery and a total meniscectomy. I never considered that it might impair my future ability to play. I just knew it had to be done so my knee would stop swelling and locking up on me.

I was in the hospital for several days after the operation. Though I wasn't aware of it at the time, Coach Mears slept on a chair outside my room. I realize now that he was keeping a sort of vigil, knowing I had no family there in Knoxville. I'll be forever indebted to him for that, God bless his soul.

After the knee healed up, I started physical rehabilitation. I'd never undergone anything like it before—the only time I was ever in a hospital was when I broke my arm as a kid—so the process was new to me.

The pace the therapists set out was very slow, and after a month or so, I decided to accelerate it on my own. I'd always done knee lifts and stretches as part of my strenuous conditioning routine, and knew I could intensify the exercises I was given. Besides that, I got a ten-speed bike and also started a running program.

That summer I rode my bike everywhere. In July or August, I got a part-time job with a local oil and fuel distributor—NCAA rules didn't allow student athletes to work during the school year, or I'd have done it sooner—and rode the bike into Knoxville to my employer's home office.

From there, we traveled all around the area to meet with his account holders.

My boss was a nice guy, and I enjoyed the various changes of scenery that came with the job. At last, I had some money in my pocket.

After a while, I was loaned a car, thanks to someone at the oil company—an old red Pontiac with a black top. Earlier, I'd learned to drive and gotten a license. With the campus deserted, and bus service into Knoxville stopping after 6 P.M., I was ecstatic to be fully mobile.

It should have been a great improvement to my quality of life. And at first it was. But the reality of the police chief's warning couldn't be kept in the back room. I could try doing that, try pushing it into the darkness and bolting the door, but I wouldn't be able keep it there for long. And it didn't help to pretend I could.

Reality has a way of letting us know we can't escape it. Eventually, it caught up to me, and I had to bear the consequences.

Inside and out.

I WAS DRIVING FROM THE STRIP one evening after picking up some takeout food when I noticed a police car close behind me.

As I turned one way, then another, it stayed in my rearview mirror.

I tried not to be too concerned. It wasn't the first time I'd suspected I was being followed. The police knew my car, and they knew me. But on previous occasions, they dropped back or turned off the road.

This one wasn't going anywhere. It kept a steady distance back.

They're out to get him. And there's nothing I can do . . .

I checked my speedometer, making sure I was under the limit. No problem there, I thought.

I drove on, slowing to a halt at a stop sign at an intersection that led to the campus entrance. Checked the mirror again. The squad car was closer now. Red lights flashed on its roof. Then I heard a voice over its megaphone ordering me to pull over.

The officer came around to the driver's side.

"What's this about?" I asked out my window.

"You ran the stop sign."

I looked at him. He'd been no more than two or three car lengths behind me. Near enough to see me halt.

"No, sir," I said. "I did not run the stop sign."

He leaned forward. "Bernard," he said harshly. There was venom in his voice. *Don't like that uppity nigger.* "You ran the stop sign."

I stared at him with a flat expression, my heart beating a hundred miles an hour. The cop had used my first name. He hadn't even asked for my license. But he'd known my name.

He stood outside my car another minute without speaking. Then he straightened up.

"I'm going to give you a break this time," he said, and returned to his cruiser without another word. He'd sent his message and was finished with me.

As I turned toward campus, my hands were shaking uncontrollably around the steering wheel. I'd been pulled over by an officer with a badge and a gun without just cause. Back in Brooklyn, I'd had bottles thrown at me because of my skin color. But being subject to harassment by an individual sworn to uphold the law . . .

It left me in a state of shock. Traumatized.

In my dorm afterward, I sat at the edge of the bed and listened to the sound of my breathing in the silence. A sense of total isolation had come over me. Suddenly, that room felt like the loneliest place in the world.

Message received, I thought.

Loud and clear.

BY THE TIME OUR TEAM BEGAN WORKOUTS for the 1975–1976 season, my knee was in very good shape. But the same couldn't be said for my psychological well-being. The police harassment was a constant source of tension. I was disconnected from everything—and everyone—around me. When I wasn't competing, I was in emotional and mental pain, drinking and smoking weed.

None of it affected me on the court; as a player, I was reaching a new level of maturity. But I was making immature errors of judgment outside the lines.

Those mistakes only compounded my other problems. The police would randomly stop my car, notice a pot seed on the carpet, search the vehicle, and discover a joint. I'd be fined for marijuana possession, and the incident would appear in the local newspapers. But when I read the stories, it was like reading about someone else. I wasn't the bad boy in the headlines. I wasn't out carousing with friends. I was self-medicating and it wasn't helping anything.

Eventually my actions would catch up to me, and threaten to take me from the game I loved. But I didn't see it coming.

In my mind, I had things under control.

8 | Game On

There was a tremendous buildup of anticipation for the start of my sophomore year with the Vols. The Ernie and Bernie Show had attracted a lot of attention in the NCAA and given Stu Aberdeen a great recruiting hand in the offseason. As a freshman, I'd played the post because we did not have a true center. But now, we gained one in six-foot-nine Irv Chatman, a New York kid with an incredible nine-and-a-half-foot arm span. We also had Johnny Darden, a pure point guard who'd go on to hold the school record for assists, and Terry Crosby, an outstanding wing player to back up Mike Jackson.

We started out of the gate at a running clip and never slowed down, lighting up the Southeastern Conference.

Two of that season's games stand out in my memory. The second, a late February game in Tuscaloosa, was against Alabama for the conference lead.

But the one I recall most clearly fell a month earlier on the schedule, on the road versus the hated Kentucky Wildcats.

Our team, coaches, and other personnel had flown to blustery Lexington on Friday, January 10, ahead of the next day's grudge match. During the flight from Knoxville on our private plane, we relaxed by playing cards, spades being the game of choice.

I'd never heard of the game before college. Back in Brooklyn, we only knew about dice games. But in Tennessee, it was part of campus life. I learned to play and became good at it.

At the airport, we boarded the bus for a short trip to the Hyatt Hotel. Coach Mears believed in first-class travel arrangements, and that meant each player had his own room.

I enjoyed the privacy that afforded. A close-knit group from diverse backgrounds, we all genuinely liked each other. But we spent an inordinate amount of time together traveling, attending publicity functions, practicing, and, of course, playing games. For a person to think clearly, he must have moments of solitude. I knew it as a fifteen-year-old riding the subway on Friday nights, and I haven't changed my view.

After check-in, we always dined as a group at the best spot in town. Well traveled, well fed, thank you, Coach. That Friday night, I dug into some great Southern cooking in Lexington. As a country singer performed, we clapped our hands, tapped our feet, and had a good old time.

Then it was back to the hotel for an early night's sleep. We aimed to be fresh for the big game.

Saturday afternoon, we had a quick pregame meal, went over the game plan, and, yes, finished off with our usual milkshakes, oatmeal cookies, and Jell-o. While an excellent team, Kentucky was no longer quite the dynamo it had been the year before. Even as we'd improved, the Wildcats were recovering from the loss of senior Kevin Grevey, who was drafted into the NBA by the Washington Bullets.

The Vols weren't going to miss him. And we still had to contend with All-SEC big man Mike Phillips, forward Jack Givens, and six-foot-ten forward Rick Robey.

We entered the game ranked ninth in the country and winners of our last two games. I'd fully recovered from my offseason knee surgery and was fortunate not to experience any loss of quickness or leaping ability. Memorial Coliseum was a new arena, a Kentucky jewel, and the Ernie and Bernie Show intended to christen it with a command performance.

The game's intensity was high from the tip-off. Kentucky held a major size advantage in the post because of Mike Phillips, their six-foot-eleven big man, who grabbed rebound after rebound as our bodies collided under the backboards. That was UK's tradition—fight for every possession.

They played us hard. But with Grevey gone, the Wildcats had no solution for Ernie. He carried us in the first half, shooting pull-up jumpers and making power drives to the basket. Our team saw what was happening and rode his hot hand, feeding him the ball whenever we could. There was no sense getting it inside to me. He was blazing past whatever Kentucky threw at him, knocking down shot after shot.

But this was Wildcats–Vols. Every game a seesaw. We got to intermission with the score 43–42 in our favor, knowing we'd have to battle for every point the rest of the way.

The second half resembled the first, the Kentucky crowd cheering louder and louder, our two teams making tremendous physical contact under the basket.

In the fourth quarter, the Wildcats surged. Phillips was a banging, crashing beast under the basket. I think he pulled down a record 28 rebounds before the game was over, and they led to several fast-break scoring opportunities for his team. At one point in the final quarter, I glanced up at the scoreboard and saw we were down 75–61.

Fourteen points. More than we had minutes left in the game. And there were no shot clocks to limit the time of possession.

We needed to get the ball into our hands and score.

A lot.

Our defense went into clampdown. Mike Jackson and Irv Chapman stayed cool and held Kentucky back from scoring by blocking, boxing out, getting their hands up in shooters' faces, grabbing hold of the ball and bringing it quickly up the court.

With seven seconds left in regulation, and the score tied at 79, we called a time-out.

The 'Cats had gone into a zone defense, giving up on man-to-man against Ernie, and I'd taken up the scoring charge in the final quarter.

"Coach, put in Austin," I shouted in the huddle. The noise around us was deafening. "Throw me a lob pass."

Austin Clark was our secret weapon on the bench in certain situations. Our best sideline lob passer. We'd made a play like it in another game; I think it was against Michigan at home.

Mears nodded. The ball was mine.

Oh, how I loved those pressure-filled moments. I could taste adrenaline at the back of my tongue.

I set up on the low right block as Austin was handed the ball. I moved up the lane quickly, faking as if I'd use a screen. I went backdoor behind the defender to our basket; the ball was in flight. Austin had thrown toward the right side of the backboard, exactly where I wanted it. But the alley-oop went high.

I skied as high as I could jump, barely getting my fingertips on the ball, then tipping it toward myself, gaining possession as I fell backward to the floor.

I'd practiced shooting while falling a thousand times. In the gym at Sands, I'd done repetition after repetition till it became muscle memory.

I released the ball as my left heel hit the floor and went flat on my back. It went cleanly through the net as time expired, giving us a 2-point lead.

But the Wildcats wouldn't quit. With five seconds to go, they ran a perfect fast break. Kentucky's guards started it, the ball going from Dwane Casey to Truman Claytor, who pushed it up the court in a hurry.

We went into a mild press, wanting to disrupt their tempo without fouling anyone and giving them a chance to win on free throws. Claytor went to Phillips, who snapped it to Merion Haskins, their forward.

Five seconds can be an eternity in basketball.

Haskins was my man. But when they started to run, I broke for the far end of the court, trying to keep the ball from going into the post.

I should have stayed on him. Should have taken care of him. Instead, he streaked past me and scored a wide-open layup.

The buzzer sounded.

Kentucky had tied the game and forced overtime. The arena shook with cheers and applause.

We didn't get down. We never thought we were going to lose.

OT was furious, our teams trading baskets and turnovers. Ernie was fouled drilling a fifteen footer and went to the line. Kentucky's coach Hall was livid, claiming nobody made contact with Ernie. Irv Chatman was hit, he argued. *Okay*. Chatman, a poor free thrower, playing with a broken cheekbone. The officials stuck with their call and Ernie made the free throw for a third point.

Score, 84–83.

But it wasn't over. Joe Holland, a Kentucky forward, got fouled and tied the game with one of two. 84–84. Then I gave us the lead with a steal and layup. 86–84. Ernie added to it, 88–84. Then Phillips with another rebound. 88–86. With just over a minute left in the game, I flicked one in from underneath, 90–86. *Still not over.* Claytor, with a long shot, pulled the 'Cats to within two.

Seven seconds left. We had possession. They fouled Mike Jackson and he missed.

Four seconds. They had the ball. The noise around us earsplitting, Givens launched a long shot from deep on the floor.

His shot went wide of the basket and the noise stopped.

Except for the horn. Everyone in the place heard the horn.

Game over, Vols won. Final, 90–88.

Afterward at our lockers, mobbed by the press, we were effusive about our teammates.

"Ernie was carrying us that first half," I told them.

"Bernard was amazing," Ernie said. "That shot he took wasn't lucky. He's hit those kind of clutch shots before."

"Give credit to Austin. He made a great pass," I said.

"I thought for a second I threw the ball too high, but I forgot how high Bernard can jump," Clark said.

As for Ernie's controversial free throw, Coach Mears laughed off Hall's complaint.

"It's like a player stepping on the opposing player's foot as he's trying to rebound," he said.

Our leader had spoken, and I'll let his be the last word.

THE VOLS FINISHED THE 1975–1976 SEASON with an overall record of 21–6, but came in second in the SEC right behind Alabama's Crimson Tide, who went 23–5, and whose conference record was 15–3 to our 14–4. For most of the season, we ran neck and neck for the top spot, but the deciding contest was in Tuscaloosa on February 28, with our schedule down to three games.

We went into that match a half game behind the Tide, with one less left to play, knowing it was probably for all the cards. The game was one of the hardest fought of the season, but we lost 90–93 in double overtime. Three points. The hardest thing was that both Ernie and I had to watch from the bench after fouling out in the last few minutes. We wondered what we could have done to change things on the floor.

It was a letdown to see Alabama move ahead of us in the standings and take the conference title. But the Vols had given their all and lost to a great team. We weren't hanging our heads.

My personal numbers that year were on par with my first. I averaged 25.2 points and 13 rebounds a game, shooting .573 from the field, leading the league in rebounds and field goal percentage. By the end of the season, I was second in SEC scoring behind Ernie, who smirked when he saw that he'd edged me out by a tenth of a percentage point.

"Twenty-five point three, B!" he gloated over the stat sheet. "Point three!"

I laughed. Ernie and I had no jealousy between us. The only stats we cared about were team wins and losses. We'd helped the Vols build on the promise of our preceding year, and that made me feel pretty good about what we'd accomplished.

Then I got a shot at every young athlete's dream.

In April, not long after the season ended, Stu Aberdeen phoned me. He said I'd received an invitation from the 1976 Montreal Summer Olympics Committee to try out for the United States men's basketball team. Trials would take place at a weeklong camp at the University of North Carolina.

Oh boy! I thought.

I jumped for joy in my dorm room, feeling like the eight-year-old kid who made his first-ever basket in P.S. 67's cafeteria. And things got better. Stu had told me Ernie was also invited to camp. I envisioned the two of us representing our nation together, competing against the best in the world . . .

But to do that, I'd first have to outperform America's best. What a challenge. This was why we played. It would be the biggest test of my basketball life.

Once my initial excitement died down, I put on my gear and immediately started to train. I went to the outdoor track where the UT sprinters practiced daily, asking to participate in their sessions. I'd run track growing up in Brooklyn and loved it. The guys happily accommodated me and were probably a little surprised to see me keep pace.

After every session, I went to the basketball gym and worked alone for a couple of hours, pushing myself harder than ever before. I left for North Carolina mentally, emotionally, and physically ready to go, filled with a burning desire to make my dream a reality. I had confidence in my work ethic, and was sure my performance at camp would show I belonged on the team.

On the flight to Chapel Hill, I thought, *I'm a two-time SEC Player of the Year. I led the conference in scoring and rebounding two years in a row. And I'm a Consensus All-American.*

The NCAA Consensus award was a distinctive honor. You had to earn it from four All-American teams: the Associated Press, United Press International, the National Association of Basketball Coaches, and the U.S. Basketball Writers Association. Only ten players in the country qualified.

I can do this, I repeatedly told myself. I would make my parents proud of me.

At the opening of camp, Dean Smith, the head basketball coach at the University of North Carolina, and coach of the U.S. team, put all the attending players through the paces to gauge our fitness, requiring us to do a timed one-mile run on the campus track.

I was glad I'd included track work in my preparations and grateful for my years of running across the Brooklyn Bridge. Now it would all pay off. The timed mile was a stiff undertaking; a few players vomited on the track and decided on the spot to go home.

I finished in fifth place. Walter Davis, a star forward from North Carolina—he would later spend fifteen years in the NBA—won the event. Walter wasn't a college All-American, but he certainly caught my attention.

Camp was very competitive, with a rigorous slate of offensive and defensive drills. We also played half-court and full-court games. After workouts, I would head straight back to my hotel, order room service, and review my performance on the court, pinpointing areas of improvement for the next day's drills.

At one point during the week, Coach Smith pulled me aside and complimented me on my defense. I was overjoyed; it was as encouraging a sign as I could've wanted. Then, on the final night of camp, the players were split into two squads for a formal basketball game, complete with referees. I knew it would be our final test, and I willed myself to dominance, outperforming every other forward on the court.

The next morning, I flew back to Tennessee. Classes were out for summer recess, and I again stayed on campus, working for the same oil distributor who'd hired me in my freshman year. I waited each day for a telegram from the Olympic committee, knowing they would have to contact me before too long. Opening Day ceremonies were July 17, with the players reporting to training camp in June.

One day, I returned from work to find a note slipped under my door—there was a telegram for me at the front desk. My pulse racing, I ran out of my room, bounded up the steps two at a time, and asked for the flimsy, yellow Western Union envelope.

I wanted to rip open the envelope right there at the reception desk. But I restrained myself, hurried back to the privacy of my room, and very gingerly opened it, careful not to tear apart the enclosed message.

Its first sentence stopped my heart in my chest:

We regret to inform you that you are not being selected for the 1976 Olympic team . . .

I cried like a baby. How could it be? I'd had the best camp of any forward there.

Slowly, I sat down on my bed, staring at the telegram, my eyes hot with tears. Waves of sadness passed over me. I stayed there for hours, not moving a muscle as day turned to night outside my window. I rationalized that the coaches must have noticed a flaw in my game, a weakness I'd somehow missed.

I would subsequently find out that Mitch Kupchak, a center, and Phil Ford, a guard, fellow Consensus All-Americans, made the cut. They played for Coach Smith's North Carolina Tar Heels. Forward Walter Davis and center Tom LaGarde were also Tar Heels selected for the Olympic team, though neither were All-Americans.

Of the twelve players selected, four—a third of the twelve-man roster—were Tar Heels. Ernie Grunfeld's selection as the only UT Vol would be stunning to me. I'd naively believed there was room for both of us.

But I was still unaware of all that as I sat with the telegram in my hands, barely noticing the room had gone dark; hours had passed since I opened the envelope. Finally I stood up, switched on the light, dropped the thin slip of paper into the wastebasket . . . and put the old chip squarely back on my shoulder.

My eyes were clear and my sadness had turned to resolve.

I resumed training the very next day. But not for the Olympics. That was behind me.

Although I would not tell anyone, I decided that my junior season would be my last as a college player. I began preparing for the next step forward in my life and career.

My sights were set on the NBA.

Game on.

IN JUNE, I WENT TO A ROCK CONCERT at the Knoxville Civic Coliseum, a few minutes from UT. I had a good time at the show and was slowly driving back toward campus with the heavy outflow of vehicles from the arena's parking lot, when the police stopped traffic so people could cross the street.

As I sat with my foot on the brake, a guy in the crowd banged his hand down on the hood of my Pontiac.

WHAM!

I looked out the windshield, startled. Was he drunk or just a troublemaker? I'd done nothing to set him off.

He slammed my hood again. And kept slamming it.

WHAM! WHAM! WHAM!

I pushed open my door and got out. It didn't faze him; he kept banging away. Thinking enough was enough, I started in his direction.

"Nigger, get back inside."

I turned toward the voice. It was one of the officers who'd halted traffic for pedestrians.

I motioned at the guy pounding on my hood. "He's bang—"

The officer interrupted me. "Bernard, get back in the vehicle."

I froze, dumbfounded. I was shocked. I had never been called a nigger before. I angrily turned toward the voice. This was like a replay of the time I'd gotten pulled over at the stop sign. And now another guy was involved and getting different treatment.

It did not escape me that he was white.

I didn't say anything to the officer. I knew better than to put up an argument.

Instead, I slid back into my car.

At last, the cop turned toward the guy in front. "All right," he said. "Move on."

The guy obeyed, but not without giving me a parting gesture. Stepping toward the opposite side of the street, he turned toward my windshield and flipped up his middle finger.

The officer didn't say a word. I hadn't expected he would.

I drove on toward the campus, the good spirits I'd felt leaving the concert gone. It was as if they'd dissipated in the hot Southern night.

I knew then that the police harassment would not go away. I'd have to live with it as long as I was in Tennessee.

I continued to train hard for the coming season and NBA draft. But my armor had thickened around me. I kept my emotions inside and allowed no one to penetrate.

Bernard King, the player, would not be denied.

But Bernard, the young man who loved the game of basketball above and beyond all else, was in icy hibernation.

THIRD QUARTER

●●● ○

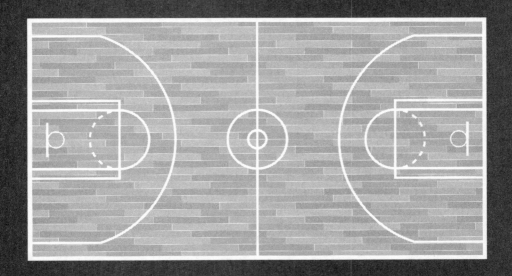

The NBA
Years

9 | Drafted

Love and passion can be intertwined. But they aren't the same.

I was eight when I fell in love with basketball. A boy. At that age, I thought it was all I needed. It allowed me to express myself, gave realization to my creativity. The court was a safe haven, a place of joy where I could block out everything around me: the crime, drugs, and desperation on the streets, and the constricting environment at home. When I had the ball, I felt complete. The world couldn't touch me.

That's the love.

My passion for the game was deeply ingrained in my spirit, burning through every tissue of my being. The passion drove me to compete, to be the best, and to overcome any obstacle, no matter what I might face.

Nothing could ever take that fire from my belly.

But when I was eighteen, in the winter of my heart, the love waned.

I kept bringing Brooklyn to the basketball. The stat sheets show my junior year at Tennessee was consistent with the previous two. I averaged 25.8 points a game and a career high 14.3 rebounds. I was once again a Consensus All-American and SEC Player of the Year. I played in twenty-six of twenty-eight games and set a school record of 22 double-doubles (points and rebounds). Nine of them came in a streak from January 8 to February 1, when our team went 9–1 against our toughest opponents.

With Ernie, I was co-captain of the team. He came into the season as an Olympic gold medalist; Dean Smith's team had squashed Yugoslavia for the prize in Montreal. Back in Tennessee, he continued the charge.

He had a lot to play for.

Ernie was a senior, graduating at the end of the year to embark on an NBA career. After three seasons, our tear through the Southeastern Conference would be over. The Ernie and Bernie Show was nearing the end of its run. Two New Yorkers, one Jewish and the other black, had changed Tennessee basketball forever. We'd had a wild ride, and wanted its climax to be a championship for Big Orange Country.

Although I didn't tell anyone, it was also going to be my last year at UT. As a sophomore, I'd submitted my name for NBA draft eligibility as a hardship applicant, which allowed non-seniors with financial need to turn professional. The hardship exemption had started in 1972, and players like Dr. J, George McGinnis, and Bob McAdoo were among the first to enter the draft as underclassmen.

NBA rules allowed you to withdraw until twenty-four hours before the start of the selection process, and in 1976 I'd pulled out at the last minute. In the end, I didn't think it wise to leave school as a sophomore. I felt I could improve my game more by staying and thought Ernie and I still had something to accomplish as teammates.

This year was different. I was leaving my name in consideration. It wasn't for the monetary gain. I never played basketball for the money. I wanted to join the NBA for the same reason I'd once sought out the court where the older kids played in Fort Greene. My omission from the Summer Olympics team had stoked my competitive fire. I wanted to prove myself, to compete against the best.

There were certainly other factors. I'd continued partying heavily on weekends. It hadn't affected my game, so no one said anything to me.

I didn't think I had a problem with excessive drinking. But for the first time in my life, basketball wasn't giving me happiness. My inner being craved something more to fulfill it. I also knew my difficulties with the police weren't going away.

I needed a change.

My decision wasn't impulsive. I'd thought it through very carefully. As a student athlete, you weren't allowed to engage a representative until the draft. But you could consult with knowledgeable people around the game and solicit their unofficial advice.

Tom Konchalski had kept in touch with my parents after I went off to college. He didn't expect anything in return. He wasn't trying to benefit financially. He just cared about young basketball players and their families, understood their struggles, and wanted to make a difference in their lives. I respected Tom immensely and sought out his guidance as a friend.

In his opinion, I would be drafted in the top eight. He'd independently assessed the needs of different teams around the league, and felt the New Jersey Nets might have significant interest in me if I remained eligible. It was just an educated guess from what he'd observed, he said. Don't count on it. But I knew him well enough to take his hunches seriously.

The Nets played just across the Hudson River from Manhattan. They weren't the storied Knicks I'd loved as a kid. But it excited me to think about performing in front of New York area crowds, so close to my home turf.

None of the Vols' players or coaches were aware of my desire to turn pro as our season barreled along. There had been speculation about it in my sophomore year, but I never really considered it. Nor did I speak of it as a junior. I didn't want to answer questions from the press and create a distraction for my teammates or myself.

On March 5, the Ernie and Bernie Show faced Kentucky for our fifth and last time. The SEC title was on the line; if the Wildcats won, they would play a first-round NCAA tournament game at home in their brand-new twenty-three thousand-seat Rupp Arena. A loss would give them an at-large berth on the road.

We entered the game with a record of 14–2 in the conference and 20–5 overall after a tough loss to Georgia. Kentucky was 15–1 and 22–2. That put us a game behind them for the SEC title, with each of our teams having one more left to play.

For us, all the chips were on the table. A win would give us a chance to tie the Wildcats up for a share of the conference title. If we went on to take the last game on our schedule, a home game against the weak Vanderbilt Commodores, we would earn sole possession of the title because we'd swept our season series with the 'Cats.

After practice the day before, Coach Mears had posed like a Bantam officer while addressing a crowd of reporters.

"This is the biggest game in my fifteen years at Tennessee, although we've had some other big ones against Kentucky," he said. "You're playing a team many people feel is number one in the country, and most others think is number two."

We were ranked eleventh, which should have made them the hands-down favorite. Except this was Vols–Kentucky. The Wildcats hadn't defeated us since my freshman year at UT. Back in January, we'd beaten them at Rupp in another overtime match, giving us a four-game winning streak against them.

Mears knew they would want revenge. During his press conference, a beat reporter asked, "Do you have any particular worries about the game?"

The coach cleared his throat. You could see him gearing up. "Its physical nature," he said. "Coaches around the league are saying Kentucky ought to be in the National Football League."

The reporters all laughed. Then a guy followed up.

"And what about Tennessee?"

Mears stood there looking like he'd rip the pad and pencil from his hands. But then he just smiled.

"We're a finesse team with grace and quickness," he said.

Our final contest with the 'Cats would play out at Stokely, giving us the home-floor advantage. "The Game" was all anyone was talking about in Knoxville. Earlier in the week, over twenty-four hundred students had slept out in the forty-degree cold for tickets; for some reason, we always seemed to face Kentucky in the dead of winter.

My team tried to block out the hoopla, but I could feel the tension in our locker room before the game. NBC was televising it nationally. We'd heard that the governors of Kentucky and Tennessee were in attendance. Ray Blanton, our state's governor, loved to brag about UT's teams.

I knew what was at stake, but didn't think about it. As I mentally prepared to play, I marshaled my concentration and visualized, exactly as I would for every other game.

Then it was time. We made our way into the tunnel, pumped up, slapping five, ready. The Pride of the Southland marching band was in big-game mode, blowing the roof off the arena with "Rocky Top." The crowd was on its feet singing along.

As I waited to be announced, I realized this would be the last chapter at Stokely for me and Ernie. But it was a fleeting thought. There was no time for it, no room in my mind. We had a game to play.

" . . . *number fifty-three, the King of the Volunteers, BERNARRRD KINNNG!*"

Like the band, John Ward was in peak form.

I went busting through the paper-covered T. The crowd cheered wildly, and I pumped my fist in the air.

Kentucky will not defeat us in our house this Saturday afternoon, I thought as Ward introduced my teammates.

The game started out at a breakneck tempo. Kentucky liked setting the pace as a plan of attack. They'd play a fast, physical eight minutes and hope to wear down the opposition. But we could match their energy and aggressiveness.

It was a ferocious dogfight under the boards, each team bumping, jostling, and crowding for position. With Robey and Phillips, the 'Cats had two powerful big men who didn't leave much open space between them. Add James Lee in relief, and they had a six-foot-five forward who could come off the bench to score and rebound if either starter got into foul trouble.

Coach Hall's second line was a Kentucky strength, and Phillips's junior year play had allowed him to use Lee in the reserve role all season. That gave Hall ten fouls in the low post, freeing Robey and Phillips to do their karate routine.

And, no, Coach Mears wasn't making that up. They would whack you whenever they thought they could get away with it. But where Ernie and I came from, if someone hit you, the thing to do was hit them back.

Karate chop us, we'll kung fu you.

I still laugh when I remember how Ernie gave Phillips payback for one of the craziest fouls I ever saw on a basketball court.

We were battling under the net in a press of bodies when Phillips bit Mike Jackson's arm. That's right. *Bit*. Sinking his teeth into it. Mike couldn't believe it. All of a sudden, he went down to his knees yelling, "He bit me! He bit me!" at the top of his lungs.

As the official's whistle shrilled, I saw a woman dive onto the court from the stands. It took me a second to realize it was Mike's mom. She ran straight over to him, pushing through the players and referees.

"My son got bit!" she screamed, crouching over Mike. *"Somebody help my boy!"*

Phillips was called for a foul, and both players stayed in the game. But the look on Ernie's face told me it wasn't settled.

I won't claim to have been shocked when, a few minutes later, his elbow found Phillip's eye. *Crack!* Right under the brow bone. Phillips staggered with his hands over his face, and there was another whistle. You could see his eye swelling up as his trainers examined him.

Finally, order was restored, but neither team let up. The Kentucky defense had keyed in on Ernie with double and triple teams, so he concentrated on pulling down loose balls and finding me with crisp, excellent passes. I dominated inside, sailing through Kentucky's front line. If I could get open for a layup, he would route the ball through Johnny Darden, and I'd break away to shoot a jumper from the key.

Ten minutes into the game, we were up 26–20. We'd done a good job holding back Givens, their leading scorer. But he and Robey made a few points late, and Ernie went cold from the free-throw line.

That gave Kentucky the lead.

At the break, we trailed 47–42. The game had been knotted eight times in the first half before the Wildcats capitalized on Ernie's blown foul shots.

I could see him seething with anger and frustration in the locker room. It wasn't just his free throws. Kentucky had keyed their defense on him all night. Double teams, three-on-ones, they were doing anything and everything they could to shut him down.

I'd scored 16 points, but knew I would have to deliver more in the second half. We wouldn't have stayed close without Ernie's rebounding. Now I needed to pick up the slack.

The second half was a test of wills. Neither team gave in. The lead changed twice, but Robey and Phillips were killing us down low. At one point, Kentucky pulled ahead by 11, 55–44.

I remember Coach Mears calling a time-out. We were going to a zone defense to try and stop Kentucky's two hulks. Ernie, me, and Reggie Johnson, our freshman center, would clog the passing lanes to keep the basketball out of their hands.

There was a risk to that approach. One of the Wildcats best players was Jack Givens, a pure shooting guard. If he got the ball on the outside and found his jumper, we were in trouble.

But we never lost confidence. We'd had several comeback wins against Kentucky and were in their heads. I knew they half expected us to do it again.

The coach's change of strategy worked. We clamped down defensively, cutting off the middle. The Wildcats' guards kept trying to get the ball to the big men, but we wouldn't allow it. That held their scoring in check and gave us an opportunity to claw our way back into the game.

I stepped it up. Suddenly I couldn't miss a shot. With eleven minutes left, Ernie made a pickoff inside and fed me the ball for a spinning layup. We retook the lead, 62–61. Then I scored another layup, and Johnson added two more points. 66–61.

The Wildcats were rattled. I saw it in their eyes and postures. Hall must have seen it too and called time.

They were tough out of the huddle and scrambled back on top, making it 69–68 Kentucky with five minutes to go. But I pulled us back in front with a pair of foul shots, and we never let them pass us again.

With forty seconds on the clock, we led 80–77. Then Kentucky got possession and fed the ball to Givens.

We began trading fouls away from the basket, neither team wanting to give up a 3-point play. Givens went to the line, missed both shots. Our ball. We dribbled and passed, running down the clock. With fourteen seconds left, they fouled Darden. He dropped in one of two from the line. 81–77.

We gave them the next shot with the clock at ten seconds, knowing it would set us up for the final possession. 81–79.

Six seconds on the clock. Ernie inbounded to Crosby and two Wildcats converged on him, forcing him out of bounds.

I glanced up at the clock, my heart pumping in my chest.

Two seconds.

One.

Crosby raised the ball into the air with both hands and our bench erupted.

The noise from the seats rolled over us like a tidal wave. Our fans were amazing. We'd packed in the biggest crowd in Stokely's history and you could hear it.

We celebrated the win by cutting down the nets, Ernie and the rest of my teammates mobbing me, hoisting me into the air, then carrying me to the basket. The next thing I knew, I was holding the scissors. I can still see them in my hand as I reached up to do the honors, jubilantly screaming, "We don't lose to Kentucky!"

If I'd paid closer attention, I probably would have noticed my old love for the game stirring in my belly. I scored 20 points in the second half for a total of 36, pulling down 11 rebounds. Best of all, I'd delivered on the promise I made after that loss in Kentucky two years before.

The Wildcats had never again beaten us while I was on the team.

Back in the locker room, a towel draped over his shoulders, Ernie played to the reporters and got in a parting jab at our rivals.

"I just hope Joe B. Hall doesn't come up with some reason why Kentucky lost today!" he said. "First it was injuries, then the officiating, then someone shooting someone else's free throws. While Hall's making up his excuses, we'll just cherish the win!"

I remember looking over at him and seeing a huge grin on his face. It put one on mine as I replied to a reporter's question about how I felt.

"Man, I'm tired," I said. "But not too tired to get measured for a ring."

Of course, I added, we still had to beat Vanderbilt in a couple of days to earn those SEC Championship rings.

But I knew we were ready.

VANDERBILT WOULDN'T MAKE IT EASY ON US. They were grittier than their record showed and came into Stokely on a full tank of pride. No one was walking over them.

It was a tough game for our team, even with the loud cheers we got when our names were announced. We had trouble getting up for it after beating Kentucky, and Ernie was still pretty bruised from wrestling with its two giants. I can't recall how many turnovers we had, but think there were over 15. We were sloppy and Vandy took advantage.

Thirty-three minutes into the game, the score was tied 45–45.

I told myself that was unacceptable. If we let things slip away and lost, the Wildcats would become SEC Champs and we'd be looking in on the NCAA tournament from the outside. Saturday's win would have amounted to nothing.

I poured it on. 24 points. 20 rebounds.

We won 65–55. It gave us twenty-two regular season victories, a Tennessee record.

The Vandys were gracious enough to give us hugs and wish us well. In a few days, we would play the Syracuse University Orange, holders of a 26–2 record, in a first-round NCAA Mideast Regional at the University of Louisiana, Baton Rouge.

But what sticks out most in my mind, in addition to the win, was the standing ovation I got coming through the T before the game. At the time, I thought it was because of my performance against Kentucky. But I've since wondered if the fans realized I might be gone after the season.

The standing Os for Ernie and Mike Jackson were understandable. They were seniors, so it was a given that they wouldn't be back. In my case, it wasn't certain, not for the fans. But under the NBA's relaxed hardship regulations, a lot of underclassmen were making the early jump from varsity hoops to the pros. I was one of the nation's best college players.

I think they knew it was goodbye. Their applause touched me. I soaked it in and filed it into memory.

The Ernie and Bernie Show had closed in Old Rocky Top.

What a ride, I thought. *What a ride.*

I WISH I COULD SAY that ride had a storybook finish. That we took it all the way to an NCAA National Championship or even a Final Four appearance. But in reality, it came to a jarring first-round halt.

The single-game elimination format is a cruel heartbreak for the loser. You play all season for an invitation to the dance. Then, suddenly, it's over. But you take whatever lessons you can and move on. It's part of competitive sports.

Syracuse University was an independent Division 1 school in the Eastern area. Eastern teams were considered the weakest in the NCAA, and their excellent season record didn't impress the odds makers. They had us as the heavy favorite.

The Orange deserved more credit than they received. Their six-foot-eleven center was Roosevelt Bouie, an All-American and one of the best players in Syracuse history. Jimmy Williams—they called him "Bug" because he was only five foot ten with his shoes on—was their point guard and top scorer. Their captain and power forward, Marty Byrnes, was a smart, physical player and solid leader on the court. Larry Kelly, a marksman from the outside, was having his best season with the team. Ross Kindel, Dale Shackleford, and Billy Drew could score twenty off the bench any given night. The exceptional reserve corps also included freshman Louis Orr, a tough, light-footed forward who would become a future opponent and my eventual teammate in the NBA. As a late-game scoring option, Orr was a deadly secret weapon.

As for their first-year head coach, I suppose you could say he was Ray Mears's opposite number. He certainly wasn't fiery or a showman. With his Coke-bottle glasses and quiet manner, he could have been mistaken for a certified accountant. But he paid close attention to detail, stressed discipline and preparation, and was popular with his players. Like Hubie Brown, my future coach with the Knicks, he believed in using a platoon system and was masterful deploying his bench. That year, its depth of talent had allowed him to utilize a ten- or eleven-man rotation.

His name?

Jim Boeheim.

If you're a college hoops fan, enough said. But for those who aren't, here's a quick career summary:

Forty-one years after our game in Baton Rouge, Boeheim's record would show ten conference championships, thirty-two tournament appearances, five Final Fours, and a National Championship. As I write these words, he's still leading his team as one of the NCAA's most successful and longest-tenured coaches.

His team came to the tournament tired of being called second rate. They were out to prove they could play with anybody. And we weren't just anybody. We were the ballyhooed Tennessee Vols. Coach Mears was so confident of our chances to start the season that he'd had a picture of the Atlanta Omni Arena, where the NCAA Championship game was to be played that year, printed on the backs of our warm-up uniforms. A month earlier, Ernie and I became the subjects of a cover story in *Sports Illustrated*.

It was supposed to be a mismatch, but I took nothing for granted. This would be the Vols' second trip to the NCAA tournament in my three seasons with Tennessee. At the close of my sophomore year, we had played Virginia Military Institute in the round of thirty-two at Charlotte Arena. But I'd been sidelined for the game.

A week or so earlier, I was running a warm-up drill with Johnny Darden and Terry Crosby. The three-man weave was a basic passing exercise. But freak injuries happen. Crosby was a burly former football player. My thumb hit his shoulder and snapped backward. I thought it was only jammed until I saw the white jag of bone poking through the flesh of my hand.

It was a compound fracture. I needed nine stitches at the hospital to close the open wound, and a cast to set the bone in place.

I couldn't believe it. I'd done that exercise countless times. How could this happen a week before my first NCAA playoff game?

I insisted I could play. But the doctors told my coaches I would risk permanent damage to my hand if I took the court.

Coach Mears and Stu Aberdeen understood what keeping me out would spell for the team's prospects. They knew they'd be at an extreme disadvantage without their leading scorer. But they wouldn't take the chance that I'd ruin my future. They put my long-term welfare ahead of everything.

I kept hoping my hand would miraculously heal in time for the game. That I could somehow contribute, even off the bench.

Of course, it was wishful thinking. Compound fractures don't mend in a week. When the coach told me to suit up halfway through the game, he made it clear I wasn't leaving the sidelines. He was just hoping to lift the team's morale and get the Tennessee fans going in the stands.

We lost 75–81. All our starters were in double digits, with Ernie scoring 36 points, and Mike Jackson, 14.

I felt helpless watching from the bench, knowing the difference I could have made for my team. I'd waited a year for us to reach the NCAA playoffs again.

The Vols team that arrived in Baton Rouge to play Syracuse on March 15, 1977, was much better than the 1976 version. More talented, more balanced, more experienced. We were a confident bunch.

Syracuse probably would have conceded that its starting five didn't compare to ours. But we let up after pulling to an early lead. For most of the afternoon, it was a four-, five-, or six-point ball game. We never gained separation, and it gave the Orange a boost of confidence.

In the final ten minutes, Ernie, Mike Jackson, and I were all in foul trouble, playing right into Boeheim's hands. He was masterful using his bench.

With under three minutes to play, and the score 72–68 Syracuse, Mike committed his fifth personal foul on an attempted steal and was out of the game. He was our third best shooter.

About two minutes from the end of regulation, our freshman center, Reggie Johnson, pulled us to within a couple of points, 74–72. Then both teams scored again. 76–74.

The clock ran down to under two minutes.

With a minute and a half left, I fouled out trying to block a short jumper by Shackleford. He made his shot and the free throw. A three-point play.

The score was 79–74. A 5-point deficit. But it felt bigger than that. I knew I could've helped make it up. Except I was relegated to the bench.

I was shaking my head as I walked off the court. There hadn't been much contact on the play—if there was any at all. But I wasn't upset at the referee. I was angry at myself. The officiating was tight through-out the game, and my team never adjusted. Our best players needed to stay aggressive and, at the same time, stay on the court. We didn't, and we paid the price.

If we'd gotten blown out at that point, the loss might sting less than it does. But we rallied in the remaining minute of regulation, and Reggie Johnson hit another jumper to force overtime.

Ernie and the guys on the floor played their hearts out, but the Vols were built around our starting five. With Mike Jackson and me sacked, Syracuse gained the advantage.

Larry Kelly probably had his best game with Syracuse that after-noon. He'd been bucketing jumpers all game and started overtime by putting one in from the key. Then Kindel, a replacement, scored an-other two.

It's hard to come back when you're down by two in limited extra minutes. Ernie started OT with four fouls. Once he was called for his fifth, it wasn't to be.

Syracuse won 93–88.

Our team was stunned. We'd let the game slip out of our hands.

It was a quiet flight back to Knoxville. Ernie knew he'd played his final game with the Vols. Secretly, I knew I wouldn't be back either.

But no one on that plane suspected Ray Mears's brilliant, inno-vative coaching career also came to an end in Baton Rouge. After the curtain fell on the Ernie and Bernie Show, he resigned his position as head coach of the Vols after fifteen groundbreaking years.

Mears had suffered from clinical depression most of his adult life, and the incessant pressures of coaching basketball could not have helped his condition. He didn't just get his bearing and mannerisms from his hero, General Patton. He had the same militant attitude. A basketball season, he'd tell us, was like going to war with the enemy. As our leader, he took every loss to heart.

Did that weigh on the coach? I sometimes wonder. I wonder if he suspected my own problems stemmed partly from grappling with institutional racism of a sort I'd never experienced growing up in Fort Greene, where the majority of people were black. We never discussed it, leaving the question unanswered.

Mears was eighty when he passed away in 2007. He'd been Tennessee's most successful coach ever and remains one of the top-fifteen winningest in the history of NCAA basketball, with a record of 399–135. After resigning from his position as the Vols' head coach, he spent a decade as the athletic director at the UT system's Martin campus outside Memphis.

We stayed in touch over the years, and I believe he was as proud of me as I was to have played under him. I wish he'd lived long enough to attend my induction into the NBA Hall of Fame. I would like to have shared that experience with him and thank him in person for helping to bridge my way from the playgrounds of Brooklyn.

Ray Mears was a great coach and better human being. He went out on top.

THERE WERE NO EMOTIONAL GOODBYES after our loss to Syracuse. When the professional basketball season ends, guys clean out their lockers and go their separate ways. It's different in college. You all live in the same athletic residence. Classes are still in session. Nobody's going anywhere for a while.

But things had changed. Ernie was about to graduate and move on to an NBA career; everyone knew he would place high in the 1977 draft. Mike Jackson was also getting his diploma, though as a complementary player, he had more uncertain prospects.

My time at Tennessee was also over. I hadn't told anyone, but my mind was made up. I was leaving my name in the draft.

I dropped out of school shortly after we returned from Louisiana. It wasn't official, but I didn't see any point in attending classes or staying on campus. Having managed to put away enough money for a few months' rent, I found an inexpensive apartment in Knoxville and left the dorm without telling anyone. I wanted to quietly cut ties with the past.

The NBA draft was on Friday, June 10, that year. Thursday morning, the deadline for withdrawing my name from the pool, I called a press conference to announce my decision to leave it in. Coach Mears wasn't really surprised. He'd suspected I might not be back and recruited for the next season based on that possibility.

That Friday, I didn't wander more than a few feet from my phone. I'd hired a sports management firm to negotiate with whoever drafted me. My representative, Bill Pollak, would call when my selection occurred.

When the phone rang, I almost dove for the receiver.

Bill informed me I'd been chosen by the New Jersey Nets as the seventh first-round pick, confirming what I was told in advance. What I did not know, and would not for many years to come, was that Kevin Loughery, the Nets's head coach, had visited Tennessee during the season to scout Ernie Grunfeld, but decided he wanted me instead. If he'd stuck to his original plan, I would have drafted eighth, one slot below Ernie, and gone to the Denver Nuggets.

Ernie was drafted eleventh in the first round. Still a high pick. But his immediate future in the NBA would be with the Milwaukee Bucks.

And that was that. I was ready to start earning a living as a pro basketball player. Except for a few all-important things.

Finalizing the contract would take time, and my cash had just about dried up. Though my landlord in Knoxville offered to hold off asking for rent till I could pay him, I felt it was time to get started on my future. That meant leaving Tennessee.

Of course, being broke, I knew it was going to be easier said than done.

10 | The New Jersey Nets

Just before the start of contract talks, Bill Pollak informed me he was leaving his firm for a position as counsel for the White House Office of Administration. Bill offered to continue representing me under the firm's auspices, but said it would be fine if I wanted to ask one of his colleagues take over discussions with the Nets. It was my decision.

I didn't have to think about it too long. He'd been a straight shooter in all our conversations before the draft, and I felt I could trust him to serve my best interests. Also, most agents worked on commission, but I preferred paying a straight fee. Bill was agreeable to that arrangement, explaining he would function solely as my lawyer.

It set a precedent I followed the rest of my career. I've always felt having an attorney rather than a traditional agent gave me greater input into the negotiating process.

One of my first questions to Bill after the draft was about my desire to move on from Knoxville.

"I want to find someplace else to live," I said during one of our calls. "But I'm not going back to the projects. I can't do that again."

He paused for a long moment. "Can you handle a lawn mower?"

I was thinking that I'd never used one in my life.

"Why do you ask?"

"Well, I've got a place with a lawn that needs mowing," Bill answered. His job change had required him to relocate to the Washington, D.C., area with his wife and kids. "We'd be more than happy to have you stay with us. But I'm warning you, you'll have to earn your keep."

The man at the center of the huddle is Gil Reynolds, my legendary coach on Bed-Stuy's Restoration Eagles. A strict but caring mentor, Gil changed the lives of all the kids who played under him.

Earning the nickname "Sleepy head" outside Ft. Hamilton High School. I'm faking the snooze, but I really like the snap brim cap.

79 North Oxford Walk, Fort Greene. My home growing up, and the court where I shot hoops by moonlight (original basket and backboard have been replaced). There's a plaque commemorating it on the side of the apartment building.

The Bernie and Ernie Show at the University of Tennessee. Hundreds of publicity photos were taken of us. This is my favorite.

My Vols (and later Knicks) teammate Ernie Grunfeld creating space. Our chemistry on the floor was unmatched throughout my basketball career.

The UT Vols' archrivals, the Kentucky Wildcats, had a bruising defensive front line. After a tough loss in my first game against them, I vowed Kentucky would never beat us again. And they didn't while I was a Vol.

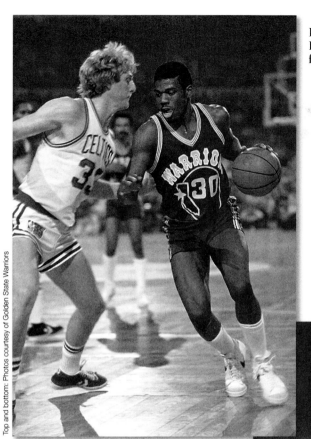

Driving downhill against Larry Bird to my King spot for two points.

Looking to pass the ball to a cutting teammate, World B. Free.

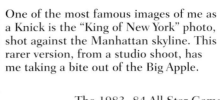

One of the most famous images of me as a Knick is the "King of New York" photo, shot against the Manhattan skyline. This rarer version, from a studio shoot, has me taking a bite out of the Big Apple.

The 1983–84 All Star Game was the start of my Season of Ascension. Here I'm getting five from Julius "Dr. J" Erving, the iconic standard bearer at my small forward position and one of the greatest basketball players in history.

LEFT: Battling my way through three Detroit Pistons, including Isiah Thomas, in the 1983–84 NBA playoffs. Despite severely dislocated fingers on both hands (our trainer Mike Saunders designed special casts) and a bad case of the flu, I averaged 42.6 points a game in our five-game series. RIGHT: In the air against the Pistons. My injured hands made it excruciating to dunk and pass the ball. But winning in the postseason means playing through pain.

After defeating Detroit, the semifinal round of the 1983–84 playoffs pitted my Knick team against the formidable Boston Celtics, led by the incomparable Larry Bird (right side of photo).

Kevin McHale was one of four future Hall of Famers we faced in the 1983–84 semifinals. It was a rough, tough, hard fought series that pushed both teams to their limits.

My Christmas Eve 1985 press conference at MSG. I was about nine months into rehab for my ACL injury and felt confident informing the media I would play again—but I didn't know exactly when I'd be ready. Pictured (L-R) are my therapist Dania Sweitzer, Knicks GM Dave DeBusschere, and me.

I spent four great seasons with the Washington Bullets after my comeback, competing against talents like the magnificent Magic Johnson.

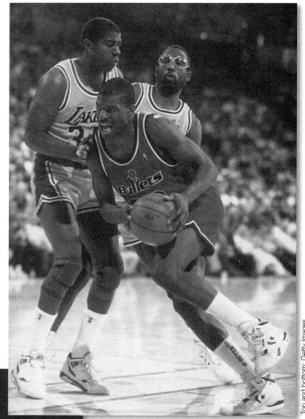

Top and bottom: Getty Images

Matching up against the worthy James Worthy in my Bullets years.

Amina, my rising star.

With my parents Thelma and Thomas King. Through their example, I learned the meaning of hard work, dedication, and responsibility.

One of the proudest moments of my life was giving my Naismith Memorial Basketball Hall of Fame enshrinement speech before an auditorium filled with basketball legends and, best of all, my amazing wife Shana, extra-special daughter Amina, and in-laws Susan L. Taylor and Khephra Burns.

GAME FACE:
I Shall Not Be Denied.

I laughed. He'd found himself a groundskeeper.

Bill's home was in suburban McLean, Virginia, eight miles from the Capital, and one of the wealthiest communities in the nation. The houses were large and stately, with tall columns flanking their doorways and taller shade trees out front.

I had no shortage of grass to trim. Bill gave me a weekly stipend, making clear it was a loan to remedy the awkwardness of paying his client. He kept track of every dollar, which was fine with me.

I had an incredible summer. When I wasn't pushing a mower on Saturdays, I worked on my game. Having represented a number of top athletes, Bill introduced me to other professional basketball players in the area. During the NBA offseason, some of the best guys in the country played in a Pro-Am league outside Baltimore. One was John Lucas, a point guard with the Houston Rockets drafted from the University of Maryland the previous year. Many people are aware of his fourteen-year NBA career, but he was also a world-class college tennis player.

John took me under his wing. He'd pick me up in his car, introduce me to friends, and, being single, would sometimes bring me to dance parties. I liked hanging out with him, and it didn't hurt that he had a gorgeous sister. Or that she had a lot of pretty girlfriends who liked to dance.

Eventually, I rented a car and was able to get around on my own, driving to Maryland to play ball in the Pro-Am league on a daily basis. Competing against NBA greats all summer was fantastic.

Adrian Dantley, one of the greatest scorers in the NBA was among the regulars. So was the late Maurice Lucas—no relation to John— the best power forward in the league. Maurice had started out in the old American Basketball Association, then spent over a dozen years in the NBA. The year before, he'd helped the Portland Trailblazers overcome two powerhouse teams—the Philadelphia 76ers and Los Angeles Lakers—and win an NBA Championship.

Maurice would earn the nickname "The Enforcer" for being an intimidating presence on the basketball court, but his personality when we practiced couldn't have been warmer. I learned not to confuse the two after joining the Nets.

About six weeks into the season, our team met the Blazers on the road at the Portland Rose Garden.

"Hey, Maurice, how you doin?" I said, shaking hands with him before tip-off. "Good to see you!"

Then it was jump ball. Game on.

I was driving across the lane in the first quarter, cutting past his six-foot-nine body, when he gave me what I call "The Forearm Shiver."

Let me tell you what I mean by that. The Forearm Shiver is when somebody slams you so hard in the gut with his arm, you tremble in pain from head to toe. Like you're standing out in zero-degree weather. Naked. And soaked to the bone with ice water.

In Fort Greene, we knew about forearm hits. Normally, when I was breaking past an opponent, I'd tighten up my muscles to protect my abdomen. But I got lax with Maurice, thinking we were friends. And he'd kind of mentored me over the summer. I didn't expect it. Rookie mistake.

It hurt. Man, oh man, did it hurt. My back teeth rattled together. The breath whumped out of me. I'd never been hit like that before. His arm was like a crowbar.

I never spoke to another player on the floor again. I hadn't done it in high school, and didn't do it in college. Now I knew I would never, ever, ever do it in the NBA.

I'd learned my lesson. Off the court, you had friends. On the court, you didn't have friends. And when you were competing against guys at a certain level, you had to be extra prepared.

But I digress. All that was still ahead when I was playing Pro-Am with Maurice and the other guys. After workouts, he would take a bunch of us to his favorite seafood house, where I was initiated into the glories of Maryland hard-shell crab. We'd find a nice, shady, outdoor picnic table, spread some newspapers on top, toss some butter into the plastic serving basket, and dive in.

I'd never eaten crabs before, and the guys had to show me how to crack open their shells with my mallet. The meat was delicious, hot and spicy from seasonings added to the water when the crabs were steamed.

I relished those experiences. It was the first time in my life I socialized with African American men of financial means—and basketball
players like myself. The first time I felt comfortable in a group. We'd all
talk and laugh as we devoured the crabs.

At night, I would head back to McLean. Bill and his wife couldn't
have been kinder or more gracious. They opened their home to me,
inviting me to eat dinner or watch television with their family. Their
kids were very small, and I would often sit on the floor and read to
them. You could see the joy on their faces when I opened their favorite
books. It was unlike anything I had ever known with my own family.

Bill's office was in the Eisenhower Executive Office Building, a
historic post–Civil War structure that held most of the president's
administrative staff. If you looked out the window, you were staring
across a walkway at the West Wing. I would visit Bill there during the
week, and its close proximity to the White House was always a kick.
He'd let me make calls on his phone, and I can't tell you how many
started with the words, "Hey, you won't believe where I am!"

So that was my summer. Spending time with Bill and his family,
practicing with Maurice Lucas and the rest, and learning the mouth-
watering pleasures of crab consumption. And, of course, Saturdays, I'd
go hard at the lawn.

In early September, Bill told me he'd finalized the contract with the
Nets. Training camp would start in Piscataway, New Jersey, later that
month. The first game of the regular season was in October.

I drove up to New York in a rental car. It was the longest trip I'd ever
made behind the wheel. I spent the night with my parents, and then we
went to Jersey together for my press conference.

I'll never forget my nervousness in the Lincoln Tunnel. The tube
ran a hundred feet under the Hudson River, and its walls seemed too
close for comfort. I kept imagining what would happen if I swerved out
of my lane . . . or someone swerved into *me*. That made me shiver like
a hit from Maurice Lucas's forearm.

I survived crossing over to Brooklyn, but was so excited about the
press conference, I could hardly sleep. The next morning, the Nets sent
a car to bring my parents and me to Newark.

When we arrived, I discovered that a major difference between college and professional basketball was the way you were prepped. The team's public relations people never told me how to answer particular questions, but gave me tips on how to collect my thoughts and phrase my responses so they weren't mischaracterized. They helped me understand that there was a certain form to dealing with the media. That it required certain communications skills. As someone who'd always idolized Sidney Poitier for his grace and polish, I soaked it up.

The press conference was overwhelming. Standing at the podium, I could have pinched myself. I was a professional basketball player in the greatest league on the planet. Soon I would compete on the same courts as the superstars I'd always admired from afar. Players like Dr. J and Kareem Abdul-Jabbar.

I looked at my parents in the front row and felt my heart swell. It was a dream come true.

There were obstacles behind me, and there would be many challenges to come. But that moment was preserved in my memory like a perfect, everlasting crystal.

Bernard King, the shy kid from Fort Greene, had made it to the NBA.

TEAM WORKOUTS BEGAN about a week after I signed my contract.

The Nets was an expansion team that had been part of the American Basketball Association before the NBA absorbed it in 1976. We didn't have our own arena and played our home games at the Rutgers University athletic center, sharing the gym with the varsity Scarlet Knights.

It would be a while before I set foot on that court. Training camp was at the Rutgers University Center in Piscataway, New Jersey. The entire team stayed at a local hotel.

Our head coach, Kevin Loughery, had led the American Basketball Association Nets since their 1974 season, when they won the first of two back-to-back championships behind Julius Erving. Loughery was known for his fiery disposition and had never met a referee he liked. But he was a former player who understood the game.

Camp lasted a grueling twenty-one days. We practiced twice a day, five days a week. I thought I was in great physical shape going in, but there was a difference between collegiate shape and professional shape. I quickly learned I'd have to dial up my training routine to be an impactful forward in the NBA.

We had some fine veteran players on the team. George "Hands" Johnson, our six-foot-eleven center, was a master shot blocker. He loved nothing more than deflecting a ball from the hoop. Our point guard, Terry Porter, could see the seams in any defense and rack up 21 assists a game. Tim Bassett was a solid power forward who'd been with the team since its ABA days and won two crowns with Dr. J. No one cared more about basketball fundamentals or fought harder for rebounds. Whether at practice, aboard the plane, or in our locker room, Tim was always willing to share his knowledge and experiences with the younger guys like me and my fellow rookie, Eddie Jordan.

Speaking of Eddie . . .

He didn't start the year with the Nets. A Rutgers alumni, he was drafted by the Cleveland Cavaliers and came to us in a mid-season trade. But we developed a tremendous chemistry on the court. All I had to do was make eye contact with him, and there was a lob. I mean, right *there*.

Eddie was great at steals. He loved nothing more than intercepting a pass, grabbing a dribble, or snatching the ball out of an opposing player's hands to force a turnover. Steals can backfire if you don't pull them off, but Eddie's percentages were high. He had gambling in his soul and larceny in his heart.

For all the talent on our roster, it was a revolving door through training camp and the exhibition season. It isn't unusual for a team's makeup to change during that period, when coaches make their evaluations, and players are cut, added, and win or lose their starting roles. But the Nets were in full transition. Since 1968, they'd moved from Teaneck, New Jersey, to Long Island, New York, and played in three separate arenas there before changing leagues and returning to Jersey for my first year.

Also, Roy Boe, the team's owner, was strapped for cash. He'd paid $4 million in fees to become part of the NBA and was on the hook for almost $500,000 more to compensate the New York Knicks, who claimed the Nets were invading their geographic NBA territory.

To raise money for operating expenses, Boe sold Julius Erving's contract to the Philadelphia 76ers for $3 million. Doc had been promised a salary upgrade after leading the team to two consecutive ABA championships, but Boe now said he couldn't afford the increase. The Sixers had plenty to spend and gave Doc a multimillion-dollar extension.

An NBA franchise is a business, and businesses exist to make a profit. As a player, I learned that's the hard, cold reality. But Nets fans mutinied, and you couldn't blame them. The bottom line wasn't their problem. Dave DeBusschere once said Doc wasn't just the team's franchise player, he was the league. And now he was gone. The move to Jersey from Long Island was done to escape the fans' anger, but it left the Nets with no real home or fan base.

When I came aboard, we were in a tough spot competitively. The Nets had nothing to spend. Being new to the NBA draft, we hadn't stockpiled any prospects as trade chips. Our older players were nearing the end of their careers, and our young players needed seasoning.

Loughery was coaching a team in flux. He had to adapt his coaching style from the ABA's loose, run-and-gun, breakneck basketball to the more structured NBA brand. He didn't have a returning ball club that had been together for a number of years. He had guys in camp who wouldn't be on the roster months later, even though they were veterans. He knew there would be a great many trades, and that he'd have to adjust his lineup and rotations practically from one day to the next.

As a player, the revolving door made you dizzy. I remember when Al Skinner, another member of the ABA Nets championship team, was sent to the Detroit Pistons for a group of players while we were flying from New Jersey to a game in Cleveland. Al left the runway a Net, and landed a Piston—he'd been traded in midair!

It was like that throughout the season. Teammates came and went. I realized early on that I'd be our main offensive weapon. I'd been drafted in the hope that I could fill Doc's shoes.

A few days before the start of camp, Loughery came up to me and asked, "What is your goal?"

I said, "I want to win. And I want to be the best player that's ever played the game."

I wonder what Loughery thought of my answer. He'd coached the peerless Dr. J through those two championship seasons. Doc was arguably the best player in the game and the main reason the NBA had acquired the ABA. People loved watching him fly through the air for a whirling, acrobatic dunk, but his fame went beyond sports. He was equally respected for his class and grace off the court.

Fill his shoes?

Nobody could have done it. Doc put an entire league on the map. My reply to Loughery wasn't egotistical. It was daunting to consider that, on any given night, I might face an All-Star, a potential Hall of Famer, or even a bona fide legend like Julius Erving. But I knew what the Nets expected of me, and what I expected of myself. I wanted to prove that my skills were as good as anyone's in the league. I felt I belonged and wouldn't be intimidated.

Our team opened the NBA's 1977–1978 season on the road against the Detroit Pistons. This was still a couple of years before Isiah Thomas, and the Pistons were a mediocre ball club. But their leader and center, a 250-pound, six-foot-ten grizzly bear named Bob Lanier, was a five-time All-Star who could dominate on any given night.

I had a disappointing debut performance, scoring only 8 points in a 110–93 loss. Lanier had a good game, scoring 22 points. I doubt he took notice of the Nets' rookie small forward.

That would happen later on, as you'll see later in this chapter.

For me, those first few games were a feeling-out process. Going from the collegiate to the pro game is a mental adjustment. You face players with offensive skills that far exceed anything you faced in college. If you're going up against a great player, and he scores a lot of points, you can't help thinking about it as you dribble down the court with the ball. As a young rookie, when you're stymied at the defensive end, you might not execute offensively, as you would after being in the league a longer period.

Meanwhile, I wasn't the only one feeling things out. The league was also getting a feel for me. As were my own coaches and teammates. On our first road trip, some of the veterans asked me to carry their bags.

"No," I said. "I'm not here to carry anyone's bags. I'm here to play basketball."

They didn't appreciate hearing it from me. But by our third game, I led the team in scoring with 26 points. My confidence was up, and I'd settled in. I was a professional athlete, not a member of a college fraternity. I would not accept their hazing.

Here's another example of rookie treatment. Back then, teams flew commercial. On the plane, the veterans and coaches sat in first class, taking it for granted as their privilege. The rest of us were in coach, with no legroom. I thought it was unfair, and spoke to Loughery about it aboard a flight.

"I'm the best player on the team, and you're playing me forty minutes a night," I told him. "I don't think I should be sitting in coach."

Before Loughery could answer, one of his assistants gave up his seat and moved to coach. He wasn't a very tall guy, and I appreciated it.

I might have seemed cocky or bigheaded. But I didn't feel getting a seat with legroom should be based on years of service. I was playing veteran minutes and performing better than anyone else on the team. We'd started off 0–4, which bothered me immensely, while some of the older players seemed indifferent.

Not until the fifth game of the season did we notch a win, playing at home against the Boston Celtics. I celebrated with an eye on the upcoming schedule.

The Los Angeles Lakers were visiting next. Then, two days later, we would conclude our four-game home stand against some stiff, big-name competition: the high-flying Dr. J and his Philadelphia 76ers were coming to New Jersey.

WHEN I WENT UP AGAINST THE GREAT ONES—Larry Bird, Michael Jordan, Dominique Wilkins, Alex English, and Julius Erving—I brought my game within the game. Although the offensive skills I used were always in my repertoire, I would ratchet them into another gear. It was not something I did nightly. The best demanded a higher mode of play.

The Philadelphia 76ers were the stars of the NBA. Besides Doc, they had power forward George McGinnis, Henry Bibby at point, shooting guard Doug Collins, plus Darryl Dawkins, and Brooklyn playground legend World B. Free.

They were a phenomenal All-Pro team, built to win. They were also in trouble.

The year before, the Sixers had made it to the NBA finals, only to lose in six to the Portland Trailblazers. They'd underperformed to start 1977, going 4–2, but the reports of discord within the team were even worse than their losing record. Right before our game, their four-year coach, Gene Shue, was replaced by Billy Cunningham, a seventeen-year veteran of the Sixers and fan favorite. Billy had never coached a day in his life, but it was hoped that he could bring the club together as a former player. He was under pressure to turn things around with a win, pitting Dr. J against his old head coach, his old team, and the owner who'd sold him to Philly.

The game was our first sellout of the season. Capacity at the Rutgers gymnasium was 8,100 people, but they somehow packed in over 9,000 that Friday night. The newspapers were advising fans to drive in early to avoid traffic jams.

I played over a thousand games in my NBA career. Many have blurred together with time. Not that game. That one was special.

My preparation was no different than before any other game—I would always stay within the framework of what worked for me—but my inner fire, my passion, my *desire*, was the highest it had ever been.

In my mind, Dr. J was the greatest basketball player on Planet Earth. We had no chance of beating Doc and the Sixers unless I had a great, great game, but it went beyond that for me. Doc was my personal measure. My standard bearer. The best player ever at my position. That night I wanted to outperform him between the lines.

I was no stranger to the big stage. What was bigger in NCAA basketball than the Vols–Wildcats rivalry? The Ernie and Bernie Show? We'd played before huge crowds. We'd been scrutinized in a

Sports Illustrated cover story. Our games were broadcast on national television.

And now I was facing Julius Erving. In the NBA. It was the biggest stage for me yet. The biggest moment.

I embraced it with open arms.

I HAD NEVER GONE TO A PRO BASKETBALL GAME as a young boy. I couldn't; we had no money for it in our household. When I signed with the Nets, I wanted to provide the experience to as many children as possible and bought twenty-five tickets a night, asking that they be given to kids who might not otherwise have the opportunity to attend a ball game. That night, King's Corner, in Section 101 where the kids sat, was the loudest cheering section in the bleachers. I can tell you I appreciated it.

Dr. J was everything I expected and more. He wasn't just a great scorer. He had tremendous lateral movement defensively and, man, he elevated like he was going to the moon.

My offensive game was predicated on power, quickness, and linear acceleration and speed. Very few defenders played me straight up, man-to-man, without help. Most forced me one way or the other to take away one side of the court.

That gave me a built-in advantage. I could attack from the left or right. As I was forced left, I'd go to the left baseline, use two dribbles max, then rise and shoot. The same thing if I was forced right. Baseline, two dribbles, rise, shoot. The defender wasn't really taking anything away. He was giving me the left or right line, and that played into my strengths.

But Doc played me straight up. He took a wide stance between me and the basket, his feet horizontal, confident he could block me in either direction. If I went left to get open, he'd go left. If I went right, he shifted right. He didn't give me anything, not an inch either way.

When Doc took that stance inside the paint, it didn't matter to me. I'd use the power in my legs to elevate for a layup. But away from the basket, on the wing, I had to employ a different attack. The instant I caught the ball, I went into high offensive gear.

There was a cat-and-mouse move in my repertoire that I rarely used against other players. They didn't usually play me straight up, so I didn't need to use it too often. With Dr. J defending me, I needed it.

The move was to raise the ball over my shoulder and up above my head, then swing it down from right to left. Depending on his reaction to the feint, I might bring the ball back right, making him think he'd read my fake and anticipate that I was going left.

But I was setting him up. If he shifted left, I knew he'd taken my bait. And I would go right.

Double fake.

Once I got past Doc, I was free to do whatever I wanted. With no one else guarding me, I could drive or pull up for a jumper.

I scored 41 points and grabbed 14 rebounds that night. Twenty-two of my points came in the third quarter, tying a team record.

The Nets should have won. We were up 104–97 with two minutes to play. With a minute left, we still held a 2-point lead. Defensively, we contained Dr. J to 11 points on 5 field goals and a free throw.

When you're that successful against him, you really should come out on top.

Someone once asked how I defended Doc over the years. I gave a three-word answer: "HELP! HELP! HELP!"

Funny as that sounds, you weren't stopping him. What you hoped was that he didn't embarrass you. That you didn't open the paper the next day and see a photo of him stuffing the ball into the rim with his knees above your shoulder.

When Doc came soaring toward the hoop on the open floor, most guys would move. I never did that. You won't find footage of me getting out of the way of a dunk. I would challenge anybody, and Doc was no exception.

But the Nets lost that game by 3 points, 107–104. We had some careless passing in the game's final minutes. We couldn't push the ball over the half court in four consecutive tries. We threw it away, let them steal it, made a bad foul . . . and they scored every time we made a mistake.

It was frustrating. I hated to lose. But I'm going to share something here.

I was a month short of my twenty-first birthday. I'd played a total of seven games in the NBA. And that night, with Dr. J in the house—the player whose role I was somehow expected to take over—I was the best man on the floor.

The truth is I felt good about myself. More than good, in fact. I left the locker room walking on a cloud.

Not that I made it out of the building without getting shot down, which is a story I should share too.

I SAW HER the moment I left the locker room.

The woman was stunningly gorgeous. Tall, slender, and finely dressed, with high cheekbones, brown skin, and hair tumbling over her shoulders in thick, loose curls.

A *model*, I thought. *She has to be a model.*

I turned down the hall, feeling good and confident, gliding six inches above the floor. I'd just scored over 40 points against the greatest player in the game. I had on a three-piece pinstriped suit and knew I looked sharp.

I smoothed down my vest and approached her. It seemed my special night was about to become even more special.

"May I have the pleasure of introducing myself to you?" I said, flashing a toothy smile.

The woman looked at me and smiled back.

"Bernard, get out of here," she said after a beat of silence. "I'm Julius's wife."

Julius.

As in Julius *Erving*.

I'd just come on to Dr. J's wife, Turquoise.

Crash. So much for walking on air.

Stuttering an apology, I turned in retreat, scurried out to the parking lot, and drove off before Doc could appear.

I wish I could say I was through with postgame embarrassment. But I wasn't. I had more in me.

The next incident happened few weeks later. Once again, I'd just left the locker room. As I walked down the corridor, I passed an attractive, mature-looking woman who said, "Great game tonight."

I stopped and thanked her. The woman added that she was there with a famous player whose name I won't mention.

"Wow," I said. "Your son's great."

The blood suddenly drained from the woman's face.

"I am his wife," she said icily.

I stood there speechless. When I could finally pry my tongue from the roof of my mouth, I apologized. Clumsily.

Out to my car.

What I can say about all this is that I learned a valuable lesson.

You can never scurry off too fast when you've humiliated yourself in front of a player's wife.

AFTER OUR FIRST GAME AGAINST THE SIXERS, I told the reporters crowding my locker that I thought the Nets could compete with anybody.

On that night, I believed those words were true. Although we came away with a loss, we'd played a solid game against an elite team, and I'd bested Dr. J on the floor.

Afterward, an article in the paper called me the savior of the Nets. That was a heavy badge for a rookie, but I was okay wearing it. When I told Kevin Loughery I wanted to be the best player ever, I wasn't being boastful, or saying what I thought he wanted to hear. That had been my goal in the playgrounds long before I'd walked into Gil Reynolds's Bedford-Stuyvesant gym. It never changed.

From an individual standpoint, I had an excellent rookie season. I averaged over 24 points and 9 rebounds a game, was the NBA's seventh leading scorer, started in all but two of my team's games, and was voted onto the league's All-Rookie Team.

I was playing at a high level with consistency, and to me, that was the true measure of excellence.

But the 1977–1978 Nets, as a team, were never consistent. We couldn't sustain any momentum. In one stretch between January and February, we lost sixteen games in a row.

It wore on me. I'd never lost. Not in junior high school. Not in high school. Not in college. But we were being defeated every night. And the worst thing was that some of my teammates didn't care. They were in the revolving door and knew they wouldn't be around at the end of the season.

At one point during the losing streak, I actually told Loughery I didn't want to play anymore. I was a young man expressing my frustration and would have handled things better later on in my career. But I was overwhelmed by the team's apathy. It was disheartening.

Loughery persuaded me that the Nets were building for the future and told me to stay with it. Things would improve, he said.

So, of course, I kept playing. When I took the floor, nothing outside the lines affected me. I honored the game too much. Playing was personal for me, and my motivation came from within. I did not give in to the losing.

But I was unhappy. Being a pro basketball player wasn't all I'd expected it would be when I left Tennessee. Going home to the New York area, competing against the best . . . I had thought it would give me the same soaring joy I'd felt as a kid in the Brooklyn playgrounds. And it wasn't doing that. It wasn't satisfying me. I knew the basis of my unhappiness was separate from my issues with the team, but I didn't know what was causing it. What was hurting me inside.

When I returned to my hotel after a game, I was consumed by emptiness. I hated to be alone and tried to avoid it, to fill the emptiness with casual sex.

I'd also fallen back on a habit from my days on campus. After every game, every night, I was drinking. I had not given in to the losing, no. But I did give in to my vices, and it nearly destroyed me.

11 | Rookie Mistakes

In the late 1970s, Studio 54 in New York was the hottest club on the planet. Anyone and everyone wanted to get through the door, and absolutely anything and everything went on inside.

On any given night, half the people there were out of control. Sometimes, I was among them.

After Nets home games, I would occasionally drive into Manhattan to hang out. I'd gone from a hard-working Brooklyn kid to making more money than I'd imagined in my life, seemingly overnight. I thought hitting the scene was the thing to do.

One particular night at the Studio, I blacked out from drinking. I don't remember it, but it happened.

Former Knicks guard Dean Meminger was there with his wife. They took me to their apartment because they knew I wasn't capable of driving back to New Jersey. If I'd tried, I probably would have gotten into a serious accident. I woke up in their home. They'd driven my car there so I wouldn't wonder whether it had been stolen or towed to an impound lot.

Years later at a Knicks event in Madison Square Garden, I walked up to Dean and said, "I never thanked you for what you did for me that night in 'seventy-seven. But I want to do it now. If you hadn't brought me over to your place, I might have died."

In 2013, we lost Dean to a drug overdose. At the time, I was enveloped in sadness. Thirty-five years before drugs took his life, he and his wife saved mine.

Dean was an angel. He offered me a hand when I needed it. And he wasn't the only one.

The clubs were occasional breaks in my solitude, the exception rather than the norm. When I was in a crowd of partiers, I was hiding from my loneliness in plain sight. Everyone there was part of my disguise; I really didn't let people get close to me.

But most often I indulged alone. I kept a bottle in my glove box and would start on it after the games. Once, when I was driving back to the team hotel, I was stopped by the cops. I'd had too much to drink, and my car must have been weaving erratically.

I tried to stay calm, but my heart was racing as they exited their cruiser and walked toward me. It wasn't only because I was intoxicated. After the harassment I'd experienced in Knoxville, I would break into a sweat whenever a police car came up on my rear. I'd been traumatized and expected the worst.

The officers approached my window. When they recognized me as Bernard King of the Nets, they decided not to arrest me. Instead, they took me back to my hotel with a stern warning.

In hindsight, I realize those guys weren't cops. They wore uniforms and badges, and they carried guns, but like Dean and his wife, they were angels. If not for their intervention, I might have killed myself and others that evening.

Sometimes, though, I didn't have angels to protect me from myself.

On the road as a rookie, I traveled with alcohol in my checked bag. Our team trainer handled the bags, bringing them from the airport to the hotel. In the lobby, I noticed my bag was soaked and knew the bottle had shattered inside.

Uh oh, I thought. *What if someone smelled it?*

The trainer didn't say anything, so I was hoping he hadn't.

I grabbed the bag, hurried up to my room and opened it. Everything I'd packed was drenched in booze.

I reached for the telephone, sent my dress clothes out to the cleaners, and prayed they could get out the strong stink of whiskey. I didn't want to include my uniform, realizing it could identify me to the press or even disappear altogether. Before doing anything else, I washed the uni by hand in the bathtub. Then I called down and asked that it be dried in the hotel laundry.

That incident was the exception to the rule. On most occasions, I had no problems. After road games, I would go out chasing women. I was an NBA player and could find pretty girls in every town.

But the sex never filled the void inside me. Once, I picked up a woman and brought her back to my hotel room. We were in bed, turned on, when I abruptly stopped and asked her to hold me. I didn't want to do anything besides lay there and know a woman's warmth. She looked at me like I was an alien.

As a rookie, I used a trick to hide the extent of my partying from inquisitive eyes. When we arrived at our hotel, I'd take my room key from my trainer and go upstairs. Rookies were assigned roommates, something I only found out on our first road trip. I liked the guy but for obvious reasons didn't want him sharing my room.

After a few minutes, I would go back down to the front desk with the key and ask to change floors. I told the team I was taking a single and would pay the difference. Cost didn't matter. I wanted my own room. I needed my own room. It was worth it at any price.

Many times I came to the arena after staying up all night. I made sure I was ready for the game and never had a drop-off in performance. I kept my body conditioned and played with passion and intensity. I'd known since college that combination allowed me to overcome fatigue.

That first season with the Nets, my partying stayed under the radar. I played well enough to set a franchise record for most points scored in a season and stay in a tight race for NBA Rookie of the Year. And I never woke up to stories about myself in the paper. In one regard, I was fortunate. But in another, it hurt me, because it gave my self-destructive behavior an opening to continue. I was in denial about my problems, sending them to the back room and shutting the door.

That couldn't last. It never does.

Sooner or later, they would break out into the open.

ON MARCH 12, 1977, the Nets played game sixty-nine of the season at home against the Detroit Pistons. Our record was 17–52 and we were on our way to finishing with the worst record in the NBA. Detroit was also having a losing year, although on that date, they were only four games under .500 at 31–35.

It was our third matchup on the schedule, but the first in Piscataway. After they defeated us in the season opener, we came back and won our second game against them in Auburn Hills, 117–112.

I'd been tied for highest scorer on the floor that day with 31 points. The Pistons' veteran star Bob Lanier had scored the same number. We'd played a tough defensive game, forcing turnovers that gave us a lot of successful fast-break opportunities.

Both teams badly wanted that third game. We knew we could beat the Pistons. Meanwhile, they didn't want to lose a season series to the worst team in the league. And their leader, Lanier, certainly didn't want to take a loss while being equaled or bettered in the stat column by a rookie forward, one who'd made his splash in the league scoring 41 against Dr. J.

In those days, every kid in the playground knew Lanier's name. If you were a tall kid, the other boys on the court would shout, "Yo, Lanier!" whenever you blocked a shot or launched one over an opponent's head. That's because Lanier was one of the biggest big men in the NBA. At the time, his name was synonymous with the word "big." His size-twenty-two feet once held the record of the biggest ever to be measured for a pair of league-approved sneakers. They might still have that distinction; I'm not sure.

That last game was a brawl from the opening whistle. My matchup was John Shumate, the Pistons' forward, but Lanier was their low-post defender, and I'd pulled down 11 rebounds against them the month before.

Eddie Jordan was hot that night. Early in the second quarter, he drained a jumper that put us ahead by 4 and got our home crowd up on their feet. Then one of the Pistons missed a shot, and I went hard to the boards, reaching for the rebound and pulling it down to my chest. That was when Lanier rattled my head with his elbow.

Now, let's keep something in mind. Lanier was 250 pounds of bulky muscle. That's almost 50 pounds heavier than I was. He was also almost seven feet tall.

His elbow felt like an oar from a rowboat. And I knew it hadn't connected by accident. When you're in the league a while, like Lanier was, you learn to send a message without the ref seeing it. Even one of the sharp-eyed best in the league like Dick Bavetta, who was officiating that night.

But have I mentioned I'm from Brooklyn?

No, I thought. *That isn't gonna work.*

I knew Lanier hit me to send a message. And I knew I had to return it, preferably without getting tossed.

All in a heartbeat, I pushed the ball forward off my chest and threw it into the pit of his stomach. I mean, I did it as hard as I could.

BANG!

To my amazement, Lanier wasn't the least bit staggered. I mean, he didn't budge.

He just glared, fire in his eyes. And then he rolled up to me under the basket. Picture an enraged bear. I started backing up.

At the Rutgers gymnasium, the stands went right up to the baseline. There was almost nothing between them and the court. But I wasn't thinking about the stands. I wasn't thinking about the occupants of those seats. I didn't even notice whether or not they *were* occupied.

I just stared at that enormous body coming toward me in the center of the lane, his right hand balled into a fist, and kept backing up behind the basket.

And backing up.

And backing up.

Right into the stands.

I fell backward into someone's lap just as Lanier charged.

"Bob! Don't hurt him, Bob! DON'T HURT HIM!"

That was Kevin Loughery, screaming at the top of his lungs.

But Lanier wasn't paying attention. He'd closed the gap between us with a couple of long strides.

I'd never be sure what made him fall on me. My legs were sticking straight out as I went into the stands, and it's possible he tripped over them. Or it could be Bavetta or the other referee, Lee Jones, threw him off balance. They were clinging to his back and arms, trying to tear him away from me. Bavetta was a scrapper who'd broken up plenty of rumbles in the Harlem summer league, so he knew how to handle himself.

The only thing I knew absolutely was that Lanier was looming over me one second and the next was sprawled top of me—all two-hundred-fifty muscle-bound pounds of him.

Talk about heavy. I grunted out a breath. It was like having a sack of wet concrete drop on my chest. Then I saw bodies close in around us, pulling us apart. Refs, coaches, teammates.

"That's it!" Bavetta hollered. He was gesticulating at the sidelines. "You're both OUT!"

We'd been ejected.

Huh? I thought. It was only the second quarter. I still had over a half game left to play!

But when you're tossed, you're tossed. You can't argue with the ref. Truth is, I was glad Lanier hadn't flattened me.

I headed for the showers, came out, got dressed. Once you've been ejected, the regulations prohibit you from going anywhere near the court. But I knew I'd have to speak to the press about what happened. So I decided to find a place to hang out till after the game.

I left the locker room stepped out into the hallway. And froze in my tracks, my eyes wide, staring at the huge form down the hall.

OH GOD, I thought.

It was Lanier. He was coming straight toward me. And there were no security personnel around. The hallway was empty except for me and him.

"Young man?" he began.

I took a deep breath. Something told me this would be interesting.

"Come on," he said, and nodded his chin toward the parking lot exit. "Let's get something to eat."

I took a long exhale.

It was an afternoon game, so we went to a local diner. I drove. Lanier picked up the check. In between, we ate lunch and talked.

I hadn't appreciated the elbow. He hadn't liked the ball getting thrown at him. We understood each other and made peace.

When we returned to Rutgers, the game was just ending.

"I like Bernard," Lanier said at his locker afterward.

"I like Lanier," I told reporters at mine.

Thank heaven for our appetites. But we both meant it. Lanier's a good guy. When we see each other these days, we laugh about what happened.

I'd still tangle with him, though.

As for the game, Detroit edged out a 130–125 win. But that doesn't really tell you what kind of rough day it was on the court.

Bavetta and Jones called 64 personal fouls, half of them against my team. After Lanier and I were ejected, the Pistons' Eric Money was also thrown out of the game on double technicals. There were a total of 10 technical fouls, 8 on the Pistons. Five players were sent to the bench after collecting 6 personals each, including Wilson Washington, my backup forward.

Eddie Jordan scored 25 in the loss. He had one of the best nights of his career.

A few fans got crushed underneath us when we fell into the stands. I felt bad about it and apologized at my locker.

"I was just trying to get out of the way," I said. "I'm not dealing with someone who's twice my size and outweighs me by a hundred-fifty pounds!"

Okay, I was inflating Lanier's proportions.

But when you're getting charged by a grizzly, you don't ask him to step onto the scale.

ABOUT A MONTH LATER, the New Jersey Nets' season came to a quiet end with a loss to the Phoenix Suns. On a brighter note, we played better basketball down the stretch, so maybe our battle with Detroit fired us up. I also think Loughery had finally found a more consistent everyday lineup that allowed us to knit as a team. I personally had a strong finish, averaging almost 30 points a game over the thirteen left on the schedule.

I had hope for the coming year, and that helped me deal with the bad taste left by our losing record. But it would be a long offseason wait till training camp . . . and long waits weren't a good thing for me.

Then I got a call out of the blue at my Guttenberg, New Jersey, condo. It was Bill Pollak. A Hollywood studio was making a basketball movie, a comedy starring Gabe Kaplan—the comedian with whom I'd posed for a photo after the Dr. J game. The director was on a fast track to start filming and wanted to know if I was interested in being in the cast. If I was, he'd asked that I come in and read for him.

Absolutely, I told Bill. Just say when and where.

I was thinking the summer might not feel so long after all.

12 | Fast Break

I'm *gonna get this part! I'm gonna GET this part! I'm GONNA GET THIS PART!"*

As I drove through the Lincoln Tunnel from Guttenberg, New Jersey, into Manhattan, I was shouting at myself in the car. Repeating those four words over and over.

That says how much I wanted the role. When I went after something, it was with single-minded focus. I didn't know any other way. It was like when I'd been an eight-year-old figuring out how to sink a basketball in the P.S. 67 cafeteria.

The reading was in a conference room at the Hotel St. Moritz on Central Park South. But to my dismay, I wasn't alone. There was a crowded waiting area outside the main room. The chairs along the wall were filled with about twenty-five people. I felt my heart sink a little. I'd thought I was the only one up for the part.

I took a deep breath, sat down, and waited my turn, giving myself a silent pep talk. *This is going to be a competition. Okay. Understood. Just means I'm in my element. I know how to compete.*

When someone finally called my name, I entered the main room to find a small group of men and women seated at a table. They smiled politely but were quiet. Then one of the men introduced himself as Lynn Stalmaster.

I didn't know it at the time, but Stalmaster was one of Hollywood's foremost casting directors. A warm, pleasant guy with eyes that looked straight into yours when he spoke, Lynn was too humble a person to

161

say he "discovered" actors. But he would accept credit for helping stars like John Travolta, Jon Voight, and Christopher Reeve achieve success.

Not that I would've compared myself to them. I was an athlete and had no delusions about being a professional actor. But it was flattering to know that Lynn saw something in me that could work in front of a camera.

He explained that he'd seen a TV interview I gave in college, and that he thought I would be excellent for his movie based on how I came across. I had no memory of the interview, but was glad he liked it. It turned out he wanted me to read for two characters. One was Preacher, and the other was Hustler.

I never knew if Gabe Kaplan had a say in recommending me for the casting call. But, in the movie, he played a New York City physical education teacher who'd been offered a chance to live his dream and coach a college hoops program. The problem was that the fictional school, Cadwallader University, was a falling-down dump of a place on nobody's map. Gabe's character, David Greene, didn't have a recruiting budget, so he pulled together a team of misfits from the playgrounds.

In the story, Preacher, a former streetballer who had become a shifty Harlem minister, was in trouble with a neighborhood cult leader after getting his daughter pregnant. The Hustler character was a streetwise pool shark David hung out with on the West Fourth Street Courts. Since he knew all the best players around, Hustler became his right-hand man and team recruiter.

I remember Lynn asking me to do a cold read at the audition, a few lines of dialogue. I couldn't tell if the group liked it; they were all deadpan. Then Lynn handed me the screenplay.

"We'd like you to do a second read, Bernard," he said, dropping it into my hands. "Please look over the whole script. Try to retain all the lines for Preacher and Hustler, and think about what their scenes represent to the story."

"Okay." The screenplay was pretty thick. "When should I be ready?"

"Overnight," he said. "We'd like you to come back tomorrow and give a recital without the script."

I looked at him. *All the lines. Overnight.*

"Sure," I said. "Not a problem."

I went back to Guttenberg and was up all night memorizing and rehearsing the lines. I obviously wasn't a trained actor, so I figured the best thing I could do was relax and try to imagine myself in the different scenes and settings. I was a pretty good pool player, giving me an instant connection to Hustler. And Preacher reminded me of a half-dozen guys I knew from the projects. I figured being able to relate to both characters couldn't hurt.

The next day I was again in the Lincoln Tunnel: *"I'm gonna get this part! I'm gonna get this part! I'm GONNA GET THIS PART . . ."*

Back at the St. Moritz, only a handful of people were in the waiting area. Five instead of twenty-five.

I suppose that made me a finalist.

I went into the conference room. This time, Lynn let the others in his group do most of the talking. One of them would be my scene partner and read some dialogue. Then I would respond in character as either Hustler or Preacher.

We were at it a while. I'd memorized all the lines, and I'm sure they noticed. But I didn't feel I had the part in the bag. Although no one in the room told me, I gleaned from their conversations that they were also having people read in Los Angeles.

At first, it felt odd having unseen competitors thousands of miles away. On the court, you challenged your rivals head-to-head. But I knew I could outplay anybody when I was on my game. The root of it was preparation. In that sense, I told myself, things probably weren't so different from basketball. I'd prepared and executed to the best of my ability. The competition was irrelevant.

Before I left the room, Lynn told me he'd give me his decision as soon as possible. Then he asked if I was okay with spending a couple of months in Los Angeles.

Certainly, I told him. I really wanted the part, and it wasn't a big deal. As an NBA player, you were on the road for half the season and got used living out of a suitcase.

The next day, I received a call from his assistant.

"Congratulations," she said. "You have the part of Hustler."

I tried to keep from whooping myself hoarse.

"Okay . . ."

"We'd like you in LA next week," she said.

"Okaaaaay," I said, thinking that was even shorter notice than I'd expected.

"We'll provide an apartment in the Beverly Hills area."

Oh shit, I thought. "Really? *Beverly Hills?*"

"Yes. And a $500 weekly stipend," she said. "In addition to your salary. If that's acceptable."

Acceptable? $500 a week spending money *plus* salary? To stay in the land of swimming pools and movie stars—rent paid—and make a movie? What a way to spend a summer vacation. *I'd made it!*

"Yes," I said. "I think that would be very acceptable."

REHEARSALS STARTED the day after my arrival. All the main cast members were at the studio. There was Gabe Kaplan, of course. The Preacher role had gone to Michael Warren, a former UCLA hoops player with an impressive acting résumé (he would become best known as a cast member on Hill Street Blues). Harold Sylvester, another great actor—and later a screenwriter—played DC, a high school basketball star gone wrong. Mavis Washington was the only major cast member besides me with no acting experience. A high school and college athlete, she played basketball, volleyball, tennis, softball, and every other sport you can name. Mavis played Swish, a woman posing as a man so she could make our team.

The movie had a tight budget, so everything on our schedule was on the fast track. We prepared every day for two weeks, going from the rehearsal studio to Gabe's home for extra run-throughs. Then we went right to shooting.

Rushing seemed a habit with these Hollywood folks.

At the time, Gabe was coming off his huge hit television series, *Welcome Back, Kotter*, a show based on a routine he'd done as a stand-up comedian. He got along fine with everyone, but you could tell he was the star. He was kind of aloof off the set, and didn't socialize with the rest of us after each day's filming.

Gabe was different at work. He loved basketball, and we played a lot of pickup games during breaks. Under head coach John Wooden, Mike Warren had won two championships playing with Kareem Abdul-Jabbar and Lucius Allen on the UCLA Bruins—one of the most famous college basketball teams in history. Harold Sylvester's varsity hoops career wasn't as well known, but he'd been the first African American to attend New Orleans's Tulane University on a hoops scholarship. And Mavis was one of the most skillful and versatile athletes I ever met.

So our games weren't for scrubs. They were tremendously competitive. Gabe was a very good shooter and held his own.

The filming of *Fast Break* went smoothly. There was no friction on the set. Everybody got along, and everything was on schedule. You could say we did our own stunts in the basketball scenes, but, because we were all athletes, they weren't really stunts.

We didn't have much downtime. I would get to my trailer early in the morning, eat some breakfast, and wait for a knock on the door. Our director, Jack Smight, didn't like you watching scenes till it was your turn, I think because he wanted you to stay within your character's frame of reference. When I got the knock, I would go to makeup and wardrobe and then appear on set.

One Friday after we'd wrapped filming for the afternoon, I was in the trailer trying to decide on my weekend plans when one of those knocks interrupted my thoughts. I frowned. I'd thought we were finished for the day. I opened the door.

To my surprise, Gabe was standing outside. He had a big, friendly smile on his face. "B, what are your plans for tonight?"

I looked at him. From that smile, you'd have thought we hung out every night.

"Don't have any yet," I said.

He nodded. "Great! Let's go out." He gave me a mischievous wink. "Hollywood after dark, y'know. It'll be fun, guaranteed. I'll pick you up at eight o'clock."

All right.

I had a bite to eat, showered, and dressed in a sharp blue blazer, cream pants, and an open-neck shirt. A splash of cologne, a glance in the mirror, and I was ready for any ladies I might encounter.

"Not bad for a kid from Brooklyn," I told my reflection.

My reflection grinned at me.

At eight on the dot I received a call from my building's concierge. Gabe had arrived.

And how.

When I came downstairs, he was waiting in a shiny black Rolls-Royce. Nice being the star.

I hopped in and complimented him on the Rolls. "So where are we going?"

"Playboy mansion," he said casually, and pulled onto the road.

I might've gasped aloud.

My mind raced as we drove through the gates of the mansion. I was about to enter the Olympus of pleasure. The palace of A-list parties. The place that made Hollywood, Hollywood.

It was everything I'd imagined in my wildest fantasies. I entered to pumping music, gorgeous women in bunny ears and cotton-tailed bikinis, and more gorgeous women in sexy outfits lounging all around the room.

Gabe and I sat at a table and a bunny brought us drinks. One of the other guests made his way over and we introduced ourselves. Then the guy walked off. I guessed he was being sociable.

After a minute, I recognized Berry Gordy, the founder of Motown Records—and the man responsible for the careers of the Supremes, Marvin Gaye, Stevie Wonder, Michael Jackson, and countless other musical icons.

As he came walking by, Gabe stood up to say hello, shaking his hand.

Gordy was a colossus in the music business. An icon. Normally, I would have jumped at the chance to meet him.

But I was twenty-one years old. Some of the stunning goddesses in the party mix were topless. I wouldn't have tried keeping my eyes off the scenery.

Then I noticed a woman in a form-fitting miniskirt. Cocoa-brown skin, hair pulled back to accentuate her high-cheekboned beauty. She was alone.

As Gabe stood talking to Gordy, I went over and struck up a conversation. She told me her name was J'Lani, and said she'd recently signed with a modeling agency in town.

I remember that her perfume was intoxicating.

We hit it off, and pretty soon were laughing it up.

It'll be fun. Oh, yes.

I was grooving to the music and pondering my next move with J'Lani when I felt a tap on my shoulder.

It was Gabe. He leaned in toward my ear.

"Let's go," he said.

My thoughts about the night ahead came to a screeching halt. "What?" I said. *"Why?"*

Gabe looked upset. "I'll explain later," he said. "C'mon. We're outta here."

I reluctantly tore myself away from J'Lani. Before I left, she took my hand and said she was disappointed. I felt like weeping. But Gabe was my ride, and I had to work with him. Besides, I figured whatever was bothering him had to be serious. Why else would anyone in his right mind bail on the mansion?

On the drive back, Gabe explained why we'd left.

"You remember that first guy who came over to us?"

"Yeah . . ."

"Berry Gordy sent him to ask my name."

I looked at him. "So?"

"*So?* Give me a break! I'm Gabe Kaplan! Christ, how can he not know who the hell I am?"

I stared at him from the passenger seat. We'd left because Gabe was angry someone didn't recognize him.

As we descended from the hills, I think I might have contemplated hitting him upside the head.

I climbed into bed alone that night, thinking about J'Lani and what might have been. But I eventually did find out.

When J'Lani and I clasped hands, she'd slipped me a piece of paper with her phone number written on it. We got together several times during my stay in Los Angeles, and it was incredible.

I didn't tell Gabe. I wasn't sure he would have been thrilled for me.

AFTER THE PRINCIPAL PHOTOGRAPHY WRAPPED in late August, we flew to New York for two-and-half weeks of location filming. In one scene, I'm going into a Harlem billiard hall. That was a real place. When you see me shooting pool in the movie, I'm taking all my own shots. In Brooklyn, we played Eight-Ball calling pockets. So you had to be skilled.

We did a scene in an abandoned apartment building uptown. It was a shooting gallery, a place where numbers runners and drug dealers squatted. We had far too many neglected tenements to choose from.

Finally, there's a scene with Gabe and me playing basketball in the West Fourth Street park. It's early in the film; we shot out of sequence. If you pay close attention to the street kids, you'll see Laurence Fishburne as a seventeen-year-old extra. Robert Townsend, the illustrious director and actor, is also an uncredited extra in the scene. I believe it was his first movie appearance. I guess you could say we had a cast of pre-stardom all-stars.

There's a scene when one of the characters says something to me, and I reply with, "Okay, *solid*." That word wasn't in the script. It just came out of me. In my old neighborhood, *solid* meant "cool" or "all right."

As the word left my mouth, I thought I'd flubbed the line. But the director signaled me to keep going.

"Use it!" he said. "Use it!"

That happened a few times afterward, and the slang always stayed in.

Blueberry Hill, the kid with the big head and mama-cut hair, was keeping it real in the movies.

Fast Break wrapped filming in the fall of 1978. It would open about six months later, in March 1979 to decent reviews and a solid box-office take. The soundtrack even produced a top-ten song, "With You I'm Born Again" by Billy Preston and Syreeta.

The movie's advance screening would be in a few months. Lynn Stalmaster had told me everyone was delighted with my performance.

Meanwhile, the 1978–1979 NBA season was underway. The ten weeks of filming in Los Angeles and New York pulled me out of my conditioning routine, and I felt it took longer than usual to get into peak shape. But I was my own toughest critic. As we entered December, I was averaging 23 points a game, putting me among the league's top scorers.

It was a good time for the Nets. We were 17–13, four games above .500, and had an upbeat vibe among us. Over a third of the way through my sophomore season, Kevin Loughery's promise that things would get better seemed to be bearing out.

One addition to the team who'd made a positive difference was our new player-coach—a former player with the Knicks, Phil Jackson.

Early in the offseason, the Nets had acquired Phil in exchange for two high draft picks and a settlement of their financial debt to the Knicks. After eleven years and two championships in New York, he was at the end of his playing career. But Loughery had convinced him that a dual role with the Nets would prepare him for a head coaching job down the road.

I liked Phil and felt his experience was a benefit. Unlike the year before, our different ingredients were coming together. Some of us were even starting to think realistically about the playoffs.

I had no idea it would be my final season with the team, and the beginning of the darkest period of my life.

13 | Hard Falls and Second Chances

Thumps.

Loud ones.

I blinked open my eyes, jerked my head upright. Then realized I was in my Corvette.

Thumpthumpthumpthump . . .

The noise had startled me awake. I blinked again, turned toward my window, and squinted into glaring brightness. Behind it, I saw a man's silhouette in the dark.

A police officer. He was rapping on the glass with one hand while shining his flashlight into the car.

I lowered the window. Cold air blasted me. It was windy outside.

"Where am I?" I asked.

"Sir," the cop said, "would you mind stepping outside?"

I realized my engine was idling. The motor was on. So were my headlights. I'd been slumped over the steering wheel.

My head filled with fog, I pushed open the door, stepped outside, and looked around. I was at an intersection. The corners of Stone and Livonia Avenues . . . in Brownsville, Brooklyn. The car was double-parked, facing a stop sign.

I had no idea how I got there. Saturday night, I'd attended a sneak preview of *Fast Break* out on Long Island, and had a nice time. Then . . .

I went to a bar. Everything after that was a blank. How long had I been partying?

Then I remembered something. I had a commitment Sunday night. That was *opening* night for the New Jersey Gems, a women's pro basketball team. The arena was in Elizabeth, New Jersey, and I was an announced special guest on the program.

I had to get to the event. Why was I still in Brooklyn?

The more I thought about things, the more mixed up I got.

"Officer," I said. Only seconds had passed since I got out of the car. "What day is this?"

The cop looked at me over the beam of his flash.

"It's Monday morning, sir," he said. "A quarter past five."

I felt my stomach drop. I'd missed the event. Lost a whole day in the fog.

The patrolman—the name tag under his badge said Lange—put me in the backseat of his squad car. It was still hours before sunrise, and the streets were empty as we drove along.

At the 78th Precinct in Park Slope, I failed a Breathalyzer test. Then I was led back to Officer Lange's cruiser and driven to Brooklyn Central Booking at the 84th Precinct, a ten-minute walk from the Whitman Houses where I'd grown up.

I was humiliated, deeply ashamed, and numb with self-disgust. Those feelings would only deepen in the coming hours, when officers at the 84th gave me a partial strip search and found a coke vial containing a small amount of the drug—about ten dollars' worth, according to the police—in my pocket.

I was not a cocaine user. I'd always steered clear of hard drugs and didn't know how the vial wound up in my possession. Could I have put something up my nose and forgotten? How was that even possible?

Later that morning, the police sent me home with a desk ticket to appear in criminal court. I'd been charged with a misdemeanor DWI and possession of a controlled substance, as well as driving without a license.

I missed the Nets' team practice the next day. I knew my arrest would make the news and couldn't handle it. Couldn't face anyone. I was too mentally and physically depleted. At a low ebb, I stayed in my condo and ignored the ringing of my telephone. I tried to sleep, and might have drifted off. But mostly I cried in solitude.

I felt that I was going to die. I'd had the thought before, except it wasn't really a thought. I couldn't have described it at the time, but it almost seemed like a premonition.

I couldn't go on the way I was.

Unless something changed, I was going to die.

OUR NEXT GAME WAS AT HOME Wednesday night against the Houston Rockets. In the locker room at Rutgers, I got pats on the shoulder, nods, and other quiet gestures of support from my teammates and coaches. I remember Tim Bassett saying everyone was behind me. He'd always looked out for the younger guys. Coming from a veteran like him, those words meant a lot.

When I was introduced before the game, the crowd gave me a standing ovation. It went on for over a minute but seemed longer. I told myself to stay in control and kept my eyes straight ahead, not looking around at the fans.

I was embarrassed. I wasn't in college any longer and was supposed to be a pro in every way. But I had failed miserably.

The Rockets won by three points, 108–105, on double-digit scoring performances by four of their five starters: Rudy Tomjanovich, Moses Malone, Rick Barry, and Calvin Murphy. After narrowing an 8-point deficit in the first quarter, we stayed close all night, but they managed to keep a half step ahead of us.

I hit 29 points and snatched 11 rebounds. My 17 points in the fourth quarter accounted for over half the 33 scored by our team. I didn't—I *couldn't*—let anything sidetrack me from my usual game.

I knew Loughery appreciated it. Once, after a very physical game, he'd said to me, "You can't play like this every night."

He meant recklessly attacking the basket, running through a screen for a defensive foul, and hitting the floor all the time.

I replied, "Coach, that's the only way I know how to play."

He understood what I meant. It went back to when I'd told him I wanted to be the best player ever.

But that night in December bothered him more than he let on. Loughery had alcoholism in his family and knew the damage it could do.

Once during practice, he rode me especially hard during the fast-break drills Jackson called ten-and-twos. In a three-man-weave drill, three players sprinted the length of the court at full speed, passing the ball between them and changing places as they ran. The player holding the ball when they reached the basket took the shot. With the ten-and-two variation, they ran the court eight times, but the player with the ball had to dunk. They were strenuous, high-effort warm-ups that were usually followed by intra-squad scrimmages.

On the day I mentioned, Loughery repeatedly called me for travels, hitting too much rim, and other things, instructing me do the drill over each time.

I later learned Jackson asked him what it was all about.

"Bernard was trying to prove to me that he was sober, and he wasn't going to quit or bitch or puke," he said. "I've got to give him credit for taking his punishment."

Jackson was taken aback. He hadn't seen any flaws in my execution, or noticed anything else that seemed off about me. And he was right.

It never occurred to me I was being punished. I'd played for Gil Reynolds and was used to coaches driving me hard. I pushed *myself* harder than anyone and didn't stop to think about Loughery's reasons.

Still, Loughery recognized I had a problem, and he was trying to come to grips with it. The entire Nets organization was. It took me years to appreciate their dilemma. I was their best player, and I was in trouble.

After my January court appearance—at which the cocaine possession charge was dropped—I was called into an office with team officials. I believe Loughery and our general manager, Charlie Theokas, were present. Maybe some others. During the meeting, I was informed the team would not take disciplinary action against me. But they were requesting that I see a psychologist.

I was reluctant to go. I'd read all those psychology books when I was younger, and in my mind, they made me as qualified as the doctor. But I appreciated the team's continued support and finally agreed to it.

It didn't help. I wasn't at all prepared to talk about what was hurting me. To discuss any of the real, essential issues I was facing emotionally. I was searching for love and using alcohol and casual sex to mask the pain I felt in its absence.

I knew how to use specific coping skills in certain settings and situations. In fact, I had mastered them. What I didn't have was the clarity to really look inside myself. I was unable to grasp the difference between coping and getting to the source of my problems.

I could not admit I was an alcoholic.

I went to one therapy session; that was it.

NEWS FLASH.

The NBA season didn't stop because of my personal struggles.

In late January, the Nets went on a long, taxing West Coast road swing that pitted us against some of the league's best teams—the Phoenix Suns, LA Lakers, Portland Trailblazers, and others. We didn't play well during that stretch and lost five in a row. Four straight wins at home got us back on our feet, but our troubles with the Pacific Division hurt us again in March, when we went on another four- or five-game losing streak.

The upshot? We had to scratch and claw for a playoff berth for the remainder of the season.

We got a break being in a weak Atlantic Division. The Boston Celtics were in transition and a year away from Larry Bird. The Knicks' two great players, Bob McAdoo and Earl Monroe, were aging and slowed by injuries. We finished with a record of 37–45, eight games below .500, a real letdown after our quick start. But it was good enough to put us in third place ahead of the Knicks and Celts, and behind the Washington Bullets and Philadelphia 76ers, the only two teams in our division with winning records.

In 1979, the first-round finals were best-of-three series (they be-came best-of-five in 1984, then went to a best-of-seven format in 2003). We would play the division's second seed—the Sixers—with the winner moving on to face the Bullets in the semifinals.

If you were reading the sports pages, you might have thought my team had a new name: the Hopelessly Overmatched Nets.

I thought we had a chance of beating Philly. Every game between us was a demanding contest for both teams. As late as March 2—five weeks before the end of the regular season—we were within two-and-a-half games of tying them for the conference lead. As Dr. J honored me by saying in retirement, I was the toughest matchup of his career. And halfway through the year, we'd acquired another offensive weapon in his former teammate and foil on the ABA Nets, John Williamson.

Super John was a power guard with great strength. At six foot two, he wasn't tall for the league, but he had an eagle eye and a killer jumper. His stocky build reminded me of Oscar Robinson.

John spent most of his career with the Nets and was instrumental in winning two championships with Dr. J, averaging 30 points a game to place him at sixth on the team's all-time scoring list. In 1976, the same year Doc's contract was sold, John was traded to the Indiana Pacers in a salary dump. He never settled in there, and you'd hear stories that he and his coach, Slick Leonard, didn't get along.

John was branded a selfish player. I did not view him as selfish. When you put up astronomical numbers, you go with your strengths.

When we got him back mid-season, John would often pick me up in his car and drive me to the arena. We'd both grown up in tough neighborhoods—he pulled himself from the Trinity projects in New Haven—and had that aspect of our backgrounds in common. I enjoyed talking to him on our way to games.

John had a signature move that always stumped the Sixers, not to men-tion the rest of the league. It was something I incorporated into my game.

John loved shooting off one leg. As a right-handed shooter, if you are driving toward the basket and suddenly stop on a dime to elevate off your left foot, the defender is caught by surprise. He's still moving and can't block the shot because he's late.

Players were afraid of John because of his physicality. He liked to wear elbow pads (they're no longer allowed by the league) and had a favorite line about them.

"I pop meat," he'd say, tapping his arm.

I always grinned. It made me delighted we were on the same side.

In my first two years in the league, the Nets and 76ers tore it up on the court whenever we met. The wildest game was a battering, double-overtime clash that began in early November, when we trailed Philly by only two for the division lead. Dr. J was sitting out with phlebitis that night. Eric Money, our starting guard, scored 37 points.

When the game ended, it was late March. We were six games behind Philly, Doc was back in great form, and 14 of Eric's points had been wiped off the books. That brought his total for the Nets down to 23. But he scored 4 against us for a new total of 27.

Confused? I'll explain.

November. The Spectrum Arena in Philly. With nine minutes left in the third quarter, and the Sixers up 84–81, I was booted by rookie official Roger McCann with two technical fouls.

I didn't often lose my cool with the refs, but that night, it happened. With Doc injured, the player assigned to guard me was Steve Mix, a broad, slab-muscled enforcer. He'd been making hard contact all night, and I hadn't gotten the benefit of the whistle. But I was assessed a technical for returning one of his hatchet moves.

I understood. We were a losing team, and they were the Sixers on their home court. But I was not going to let a player take hits on me.

I was taking a shot in the third quarter when Steve body-bumped me in the post to knock the ball out of my hands. A defensive foul. It wasn't called.

The next play, he moved the ball down court and pulled up for a jumper. I gave what I got and bumped him.

McCann blew his whistle and called me for a foul. *What?* Steve had been getting away with it all night. The same play.

I had some words for McCann, and he hit me with my second technical. I'd been ejected.

Loughery saw red and ran onto the court. Whatever he screamed earned him two technicals of his own. McCann was hearing it that night.

Meanwhile, I was headed for the showers. On the way, I kicked a chair in disgust. The senior official on the floor, Richie Powers, slapped a third technical on me. For some reason or other, Richie gave Loughery a third, too. Maybe he liked handing them out in threes.

Our general manager, Charlie Theokas, had accompanied us on the road. As we left the court, he went rushing onto it from the sideline. Charlie had been around the game a while and knew the rules. The NBA only allowed *two* technicals to a player or coach for misbehavior. That meant my third came after I was officially ejected. So did Kevin's. If you aren't in the game anymore, Charlie argued, how can you be assessed a technical?

Powers didn't see it that way and ordered him off the court. Charlie yelled some more. Then somebody calmed him down and he left. When the dust settled, Phil Jackson stepped in to coach the last twenty minutes of the game. For the record, it was the first game Jackson ever coached.

We lost 137–133.

But that wasn't the end of things. After the game, Loughery filed a protest with the league. Commissioner Larry O'Brien upheld it, and Powers was suspended five games without pay for misapplication of the rules. As soon as the schedule allowed, the two teams would resume play from the time of his first botched call.

Cut to March. The Spectrum again. It was the Nets' last visit to Philadelphia that season, and we'd already played and lost our regular game. After a short break, we picked up the game from back in November. The score reverted to 81–84.

It was strange. And not only for all the points dropped off the scoreboard.

In February, our teams had made a four-player trade. Eric Money and poor Al Skinner—who'd resigned with us as a free agent after being sent to Detroit in midflight the year before—went to Philly for Harvey Catchings and Ralph Simpson. The NBA had decided we could use any players on our active rosters, regardless of whether they were in the original game lineup.

With a single exception.

Me.

Since the last legal call of the game was my second technical, my ejection stood. Loughery's second technical came after the point of protest, so it was vacated, and he was allowed to coach the rest of the game.

Before it started, Loughery said he'd have preferred that I was the one on the court. But the commissioner wasn't bargaining with us. He wanted a headache put to rest.

Action resumed at the whistle, with 5:50 left in the third quarter. Having been tossed, I wasn't allowed courtside and waited in the locker room for the replayed portion to conclude. They didn't have it piped in, and I had to wait till the game ended to find out the winner.

The Sixers had a healthy Doc that night. Eric Money also played, but as a Sixer. That's how he got his points on both sides.

They won the replay. New score, 110–98.

It wasn't fun getting beaten twice in a single night. Eric probably liked being on the winning team, but I bet he wasn't happy losing 14 points. No player likes his numbers messed with. That game was one for the books.

As I've said, I felt we could give the Sixers a run in the playoffs. If you were measuring us up, you had to look at the small forward position first. Dr. J was their best player, and I was ours. It was a good matchup for us. I'd been very successful against Doc. And let's not forget Super John. I hoped that we could win by staying close going into the fourth quarter, then taking the game down to the wire.

I was still young and had a lot to learn about playoff basketball in the NBA.

THERE ARE DIFFERENT ELEMENTS that make for a dominant basketball team. Experience, mental and physical toughness, the determination to defend and rebound, and the ability to close out games are crucial. You also need players with complementary skill sets who can distribute the scoring among them. If two players on a team are your primary scorers, the opposition can strategize a defense that focuses on them.

If you have multiple players who can score with proficiency, it creates a defensive nightmare for the other team.

When the engine that drives your players is a collective will to win, you have a team that can go far into the postseason.

The Philadelphia 76ers had been built for dominance. Julius Erving was in a class of his own. Add Maurice Cheeks, Darryl Dawkins, Bobby Jones, Henry Bibby, Caldwell Jones (whose brother Charles I'd later play with on the Bullets), and Steve Mix, and they had seven players—starters and reserves—who averaged in the double digits. They were a seasoned group loaded with All-Stars and future All-Stars.

On the Nets, John Williamson and I had been the two leading scorers all year long. Besides us, only Eddie Jordan and Eric Money put up double-digit numbers, and Eric had gone to the Sixers.

The 76ers had home-court advantage, and the series opened in Philly on April 11, 1979. Eddie Jordan's dad had passed away only a day before, but Eddie returned from Washington, D.C., to play with a heavy heart. Super John made good on his nickname, nailing jumpers from all over the court to score 38 points, and giving one of the most memorable postseason performances ever for the franchise. I scored 25 with the defense keyed in on me, feeding him the ball at every opportunity.

We did a good job putting up points, with help from Eddie and our center George "Big Hands" Johnson. But the Sixers took an early lead and never let go, beating us 114–122.

None of us hung our heads. We knew the quality of our opponent. We knew the odds of coming back from a Game 1 loss in a best-of-three weren't good. We knew all of it, and didn't quit.

Game 2 was at home a couple of days later. Rutgers Athletic Center was packed wall to wall, the Jersey Turnpike backed up. I felt we had the right mind-set. We were ready for a fight. We just lacked the weapons.

The Sixers put defensive pressure on Super John and me from the opening tip. Although we succeeded in holding Dr. J down to 19 for the night, they had other go-tos. Caldwell Jones, their center, had an exceptional night under the boards. So did Daryl Dawkins, the Mad Dunker. Seven of their players made good on their season averages to score double-digit points.

We couldn't match that. I dropped 28 points, and Eddie Jordan stepped up for 22. But the Sixers' had done their homework on double-teaming Super John. He was frustrated all night and only managed 21 points—a good number for many players, and against most teams.

In the postseason against Philly, it wasn't enough.

They defeated us 111–101 to sweep the series.

Super John was hard on himself after the game. He shouldn't have been. At the start of the season, we were nobody's pick to make the playoffs. We wouldn't have gotten that far without him.

I left the arena disappointed but proud of what we accomplished. We had an excellent foundation for our team. I'd helped turn us into contenders and saw promise and possibility for the following season.

I never imagined I would be gone before it opened.

IT WAS TUESDAY MORNING, OCTOBER 2, a few games into exhibition season for the 1979–1980 Nets. The beginning of the third year in my five-year contract.

I'd suited up and stepped out into the gym when Kevin Loughery came over in his sweats.

He had a stony look on his face.

We stood there as the other guys got into their warm-ups. His expression didn't signal anything good to me.

"Bernard," he said after a minute, "you've been traded."

I stared at him. Around us in the gym, guys were easing into their warm-ups. I heard them jumping rope, dribbling, and taking their first lazy shots.

"This was a front-office decision," Loughery said. "They got a center. Kelly. From Utah. He's been putting up big numbers."

I was quiet. The Nets had picked up a kid named Calvin Natt in the draft. A small forward. But there was never a competition between us—I was one of the top young players in the league. Natt had been showcased that fall as a trading chip.

A ball crashed off a backboard. I heard the rim quiver. Somebody said something in a loud voice. Somebody else laughed. My teammates were picking up the pace.

No, I thought.

They weren't my teammates. Not anymore.

Just like that, they weren't my teammates.

I didn't know what to say. I realized I hadn't played well in our first few exhibition games. For the first time in my life, I didn't train during the offseason. I'd been partying all summer long. Going to clubs in Manhattan and staying out all night.

I hadn't stopped going out when I got to camp. We didn't have clubs nearby, except for one in my hotel. It wasn't anything like the New York in-spots, but all the ladies were there, and I'd go out and have a good time with them.

Every night.

I wasn't playing well, no. But I didn't think it was because of my lifestyle. Should I have worked out more in the summer? Sure. But I told myself it was just the preseason. Told myself I still had a month to get in shape. Told myself anything I could to avoid facing up to my problem.

Traded. To Utah.

I was wounded and angry. The team knew about my partying. They had known for a long time. If they wanted to get rid of me now, it was their choice. But I knew it wasn't for the reason Loughery gave me. I also knew he must have had input into the decision. You don't trade your franchise player without consulting the head coach. He would have had a major say in it. Maybe the final say.

"You are going to regret this," I told him foolishly. Then I turned, walked off the floor, and took off my uniform.

Years later, I would thank Loughery for saving my life.

I NEVER ADJUSTED TO UTAH.

The Jazz were new to Salt Lake City after moving from New Orleans in the offseason. The year before, they finished dead last in their division with a record of 26–56. Now they were in a different division, and a different town.

In many ways, they were like the Nets when I signed with them. An expansion team searching for an identity.

It was a struggle to get comfortable. I'd spent two years working to bring a team from last place to the playoffs. In my mind, I was one of its main building blocks for the future. But it wasn't to be.

Now I felt back to square one.

I tried to see the positives. Tom Nissalke, the Jazz's coach, had stayed closer to his ABA roots than Loughery. Over time, Loughery had abandoned his freewheeling style in favor of set continuity offenses, partly because we didn't have much speed on the team. But Nissalke was integrating younger players into his roster and able to be more of a run-and-gunner. I thought that would be good for my passing game.

I also felt the Jazz had a better roster than the Nets during my rookie year. Adrian Dantley, who I knew from my summer in the D.C.-Maryland area, was a teammate, and I felt he could share the scoring with me in the low post; on the Nets I was the only true inside scorer. Their star player, Pete Maravich, was in his ninth year in the league and injury prone. But in his prime, he'd been a magician handling the ball. Maybe he had some of the old magic left in him.

And maybe, at some point, I wouldn't feel banished.

I went about all the steps of getting settled in. One of the first was finding a place to live. I rented a condo in a high-rise called Zion Summit that was owned by the Mormon Church. It was only a few blocks from the Salt Palace, where we played, and I could walk there before games. My apartment had a clear view of the Wasatch Range, and it relaxed me to look out at the mountains. At night, the stars were very bright.

When I moved into the place, I asked the building manager if there were other African Americans in the building.

"You're the first," he said.

I smiled. It felt a little forced.

"Guess I integrated it," I said.

When I'd tell friends about that conversation, it was always with that same forced smile. My years in Tennessee had prepared me for an environment where people were unaccustomed to nonwhites. But being a minority of one hadn't been in my expectations.

We started out the season 2–10, putting us in the cellar right off. Maravich's bad knees limited his playing time. I didn't sense an urgency to win. Because I'd missed camp, it took me a while to get used to the offense. I was putting up points, but not to my standard. Then, just as I started to improve in November, I suffered a severe foot injury that sidelined me for over a month. Initially diagnosed as an ankle sprain, it was later discovered to be a foot fracture.

With the team continuing to lose, I tried to come back before the foot fully healed and wound up playing uneven minutes. By then, our record was something like 7–21 in a tough division that included the Milwaukee Bucks and Kansas City Kings.

Early in my Nets career, I'd been on a team in which the players stopped caring. This felt worse.

I drank. I won't blame that on the losing. I won't blame it on anyone or anything but myself. With the injury keeping me out of the gym, I had a lot of time on my hands and slipped into my old patterns. The days ran together. I was depressed, and isolated, and sought to dull those feelings with alcohol. The premonition that I would die overtook me like a sinking wave.

I felt lost. Hopelessly lost.

New Year's Eve, 1980, was the low point of my life. Filled with anguish and despair, I phoned Bill Pollak. Beyond being a lawyer, he was a friend. He'd always been frank and open with me.

"I need help," I said.

They were three words I'd never spoken before. Not to anyone.

Bill advised me to seek treatment for alcohol abuse and told me he would look into possible options. We chose a medical center in Santa Monica, California, where I began six weeks of intensive rehabilitation. Once there, I enrolled in Alcoholics Anonymous.

I remained at St. John's for six weeks of intensive rehabilitation. I felt God had given me a last chance to deal with my problem.

I was still a long way from salvaging my career.

14 | The Golden State Warriors

Rudy Hackett isn't a household name among basketball fans. Born in the poor African American neighborhood of Mount Vernon, New York, he was a right-handed forward at Syracuse University who played with the ABA Spirits of St. Louis in 1975–1976, and split the next year between the NBA Nets and Indiana Pacers.

With the Orangemen varsity team, Rudy was a bona fide star, his name high on its all-time scoring and rebounding lists. As team co-captain in his senior year, he led them to the NCAA Final Four tournament.

When I joined the Nets in 1977–1978, Rudy was out of the league. For one reason or another, his natural abilities did not translate to the NBA. It happens with many great college athletes.

In 1979, Rudy began playing professionally in Italy, where basketball was a highly popular sport. He would spend a decade in the Italian leagues. I met Rudy in the summer of 1980, during my period of recovery in Santa Monica.

He was the hardest-working player I ever saw. I always thought I prepared with greater intensity than anyone. I was wrong. Rudy broke the mold. He taught me how to train at a whole new level.

That year, Rudy was back in the United States playing with the Southern California Summer Pro Basketball League—now known as the Summer Pro League. It was a league where young up-and-comers looking to hone their skills, or unaffiliated veterans looking to stir up interest in their availability as free agents, could showcase themselves

184

on teams sponsored by NBA ball clubs, led by NBA coaches, and offi-
ciated by NBA referees.

There were three games a night, five nights a week. At forty minutes long, the games were shorter than the NBA's. But the rules were
identical and there was a high caliber of play.

Four or five months after checking into St. John's for treatment, I
signed up for the SoCal Summer League. I wasn't the type of player
you'd normally see on its rosters. Most of the guys were hoping for a
spot as an NBA team's tenth or eleventh man. Billy Ray Bates, Larry
Demic, and Brad Holland were some of the guys playing that year.

I was a star forward in my prime. I'd gone toe-to-toe with Julius
Erving. Not once, but for two full seasons.

I'd also made some terrible mistakes. I knew I still could be one
of the best players in basketball. But first I needed to win back the
league's respect. I had something to prove, like when I'd been a kid
playing with the older players, demonstrating I should be on the court.

I committed myself to achieving that goal . . . to resurrecting my career, whatever it took. Besides playing summer basketball, I started working out at Pete Newell's camp for forwards and centers—his famous Big
Man Camp. Newell had been one of the great college coaches in the game
during the 1950s and 60s, led the men's U.S. basketball team to a gold
medal in the 1960 Olympics, and was general manager of the LA Lakers
when they traded for Kareem Abdul-Jabbar. He had a well-deserved reputation as a master of footwork in the low post and on the wing position.

It took Newell a little while to warm to me. He'd heard stories
about my problems off the court and had been hesitant to even let me
attend camp. But he spoke to some players who knew me personally
and changed his mind.

Camp ran for a week or two, and one of the guys with whom I became friendly was Kiki VanDeWeghe. A small forward, Kiki was a star
of the UCLA Bruins under Larry Brown from 1976 to 1980. He'd been
a top pick for the Dallas Mavericks in that summer's draft, but would
be traded to the Denver Nuggets later in the season.

I didn't have a car in California, so Kiki used to drive to my apartment
and give me a lift to camp. Later on, we practiced at the UCLA gym with

other NBA players in the Summer League. Kiki had grown up in the area and still lived with his family. Sometimes after our sessions with Pete Newell, he'd bring me over to have dinner with his mom and dad.

It was a time of healing and rejuvenation for me. Mentally, I'd never felt healthier. I hadn't had a drink since Utah. You take things day to day with alcohol problems. It was too soon to declare I'd beaten them. But I felt I *could* and was making great strides in my recovery.

My training with Rudy Hackett laid the groundwork for my return to the court. Every morning, I would bicycle out to the UCLA campus and meet him for workouts. He always took the lead. We'd run the steps at Drake Stadium, do sprints on its track, train on the soccer field. I never lifted weights during my career, but kept him company in the weight room. After we had a bite to eat, I'd hop on my ten-speed again, pedal home, get an hour's rest, and then ride back out to Santa Monica on the bike path, going past Venice Beach and the Pacific Ocean to the marina with its sailboats and motor yachts.

I couldn't have chosen a better place to be noticed than the SoCal Summer Pro League. The games were at Cal State, Dominguez Hills, in the South Bay area, a half hour's drive from UCLA on the freeway, and only minutes from the Big Man Camp in Long Beach. I remember an LA newspaper article that said you'd see more NBA scouts and coaches in the stands than spectators. I'm not sure it was meant literally, but it seemed that way to me. There were executives, too. General managers, team presidents, even owners.

When I wasn't playing in a game, I would sit in the stands and take notes about what was happening on the court. I wanted to demonstrate my seriousness about reviving my career, and knew people were watching me carefully.

One of those individuals was Al Attles.

Al was a former point guard who'd spent his entire playing career with the Warriors, then become the team's head coach and general manager in 1970. With pioneers like Bill Russell and Lenny Wilkens, he was among the first African American coaches in the NBA.

Everyone respected Al—fans, players, coaches, executives. As a competitor, he'd been as tough as anybody in the game. His background as a professional athlete gave him an understanding of what made them tick. But he also held a master's degree in curriculum and instruction, and knew how to run and organize a team. Knowing both sides of the game firsthand made him a perfect bridge between ownership and talent.

Al and Pete Newell had a friendship that went back years. Besides running the Big Man Camp, Newell had been a longtime advisor for the Warriors. I don't know if it's true, but I've heard it was his idea to change the name of the franchise from the "San Francisco" to "Golden State" Warriors when they moved across the bay to Oakland.

After the first few days of Summer League, Al was there for every game. I saw him, but didn't know he'd come especially to see me perform. I was on a tear that would earn me MVP of the league, and Newell had phoned him and said he'd better get down to Dominguez Hills before somebody else made an offer to the Jazz.

Al didn't waste any time contacting the Warriors' owner, Franklin Mieuli. They were building a team to compete for a championship and wanted me to be part of it.

But there was only one problem.

I was still under contract to Utah and would be for another year.

AL ATTLES HAD A PLAN for rebuilding the Golden State Warriors. Not over many years, but within a season or two.

When he'd begun thinking about how to do it, Al didn't have to check out other teams' blueprints for success. He could look straight back over his shoulder and see the answers in his own footsteps.

In 1974–1975, Al had coached the best Warrior squad in memory to a 48–34 regular season finish and then swept the Washington Bullets to win an NBA Championship. The next year, the Warriors surpassed their previous season's win total by going 59–23, but lost to Phoenix in the conference finals.

There was a steady decline over the next three seasons. In 1979–1980, the Warriors' 24–58 record sank them to the bottom of the Pacific Division.

People didn't talk about hustle stats in those days. But the team's numbers for rebounds, free throws, and inside scoring couldn't have been worse. They weren't stopping anyone from scoring points or capitalizing on opportunities under the basket.

Al realized he'd made some mistakes putting together his recent squads and went back to the drawing board using his 1975 championship team as a model. It had been led by Hall of Famer Rick Barry, a well-rounded player who could score and defend, and was one of the highest percentage free-throw shooters ever to play the game. The center, Clifford Ray, wasn't in the lineup to put up points, but nobody in the league could out-rebound him. Jamaal "Silk" Wilkes, the other starting forward, was known for his agility and soft hands. On defense, he buzzed opponents like a wasp with his speed and nimbleness. On offense, he was always ready for a pass.

The team was like that from top to bottom. Barry drew the spotlight because of his scoring ability. But he was surrounded by steady, unselfish role players.

Al envisioned getting back to that kind of game and was already on his way to accomplishing it. He'd brought in some solid rookies using a combination of high draft picks and trades, but still needed one or two experienced guys.

After seeing me in the summer league, he'd decided I could fill Barry's role of primary scorer and bring added defensive and low-post ferocity to the floor. He was also eyeing another move—a trade for the Jamaal Wilkes of his new team.

That player turned out to be one of my old buddies from Brooklyn, World B. Free. World was born Lloyd Bernard Free and legally changed his name in the 1980s, but "World" was always his nickname. Some people say he earned it when he did a 360-degree dunk in junior high school. Some say it was because he could score from anywhere around the court.

I don't know how it got started, but I'd called him by that name since we were twelve or thirteen in the playgrounds. He was flashier than I was and loved to dunk the way honeybees love flowers. Some coaches thought he hogged the ball. I'd played with him before and knew we could work together without problems.

A couple of weeks before trading for me, Al acquired World from the San Diego Clippers in a two-player deal. I'm not sure when I heard about it. While Al was focused on rebuilding the Warriors, I was re-building myself.

There's a saying that the past is another country. That was how I felt about Utah. I didn't want to go back there. I *couldn't* go back there. I was sober and in a good place and wanted to be traded.

When I went to the Warriors for power forward Wayne Cooper and a draft pick, I was as happy as I'd been the day I was drafted into the NBA.

I knew it was my last chance and did not intend to waste it.

BASKETBALL IS ALL ABOUT COMPETING, and not only against other teams. You compete for jobs, playing time . . . everything. As a competitor, you need a cold-blooded mentality. You need to be clear on what you want to achieve and pursue it with absolute, unswerving determination.

I wasn't guaranteed a starting role on the Warriors. Purvis Short had been the starting forward for a couple of years, and Al wasn't about to just hand me his job.

I'd been a starter since I was a teenager. In high school, the youth leagues, Tennessee, and with two NBA teams. I still intended to be one. But I had to prove I deserved it. I had to compete.

The very first day of training camp, I destroyed Purvis in an intra-squad game. Completely outplayed him. Several of his friends were in the gym. They left in the middle of the scrimmage, and I can still see them marching out the door.

Ouch.

The next day, I became the starting small forward.

I knew I'd flat out embarrassed Purvis. I hadn't really wanted to. But I'd really wanted to.

I'm sure if you asked him about it, Purvis would tell you he'd have done the exact same thing to me.

That's the NBA.

I WAS ACCEPTED by the Golden State organization with open arms. No one questioned my past. No one brought it up. Players, coaches, and management made it known right off that they were glad I was there.

Al set the tone early on. He made me feel I was finally where I was supposed to be.

"A lot of people are giving me credit for all this 'last chance' stuff, but I think that's garbage," he told the press. "It's Bernard and World who deserve the credit. We're just the recipients of their talent."

I can't speak for World, but I was grateful to Al. Joining Golden State was *more* than my last chance as a professional athlete. It rekindled something I had lost: My love of the game.

I can't stress enough how different playing with love is from playing strictly with passion.

When you play with love, there's joy.

For the first time in my life, I had a measure of inner peace.

We had a great bunch of guys on the team. Joe Barry Carroll and Rickey Brown were rookies who came over in a deal with the Boston Celtics. Golden State had traded for draft picks that they used to sign Carroll and Brown, and the Celtics got Robert Parish, a veteran center, and a draft pick they turned into forward Kevin McHale from the University of Minnesota.

Let's pause here to examine that trade.

Joe Barry was a durable seven-footer who averaged over 20 points and 9 rebounds a game in his four years with the Warriors. Rickey was a versatile center-forward off the bench.

I loved playing with them. But Red Auerbach, the Celtics' general manager and head coach, must have had one hell of a poker face to match the thick Cuban cigars that were always poking out of his mouth. With Parish and McHale joining Larry Bird on Boston's front court, he'd locked his hand around a championship dynasty.

But I'll get back to the Celtics. I don't want to take anything away from Golden State, or fail to recognize the team's impact on me.

Our players had incredible chemistry. I felt it in training camp, and you can't bottle that. A team either has it or doesn't. And if you have a talented team, chemistry, and guys who want to play every single night and are willing to be unselfish, if you have all that *and* you're well coached—I don't want to overlook what Al's soft-spoken encouragement meant to us—then you have everything it takes to go far in the league.

The Warriors were a transition team. We ran. We opened the floor up and we ran.

I was up for it every night. Lorenzo Romar was our rookie point guard. He was drafted out of Washington State, where he eventually returned to become head coach of the Cougars before moving on to an associate coaching position in Arizona. In my first year with Golden State, the veteran John Lucas started at point, and Lorenzo got limited minutes. But he moved like a colt, and I'd have fun sprinting down the court with him.

Lorenzo was quick with a wisecrack and a smile, a very likable guy. I kind of took him under my wing, and we developed a locker room routine before games.

I'd say, "I'm running tonight, Lorenzo. I'm running!" Pumping my arms to illustrate.

Lorenzo would make a face. After a while, he'd see me coming up to him and beat me to the punch.

"I know, B. You're running. You're *running!*"

Lorenzo and I were good friends. Before road trips, I occasionally invited him to my place for dinner. Afterward, we would drive to the airport together.

I was also close to my Brooklyn brother, World B. Free. But we were never above some friendly competition. World was a deadly scorer. That was his forte and his role on the Warriors.

Once, at practice, World shouted, "I got the rebounds. Bernard's our wing guy. Leave the rebounds to me, and I'll get the ball to him." He grinned. "*Run B!*"

World knew I loved to rebound. To position myself under the basket when someone took a shot, follow that shot, and dunk it.

I could have compared my rebounding *and* scoring stats to his, but for the sake of team chemistry, I let him lead until January. Besides, I loved a challenge.

During the intra-squad scrimmage, I waited to go up against him, outfought him for the rebound, beat him down the floor in a fast break, *and* made the layup to score.

We both laughed. It was like that between us.

But I can't talk about rebounds without mentioning Larry Smith. A power forward from Mississippi, Larry was another team rookie. As the season wore on, Al kept increasing his time on the floor, mostly because of his amazing rebound totals.

We called him Mr. Mean. I think he got that nickname in college because he never smiled, on or off the court. But it wasn't that he was unhappy. He was just quiet and serious about his rebounds. He'd pull one down and you'd see satisfaction in his eyes.

Larry was amazing. He used to say he was a "hard workin' working-man." Maurice Lucas and Kermit Washington were the two best power forwards in the league back then. I may have gotten 30 points on a Friday, and 50 against Dr. J on Saturday. But Larry grabbed 25 rebounds back-to-back nights against Kermit and Maurice, the two best power forwards in the league. Unbelievable!

It seemed like Larry beat me to every rebound. Not that I ever complained. I got a kick out of watching him work. He was the most dominant rebounder I ever played alongside.

Larry was fearsome in the paint, but when we traveled to New York for a game, he wouldn't leave his room other than to go to the arena. Larry came from a town called Rolling Fork, population two thousand. The big city scared him to death. Guys would stick around the hotel to play cards with him. We were a close-knit bunch.

I'd socialize a lot with the guys during home stands. That wasn't the case when I was on the Nets, or with any other team I played for. Rickey Brown and I would spend afternoons in the park with our girlfriends; we'd all grab ice cream cones and toss around a Frisbee. Joe Barry Carroll shared my appreciation for music, and we sometimes went on double dates. I remember driving across the Golden Gate Bridge to San Francisco, hitting the jazz clubs, then enjoying seafood dinners in the harbor.

The scenery was breathtaking. I'd bought a new car and would drive over the bridge to Sausalito after every practice, soaking in the beauty around me. I can still picture the low green hills climbing above the harbor in shelves, million-dollar homes perched on their edges like Monopoly pieces, houseboats floating off the piers below. The glints of brilliant sunlight on the water reminded me of sequins on a woman's gown.

I loved the Bay Area. I'd gained a sense of who I was. This does not mean I'd dug down to the root of all my problems. Some things can't be solved overnight. But I was no longer on a self-destructive course. My recurring visions of a premature death were behind me. After moving to California, I never had them again.

In my first year with the Warriors, I felt we had one of the most talented rosters in the league from top to bottom. We had our share of losses. But even with three rookies on the team, we were in every game. We'd rarely get blown out.

We would have made some noise in the playoffs. We played our hearts out for Al Attles and had all the ingredients to make a run. Nobody wanted to face us.

We were in the hunt late into the season. The Phoenix Suns and San Antonio Spurs had locked up the top spots in the Western Conference, and we were one of eight or nine teams scrambling for the last four berths.

On March 18, 1981, we hosted the Houston Rockets for one of the biggest games of our season. We were two-and-a-half games ahead of them in the standings, with eight left to play. The Rockets had one less game than we did on the schedule.

John Lucas was our starting point guard. For years, he'd been one of the best, a truly outstanding player. Lorenzo Romar and a few others had rotated as backups all season, but John provided the veteran leadership we needed at that position.

Unfortunately, he didn't show up that night. John had already missed five games during the season. We were all aware he was struggling with personal issues.

John and I both loved soul food, and we occasionally went out to eat at Lady Esther's restaurant in downtown Oakland, where the Southern cooking was second only to my mom's—and she'd long since hung up her iron skillet. Otherwise, I saw very little of John off the court; our lifestyles were very different.

His absence against Houston made things difficult. The Rockets had defeated us the week before in their arena and were looking to overtake us. Their two best players were Calvin Murphy, an All-Star, at point, and Moses Malone in the center position. Calvin was near the end of his career and pushing to go out with a bang.

We didn't know what happened to John. Nobody in the organization could find him.

I think Houston smelled blood.

The game was close. We ended the third quarter with a 92–84 lead, but Houston made a run in the fourth and we couldn't stem the tide. They won by a single point, 117–118.

Both teams left the arena alive in the Western Conference, but the game foretold how we'd wind up in the standings.

The Rockets finished with a record of 40–42. We were 39–43. They beat us by a single game to make the playoffs.

Yes, I know. Neither team had a winning record. But guess what?

The Rockets went all the way to the NBA Finals, defeating the Lakers, the San Diego Clippers, and the Kansas City Kings before losing to the Boston Celtics in the championship round.

I had a long career with many successes. But some things will always sting, and missing the playoffs by one game is one of them.

I never would have guessed it would happen again the very next season.

15 | Knick Time

Preparation.

In translating talent to performance, nothing happens by accident. It's planned. But I'll go deeper. Every experience you gain, and obstacle you surmount, prepares you for the next step in your journey. You may not even realize when you're being readied to take that step. It isn't always immediately clear.

I developed my Game Face to shield myself from the pain of my mother's belt strap. Though I didn't know it, I was preparing myself for coming challenges, gaining the toughness to fight off the bullies on the street, then stand up to my father so I could play the game I loved. That ignited the spirit and determination that drove me out of the playgrounds of Fort Greene and fueled me to climb and climb in life.

At some point, you need to take charge of your progress. Preparation has to be deliberate. *Active.*

As an athlete, I prepared for every aspect of the game. Through analysis and planning, I sought to achieve perfection. My goal was to be nothing less than the best. I had to make sure I was ready to play forty-eight minutes. That I was putting myself in the right mind-set from the moment I sat down in front of my locker, bowed my head, and closed my eyes, until the final buzzer sounded.

The Golden State Warriors had great talent. But they were young and raw. Going into my second year, I understood I'd have to provide more leadership for the team while it developed. But I never saw it as shouldering a burden. I believed my heart, soul, and desire to achieve—along with hard work and preparation—made me well suited for the role.

In Oakland, I came of age. I relished leading my team, relished being someone they could depend on, relished coming through in the clutch. My coaches and teammates could mark down what they'd get from me each night, knowing I might do even better.

When I was a kid, there was a cartoon series called *Felix the Cat*. The theme song had a line that went something like, "Whenever he gets in a fix, he reaches into his bag of tricks." I had my own offensive bag of tricks on the basketball court. No matter how difficult the situation, whatever offensive stopper a team or individual player designed for me, I'd have something in the bag to offset it.

Unless you prepared, as I would in the offseason, you would disappear as the year went on. Teams scouted you and tried to neutralize your strengths. If you had nothing left in the bag, you fizzled. You'll see this time and again in the playoffs. Guys have no answers to the defenses used against them.

You shouldn't just prepare to play. You have to prepare for *successful* play.

I would teach myself at least one new move every offseason. This was true without fail. I never told anybody. I didn't want to share the full contents of my bag with the league.

Of the more than one thousand games I played in my NBA career, there are many I can't remember because I was so focused on how to succeed each night. *The game within the game.* I'd come out of the huddle asking my teammate what play our coach called. I didn't want to sit there listening in a relaxed state. I could not be relaxed and in a dominant mode at the same time.

If you study my numbers, you'll notice I always had a strong second half to the season. Part of my secret was to lose five pounds in January. In the first half, the extra weight would help me endure the physical battering I'd take on the floor. But in the second half of the season, I would shed the weight. It helped me perform better. It gave me the speed, athleticism, and vigor I needed to up my game. As a leader, you expect your preparation to rub off on your teammates.

I was also paying attention to an impending reality. Professional sports is, by definition, a business, and my contract was expiring at the end of the season.

I wanted to be a Warrior for the rest of my career, and signaled management that I was interested in negotiating a new deal. I'd tried to initiate talks the year before. In early January 1981, we played the Celtics at home on a Friday night and the 76ers on Saturday. That meant facing Larry Bird and Dr. J. I was determined to put on a show against them and arranged for Bill Pollak to fly in from Washington, D.C., to begin contract discussions with Frank Mieuli.

You could have felt the heat of my desire radiating off me that weekend. On Friday, I put up 30 points against Bird. The next night, I scored 50 versus Erving, and made falling-down shots barely realizing I'd hit the floor. I was in the Zone.

I remember one defensive play against Doc. He was going in for a breakaway layup, one of his spectacular dunks, and as he took off into the air, I went up to block the shot and met him at the apex of his jump.

He posterized me, going right up to the hoop. I stopped him from scoring and was called for a foul. Most guys in my spot wouldn't have tried.

The Warriors surprised Bill and me afterward and backed off from negotiations, saying they preferred to wait until after the season. Bill and I concluded they did not want to buy high. If they delayed, it was possible my value would level off.

That taught me something. I became more hard-nosed. When you play for the love of the game, you can sometimes forget the NBA is like any other business entity. But you can't let yourself forget it when you're off the court.

The delay proved a tactical mistake for Golden State. In 1981–1982, I led the Warriors in scoring with 23 points a game and was voted to my first All-Star Game, representing the Western Conference alongside Kareem Abdul-Jabbar, Magic Johnson, George Gervin, Moses Malone, and other great players. After the season, I was selected as an All-Pro, just in time for free agency.

The Golden State Warriors had a solid run that year, going 45–37, a major improvement over the previous season. But we again wound up with one less win than the Houston Rockets, who went 46–36 to beat us out for a playoff slot.

I attributed this disappointing finish to our relative inexperience. An overlooked aspect of a championship-caliber team is the ability to play well two nights in a row. It's difficult for a player. But you can't let yourself tire out. You can't have a letdown. You have to find ways to perform with the same energy level on consecutive nights, particularly near the end of the season when teams are in heated battles for playoff berths. Those who can best handle the rigors of the schedule come out on top.

In a typical NBA season, a team might have between sixteen and twenty back-to-back games. The Warriors had eighteen in 1981–1982, and we handled them well early on. But a quirk of the schedule gave us almost half of them in March and April. We faltered down the stretch, losing the second game in six out of eight back-to-backs.

The worst losing streak of our season began on March 10 with a defeat to the Sixers in the second part of a back-to-back on the road. It lasted five games and included two consecutive-night losses to the Portland Trailblazers and Kansas City Kings.

I knew the team was exhausted. It wasn't hard to tell. When guys are on the floor tired, you can see the heaviness in their arms and legs.

But a single game. The Rockets. Two years in a row.

It was demoralizing. As the Warriors' leader, I felt responsible and wondered all summer long what I could have done to effect a different outcome. We had bested many of the league's premier teams through-out the season. Who knew what we could have accomplished if we'd entered the playoffs?

It's something that will stay with me for the rest of my life.

I began the offseason with question marks swirling around my mind. I'd flourished in Oakland. In my two years there, I transformed my life and career, went from being someone widely thought to have squandered my early promise to being an All-Star. But now I was a free agent. It's an exciting time for a player, but there's trepidation. You don't know your future. You don't know where you'll be living in a few short months. You believe in yourself and are confident you've established your value with a distinct body of work. But you're still on your own.

The free agency period doesn't officially begin until the conclusion of the NBA Finals. In 1982, that was June 8, with the Lakers defeating the Sixers four games to two, and Magic Johnson winning his second MVP award.

While Los Angeles celebrated the victory, Warriors fans wanted to know whether I would return to the team and help finish what we'd started over the past couple of seasons.

I shared their hopes . . . and their uncertainty. I was convinced we were only a few steps away from bringing a championship to the Bay Area. But I didn't know the thinking of team ownership. They still hadn't reached out to Bill Pollak, nor given any other concrete indications that they wanted to retain my services.

I felt I needed to say something publicly and decided to hold a press conference at the Oakland Coliseum. I told reporters I didn't know the team's intentions, and that my own preference was to suit up as a Warrior in the fall. It was important for me to know the team was serious about competing for an NBA crown. I was twenty-five years old and expected to make a long-term commitment spanning the prime of my career. I wanted whoever signed me to be equally committed to winning.

Time passed and I heard nothing from the Warriors. Then Pollak called. He'd been contacting teams around the league to gauge their interest in me, and one in particular was prepared to make a very substantial bid.

Pollak was a fellow New Yorker. I could hear the excitement in his voice. Even before he named the team, I knew it was the Knicks.

Their formal offer sheet came in September and was designed to blow other teams out of the water, including Golden State, which had the option to exercise the right of first refusal and match. The contract was for five years, and included signing bonuses and other clauses that would significantly raise my base salary over its full duration.

The Knicks want me, I thought. The team I'd grown up watching. The team I always dreamed of playing for.

The Brooklyn boy in me itched to sign the deal.

The analytical part of me said to hold off and think about some things.

I listened to that cautious voice and waited ten days.

The Knicks were going through an upheaval. Red Holzman, the illustrious head coach who led the franchise to two championships, had retired after failing to make the playoffs. All kinds of rumors surrounded them, attendance had plunged, and Michael Ray Richardson, the team's point guard and a four-time All-Star, was struggling with addiction.

"This ship be sinkin," he famously said when asked about their miserable thirty-three-win season.

Now ownership was trying to right the ship. Dave DeBusschere, my favorite player as a kid, had returned as the Knicks' executive vice president with the mission of restoring the team to greatness. His first move was to hire Hubie Brown as his new head coach. His second was to present offers to me and Ernie Grunfeld. After two seasons with the Milwaukee Bucks, Ernie had played for the Kansas City Kings and become one of the better swingmen in the league.

DeBusschere knew what Ernie and I had done in Tennessee. He'd followed my career in Oakland. And he knew what it took for a player to thrive in New York. With both of us available, he formed the idea of bringing us home to recreate our winning chemistry and excite the Knicks' fan base.

The fan base?

My God, *I* was excited.

But I had doubts about playing for Hubie Brown.

Hubie had coached the Kentucky Colonels in the ABA and been head coach of the Atlanta Hawks for six seasons. In 1978, he was voted Coach of the Year by sportswriters. He was very respected among his peers. With players, not so much.

The NBA is a small community. You hear how guys are treated on other ball clubs. And I knew Hubie was very disparaging to members of his team.

Hubie was a screamer. He shouted profanities and insults. In practice. In the locker room. Publicly during games. Anywhere, anytime, Hubie screamed and cursed at his players.

I wanted to play in New York. I wanted to play for the Knicks. I'd had the opportunity presented on a silver platter and been offered a lot of money.

But the thought of having to put up with Hubie Brown's abuse made me seriously consider turning it down. I did not want to play for a coach like that. I believed Golden State would present a respectable offer. If not, I'd find a home someplace else. Wherever I went, I would be fine financially.

I could walk away from the money. Walk away from it without regrets. But I couldn't walk away from my dream. In the end, that made me push aside my reservations. Nothing should ever deny you the fulfillment of a dream. Not a coach, not anyone, nothing.

It's Knick time! I thought, my mind made up. Those were the exact words, I swear. I remember them perfectly to this day.

Calling Bill, I told him I would accept the Knicks' offer. A few days later, I flew to New York City and signed.

THE WARRIORS' OWNER, Frank Mieuli, would have something to say about it.

Under his right of first refusal, he had fifteen days after I signed the offer sheet to choose whether to let me go to the Knicks or match their terms and keep or trade me to another team.

He waited until the eleventh hour to make his decision. By then, it was almost mid-October. Knicks training camp was underway, and my future was up in the air.

Frank was a smart businessman and self-promoter. He'd made a fortune in television and radio, and was the originator of the audiotape duplication technique that allowed major sports events to be broadcast in different markets. A portly man who loved food and drink, he had long, dark hair that never looked combed, and a dark, shaggy beard that usually covered his cheeks and chin. Frank wore a deerstalker hat and safari suit, and rode a motorcycle when he wasn't sailing the world aboard his yacht.

I'd always liked and respected him. He felt Golden State had contributed to my comeback, and I wouldn't have disputed it. But I'd waited two years to discuss a contract and given him every opportunity to initiate discussions. I had to be fair to myself.

Frank flew to Manhattan for the announcement. When he was young, he'd been a radio pitchman for a San Francisco beer company, and he loved to make a splash. He convened a press conference at the Sheraton Center on Seventh Avenue, not far from Madison Square Garden.

Sports reporters and stringers from both coasts showed up in droves. It was just what Frank wanted. He gave a command performance, declaring he'd chosen to exercise his right and match the Knicks' offer. But he took issue with the bonus clauses they'd included in the contract, claiming the Knicks' financial advantages made it difficult for him to match.

The quotes he tossed the press like sirloins made it clear he was furious.

At the Knicks: "The Knickerbockers used to run with dignity, but now they are a carpetbagging conglomerate!"

"It would be unthinkable of me to let Bernard King go! He is part of our inventory! We developed him, we found him, we own him! *He belongs to us!*"

On whether he would keep me on the team or sign and trade: "I'll put King in a Warrior uniform and run him up and down the court. Or, put two bodies he will bring in a trade in Warrior uniforms, and run *them* up and down the court. And maybe trade him for a draft choice!"

Frank wound up bringing his case to an arbitrator for the NBA and players' union. His argument was an expanded version of the one he'd made to the press. The Knicks had written in a large salary bonus if the Warriors matched and dealt me to a third team. That, he insisted, limited his ability to trade me to teams with lesser resources or facing salary cap issues. To put it another way, it weakened his bargaining position and made it more likely he'd have to deal with New York.

He was correct. One facet of the NBA as a business is the brinksmanship between team organizations. The Knicks had outmaneuvered Frank and were ruled to be fully within their rights.

But the Warriors still had a hand to play, and they used it by matching New York's offer. Frank Mieuli hadn't been bluffing to the press. He did not intend to let me go without getting something in return.

It left me in limbo.

Frank negotiated with the Knicks, but the talks seemed to reach an impasse. At one point, I heard I might be traded to the Seattle Supersonics. Lenny Wilkens was head coach there and had won an NBA Championship in 1979. He was a players' coach, a fellow Brooklynite, and I would have enjoyed being on his team. But that never materialized.

Late October came around. Within days, the NBA's exhibition games would give way to the regular season. Since a trade hadn't been completed, I decided to call a press conference to announce that I was ready to sign with the Warriors. I personally phoned every sportswriter in the area to once again invite them to the Oakland Coliseum.

I had mixed emotions. Golden State was entitled to retain me, and I understood their decision. My respect for Al Attles hadn't diminished. But my heart had been set on going home to New York and playing at the Garden in front of my mother and father.

As it turned out, that dream became a reality after all.

I never suited up in a Warriors uniform again. The next day, Bill Pollak called. I'd been traded.

I was finally going to the Knicks. In exchange, Michael Ray Richardson would be sent to Golden State.

I had surprisingly mixed emotions. Oakland changed my life. I cherished my two years there. I'd even picked out a home overlooking the Bay that I would have bought if I'd stayed with the Warriors. The realization that it was all about to be in my past came with bittersweet finality.

As I told one reporter, I couldn't have guessed my news conference would turn out to be a farewell. That weekend, I took out a full-page ad in the local paper expressing my appreciation to the fans. They'd supported me from the beginning and shown their appreciation and enthusiasm at every game.

But I didn't have much time to examine my feelings. I'd learned about the deal on a Friday afternoon. NBA rules state a player must report to his destination team within forty-eight hours of an in-season trade.

I flew to New York on Sunday.

16 | In Transition

I clearly recall my thoughts aboard the flight from San Francisco to New York.

I'd been ready to move on from the Warriors for some time. I *wanted* it. But I felt uprooted all the same.

It's uncomfortable, even disorienting, when you relocate from one city to another. I didn't have a house waiting for me. I didn't have an apartment. Training camp was over. The exhibition season was over. I would be walking through the door cold, trying to integrate myself into a new team, with new personalities, a new coach, and a new system. My reporting date was Monday, less than twenty-four hours away. Our first game on the season schedule was Friday night at Madison Square Garden. We were playing the Philadelphia 76ers, who'd added Moses Malone to complement Julius Erving and a formidable roster that included Maurice Cheeks and Andrew Toney.

We. My team. The New York Knicks.

It still seemed unreal.

I didn't feel pressure. But I had a tremendous sense of responsibility. I wasn't brought to the team as a complementary player. I was expected to lead them back to their former eminence in a conference with Dr. J and Larry Bird, the two best forwards in the league—athletes at the pinnacle of our sport—as my competitors.

Beyond that, I was a hometown kid. I would be representing the city, Brooklyn, my family and friends, and the storied legacy of the Knicks. When I was on other teams, I'd always looked forward to playing at Madison Square Garden, felt my adrenaline flowing the moment

I stepped on the court. Performing there wasn't just playing basketball. It was something indescribably special and singular. For me, New York *was* b'ball, and I'd always brought my A-plus game as a visitor.

Now I was a Knick, and the challenge was ready to be met. If our team got off to a good start, the city would be galvanized. If we failed, I knew all eyes would be on me.

We lost our first seven games.

I REMEMBER GARDEN FANS WELCOMING ME as if I'd been there forever. The cheers when I was announced for the first time made it feel like a homecoming.

I could tell the crowd was charged up. New York basketball fans are very knowledgeable. They'd seen me play at Madison Square Garden over the years and knew what I'd achieved with the Nets and Warriors. I was arriving after an All-Star and All-Pro season, and they were excited by my presence as the team's elite player.

Despite losing our first game to Philly, I felt we gave a strong effort. But we had seven new players on the squad, and many of us had never played together before. I'd only had a few days of practice after flying from the West Coast. Our backup forward Louis Orr had been acquired in trade the same day I was. We were disjointed on both sides of the court.

The roles Ernie Grunfeld and I had on the Knicks were different than they'd been in college. But we had an unbreakable bond, a special kinship. We were friends for life and would eventually move to the same town. As New York kids, we found it incredible to be playing together on the Knicks and often driving together to Madison Square Garden, where the greats we'd emulated on the playgrounds had left their indelible marks on the game and our souls.

But playing in the wake of greatness comes with expectations. The loss to Philly was the first of our 0–7 start, with a rocky cross-country road trip following our season opener.

New Yorkers aren't known for their patience. The fans are passionate. The tabloids and local news programs are fiercely competitive. The big-city sportswriters traveling with a team have deadlines to make and editors to satisfy, and saying the players just need time to get comfortable isn't going to make for a splashy headline.

When you're the Knicks, you are going to be assessed on a nightly basis. The team is critiqued. Every player is critiqued. Each game on the schedule is treated like it's a must-win.

Our fifth game was in Portland, Oregon, against the Trailblazers, a team that had lost its best players and was trying to find its bearings. They defeated us 110–102.

I hadn't played well for a variety of reasons. I wasn't in peak condition. I was adapting to a new system, and my timing was badly off. With Golden State, I'd been a transitional, open-floor type of player. Now I was being pegged into Hubie's set offense.

I knew I would adjust, but it all added up to a slow start.

Meanwhile, Hubie was taking heat from the press. As the team's new coach, he was under a magnifying glass. They were on him like we'd lost forty games instead of seven. It put him in a foul mood. And as the team's major acquisition, I became the target of his fouler mouth after the game.

The locker room door had barely closed when he lit into me.

"You worthless piece of shit! You're no fuckin' All-Star! You're no All-Pro! You ain't shit! *You're a dog!*"

He went on like that for a while. A long while. When Hubie unleashed, he could go on for twenty minutes without a breath.

I listened but didn't say anything. His reputation being what it was, I had thought about how to address that very situation if it occurred, knowing it probably *would* occur sooner or later. And I'd concluded that I would never respond in front of my teammates, no matter how mad I got. If I did, the press would pick up on it, and it would be all over the tabloids.

I imagined the morning headlines:

KING VERSUS THE COACH. IS STAR FORWARD THE REASON FOR KNICKS' TROUBLES?

I did not want that kind of thing tagged on me. I refused to be the scapegoat.

Ignoring his tirade, I took my shower and dressed in silence. But I knew I was going to handle it later. I knew that.

On my way out of the locker room, I saw Hubie holding court with a group of reporters. Most were beat writers from the New York papers.

As I passed him, he said, "Goodnight, Bernard."

His tone was strictly for the reporters' ears. It couldn't have been friendlier.

I looked straight ahead and left the arena without a word.

The next day we were at Upsala College in New Jersey, where our team held its practices, getting ready for a two-game home-and-away series with the Nets. Hubie approached me in the gym, acting like nothing had happened.

"Good morning," he said.

I didn't acknowledge him. I just went through our practice, not even looking at him if I could avoid it.

We had a second team workout the following day. I was going through my drills when Hubie again walked over to me.

"I said good morning to you yesterday," he said. "Why didn't you answer?"

That was all I needed. I looked him dead in the eyes.

"Let me tell you something, Hubie," I said, and then paused. He had this shocked expression on his face. I realized he'd heard the anger in my voice and tempered it, starting over. "Let me tell you something. I just signed a five-year contract. I'm not going anywhere. Now I'm not yet in the kind of shape I want to be. But at the end of the day, you will have coached the best player you have ever coached."

Hubie seemed stuck in place. And I was just getting warmed up.

I kept my voice firm but didn't raise it. I didn't want to humiliate him in front of the guys. This wasn't for the rest of the team to hear. It was going to stay between the two of us.

"One more thing," I said. "Don't you ever, under any circumstances, *dare* to speak to me in the manner you did again. Do you understand?"

He stared at me.

I waited.

He opened his mouth, hesitated.

I waited. I was sure no one had ever spoken to him like that before. "It will never happen again," he said finally.

And it didn't. Not with me. But he continued talking to my team-mates like that. He saw nothing wrong with it. To him, it was perfectly acceptable.

Hubie Brown was a great coach. Not a good coach, a *great* coach. I consider him to be without peer in terms of how he saw the game, felt the game, preached the game, and conveyed the game.

The reason Hubie and I meshed so well was that we shared an analytical approach to basketball. He saw the court like a chessboard and was always three moves ahead of the opponent . . . *the game within the game*. But his treatment of players kept him from reaching his full-est potential. These were grown men. You don't speak to grown men that way. To me, that's not coaching. It's degrading them.

You might wonder, what about Gil Reynolds? Wasn't he also tough?

Yes. Tough as nails. But ask anybody who played under Gil, and they'll tell you how much they loved him. They needed his strictness. They needed his discipline. They needed to be motivated, taught how to focus, shown how to prepare. The things you learned under Gil were qualities you took through life. A lot of guys became very successful as a result of playing for him.

But the NBA wasn't youth league basketball. The players weren't inner-city kids looking for direction. They were professionals. As a pro-fessional athlete, you want to win. And so, as a team, you band together for that common objective.

Hubie's ability as a coach was unchallenged. But his treatment of the players created morale issues.

After one early-season loss, a member of the press asked my assess-ment of what was wrong with the team. There was no single reason. We were falling short in every facet of the game—defense, offense, rebounding. I realized it was all part of our learning curve, and that things weren't going to turn around for us overnight. But I'd repeatedly told reporters they would. At that moment in time, though, we were simply a bad team. It was the best answer I could give.

Now, Hubie loved to read the newspapers and attempt to manage what his players said in the press. If he saw something he found troublesome, he'd bring it up at the next team meeting. The day the article appeared, he said he was bothered by my comment without naming me.

Everybody knew I was the source. Our lockers were right alongside each other. I'd spoken on the record. I told the reporter the truth and didn't exempt myself from our poor play. I had nothing to hide from my teammates. But Hubie wouldn't say he had a problem to my face. He wanted to embarrass me and pretend it was unintentional.

I called him on it.

I said, "Hubie, why don't you indicate who made that comment?"

He just stood there dumbstruck.

"Come on," I said. "If the comment bothers you, tell us who made it."

Well, he wouldn't. I gave respect and expected it in return. Nothing more, nothing less. And he'd learned back in Portland that I wouldn't let him disrespect me.

I was very forthright with Hubie. But he was the coach, and I was the player. I never overstepped that line or interfered with his control of the team. Over time, we came to understand each other and developed a lasting mutual respect.

Hubie will tell you I played every practice like it was a game. That he never had anyone who worked harder than I did. That he never had anyone who performed as I did. He'll tell you I was a leader, and that's partly because I was coachable. And when your best player's coachable, then everyone else has to be coachable.

Nothing is more damaging to a team's cohesiveness than a coach killer. Whatever our failings in that adjustment period, I had to be a stabilizing force for the team. I could never allow myself to fall into a space where I was part of the problem instead of the solution. Hubie was learning about his players even while we learned his playbook. We were all in the cauldron together.

Our skid finally came to an end in mid-November, but we couldn't manage to go on a sustained run. We won three, we lost four. We won two, we dropped three. Still, I saw positive signs. We were asserting ourselves under the boards, showing defensive resolve, and playing more cohesively as a unit. I'd also grown much more comfortable with Hubie's schemes, and saw my scoring totals rise toward my career numbers.

I felt we were close to hitting our stride and tried to urge the team on, pumping my fist on the court, encouraging the guys as I'd done back in Tennessee. But we entered December with a dreadful 5–11 record.

On December 3, the Washington Bullets handed us our twelfth loss of the season at Capital Centre in Maryland. We'd blown the game in the third quarter when Washington's defense shut us down under the boards, and their offense outscored us 28–16.

After the game, we called a players-only meeting in the locker room. Something had to change.

That night, my teammates named me captain of the New York Knicks. I was elected by unanimous vote. It was an indescribable moment. So many memories came rushing back to me. Being a kid on the playground in Brooklyn, scraping snow off the courts with my sneakers in the winter, running across the Brooklyn Bridge on the hottest of summer days, all the hard work and commitment I'd put into climbing to where I was . . .

When I was back at home in New York, away from the team, the emotions welled up. In my final year with the Nets, I'd locked myself away and cried in shame and despair, thinking my life was near its end.

Now I cried with pride and thought about how far I'd come.

Captain of the New York Knicks. The franchise Willis Reed once led. The team of Walt Frazier, Dave DeBusschere, Earl Monroe, Dick Barnett, Bill Bradley, and so many others.

I dedicated myself to honoring the responsibility and went into overdrive.

THE TEAM SHOWED SIGNS OF IMPROVEMENT. I grew more comfortable on the floor, and that made Hubie more comfortable drawing up plays for me. Over the next six weeks, I got into an offensive rhythm and averaged almost 27 points a game.

In his fourth year with the franchise, Bill Cartwright would emerge as a solid defensive center. Truck Robinson, our power forward, also began to adjust to Hubie's play calling and my presence on the Knicks. It took him a while. Truck had been the go-to guy in Phoenix, but once I joined the team, Hubie centered the offense around me, asking him to concentrate on defense and rebounds. Truck had trouble with it. He'd expected to play a very different role. My arrival must have been a bitter pill to swallow.

For the first few weeks of the season, he didn't say a word to me. He'd pass me in the Garden hallways without so much as nodding hello and do the same thing at practice. His resentment even surfaced on the court, where he would refuse to throw me outlet passes up the floor. He didn't like me being the playmaker. That was the worst of his attitude, because it reduced our scoring opportunities.

But in the end, Truck wanted to be part of a winning team. As we all came together around our common goal, he provided rebounding and scoring support. I saw him as an asset.

Little by little, game by game, we improved. Still, our record in December was uneven, and that did nothing to take the edge off Hubie's tongue lashings. I was spared, but the other guys heard them all the time. It became so bad that they had their families moved further back from courtside to prevent them from being exposed to the cussing.

As captain, I felt it was my responsibility to speak up on the team's behalf.

One day, I pulled him aside. "Hubie," I said, "I think you need to ease up on the guys. Particularly how you talk to them. A lot of them don't like you because of it."

His response?

"I don't give a shit. I couldn't care less. I really don't care if they like me or not."

I thought for a minute about how to answer. "You know what your problem is?" I said finally. "You *do* care if they like you. But you know they don't. That's your problem, Hubie."

He didn't comment or stop insulting everyone. But we kept improving under his coaching. The double-edged sword of Hubie Brown.

Meanwhile, I was settling into being back in New York. A friend of mine was into real estate, and he'd owned a place on Staten Island's Victory Boulevard. Traffic was a nightmare, but I would smile when I passed my old high school on the drive and get goose bumps on my arms and neck as I neared the city. Being a Knick was personal for me, not merely my job. There was no better place to play than Madison Square Garden, where I could fly down the left-hand side of the court as if on wings.

I could have gladly done without a mid-January game against the Atlanta Hawks at their home arena. With about four minutes left in the second quarter, I slipped on a fast break to the basket and crashed to the hardwood, my ankle twisting under me. As I limped off the court, it was already swelling up. The injury was diagnosed as a moderate ankle sprain and kept me out of action for twelve games.

The team played very well in my absence, going 8–2 in the last ten games before the mid-season break. As much as I hated to watch from the sidelines, I was delighted to see us making progress with each game.

Our defense was super. Guys were grasping the nuances of the system. Hubie's ten-man platoon gave everybody a lot of playing time, and that kept them in game shape.

I acquired a profound respect for our second unit. Hubie kept his eye on the clock and based his deployment of the bench strictly on minutes. Eight minutes in, the starters were coming out of the game. It didn't matter how well we were playing. We were coming out. That was Hubie's coaching style. He believed it helped us stay fresh and threw our opposition off balance. Unless a starter was in foul trouble and forced his hand, Hubie would put in all the reserves at the same time. By January, they'd meshed together well and were their own functional team. I thought they could hold their own against many starting fives.

Although we lost our last game before the break, the team ended the first half at 22–28, positioning us to make a second-half charge. My ankle felt better, and I was eager to get back into uniform and lead the way.

Even before the injury, my slow start—and the team's below .500 record—would have taken me out of consideration for the All-Star Game in Los Angeles. But the trade-off was that missing it gave me extra time to heal.

I decided to take my first wife on an in-season vacation to Montego Bay, Jamaica, and looked forward to reenergizing on the island's white sand beaches.

As luck would have it, I'd booked our flight for February 10, the same day a blizzard came sweeping up the East Coast to bury New York in two feet of snow. Our scheduled departure was slightly before the full brunt of the storm struck, so the airline had us board our plane in hopes we'd get clearance for takeoff.

We sat at our gate for deicing as snow fell heavily over the runways. When the captain announced we had been okayed to leave, all the passengers broke into spontaneous applause. I don't know anyone who likes flying through a storm, but there's no better incentive than the promise of Caribbean sunshine.

As the plane climbed into the sky, I went to sleep with a smile on my face. We were the last flight out of LaGuardia before it was shut down.

The weather in Jamaica was clear, sunny, and blissfully hot. As I waited for my bags, I felt the trade wind brush my cheeks. It smelled like the ocean. Or heaven.

In the taxi heading for the St. James Club, that scent gave way to something more pungent. I leaned forward in the backseat.

The driver was chomping what might have been a huge cigar.

"Excuse me." I sniffed. "What's that you're smoking?"

He broke into a smile.

"Ganga, mon!" he said, waving the spliff at me. "It's religion, yah know!" I saw his grin widen in the rearview. "Yah want some?"

I told him no, and lowered all the windows.

The scenery on the resort grounds was spectacular—white sand, flowing royal palms, the blue sea and sky meeting at the horizon. As I entered the lobby, I noticed people with suitcases everywhere.

Busy! I thought. *This place must be excellent!*

But I was in for a surprise at the desk. As I gave my reservation information, I was told the room was unavailable.

"Excuse me?"

"I'm sorry, sir. This is terrible! Truly terrible! But no one has left!"

I realized why before the flustered clerk was through explaining. With every airport in the Northeast closed, all the guests who were supposed to check out had stayed on.

I glanced around the lobby. Now I knew why so many people were waiting around with their bags. They'd landed in Jamaica to find their rooms unavailable.

"Excuse me." It struck me I'd said that way too often since my arrival. "Are we supposed to sleep on the beach?"

"A thousand apologies, sir—"

"Thank you. But I left a deposit. I made a confirmed reservation. I am a member of the New York Knicks, and this is my one chance for a vacation. Do I need to call my attorney and the U.S. embassy to get a room?"

A manager whisked over. He said that some accommodations were open after all. "Please forgive us, Mr. King!"

Before I knew it, a staff member gathered our bags, put them in a car, and drove us to an expansive villa home overlooking the golf course and ocean.

It came with a private cook. And a rental car. At the same rate as the standard room I'd originally booked.

I wasn't sure whether my playing the Knicks, lawyer, or embassy card did the trick. But all those games of stud with the Warriors had taught me when to show my hand.

Things were looking up.

Jamaican woodcrafters have been renowned for their artisan mahogany furniture for centuries. The morning after our arrival, we drove out to a furniture manufacturer specializing in dining-room tables. The place was in the coastal uplands, its outdoor parking area notched into a mountain that rose hundreds of feet above the sea. The narrow blacktop road hugged the edge of a cliff, and it was dizzying to glance over my shoulder at the sheer drop into the waves. After taking a look at the furniture maker's inventory, we decided to find a place for lunch.

The island being a former crown colony, you drive on the left-hand side of the road, as they do in England. As I left the parking area, I pulled out onto the road and started to accelerate.

At that instant, a sports car tore around the bend in my lane, coming head-on toward us. The driver must have been doing three times my speed.

As an elite athlete, I'd trained my mind and reflexes to react in milliseconds. In clutch moments, time stopped. The other players seemed frozen in place. Only I was in motion.

I know that's what saved our lives.

Suddenly, I was in the Zone. There was nothing but the sheer drop to my left.

I wrenched the wheel hard to the right, toward the shoulder of the hill, and jammed up against the embankment. The other driver also swerved toward the hillside to avoid the cliff and overcompensated, barely missing my car. Then he hit the hillside and went careening off it for about fifty yards. I heard the screech of his brakes and a loud, sickening crunch of metal.

I sat behind the wheel, gripping it with both hands, shaking like a leaf. Beside me, my first wife's eyes were wide and shocked. The sports car driver had almost killed us.

After a minute, I looked around and saw someone crawling out of the sports car's crumpled passenger door. He was bleeding profusely. Something about his leg wasn't right.

Then I saw the driver walking toward us on the blacktop. He looked unhurt. I realized he was shouting something and pushed open my door.

"Why didn't you stay in your lane?" he screamed.

"What?"

"I'm a professional race car driver and was testing the car. *You should have stayed in your lane!*"

My heartbeat quickened. I could hardly believe my ears.

"Stay in my lane?" I repeated. "So *you* could decide whether I lived or died?"

I stamped down on my anger. It wasn't going to do any good. I could already hear the warble of sirens. There were people gathered outside in the parking lot. Eyewitnesses.

I'd let the police handle it.

They arrested the driver on the spot, handcuffing him.

"You had a close call," one told me. "We know this man. He drives through the streets like a reckless maniac."

A close call.

No kidding.

We stayed in Jamaica four more days. You could say we enjoyed the rest of our vacation. But twenty years would pass before I could bring myself to visit to the island again.

I returned to New York knowing I'd almost lost my life, but never told anyone. When you're captain of the Knicks, things get amplified. I didn't want to spend time reliving that moment for reporters. It would be a distraction.

The season's second half was coming up, and it was time to turn my full attention to hoops.

IN NEW YORK, avoiding distractions is easier said than done.

I'd no sooner returned from the Caribbean than I was blindsided by something I read in the newspapers. In a piece about the Knicks' improved performance during my injury, one sports columnist suggested that they might be better without me. According to an anonymous source within the team, he wrote, some guys had complained to Hubie about the number of shots I took each game.

The columnist's speculation about the team's improvement didn't bother me. I could not control what was written in the papers. But it was hard to believe any of the guys had an issue with my scoring.

I prided myself on being a very unselfish player. I averaged 3 assists per game over my career, which wasn't bad for someone who also scored 22.5 points. However, if I had the ball, and another guy was in a better position to score, I passed it over to him unless the game was on the line. Then I would do what was expected of me.

You try to refrain from making on-court statements against your teammates. But at our first practice after the winter break, I drove the lane, rose up so high to the basket you would have thought Dr. J was defending me, then threw the ball down with an emphatic rattle of the hoop. It was an unspoken message to everyone on the floor.

I was convinced the source of the comments was Truck. His attitude toward me hadn't changed, and he was later openly quoted as saying my absence had benefited him.

That night at the Garden, I played a different game. I looked to pass first, no matter if I was in position to make the shot.

Paul Westphal was a veteran guard on our team, a five-time All-Star nearing the end of a long, extraordinary career. It was obvious to him that something was wrong, and he came up to me during a time-out.

"Listen, B," he said quietly, "we need you to play your game."

I just looked at him. *That* was leadership. I never forgot what he did for me.

When the whistle blew, I went out and played my game.

I never changed it again.

WE ENDED THE REGULAR SEASON 44–38, and had the second-best record in the league after the All-Star break, capturing a playoff berth despite our slow start.

I was very proud of that accomplishment. We'd overcome our growing pains to catapult our newly rebuilt team from the embarrassment of the previous year to the postseason. Knick fans appreciated our hustle play and embraced us. From a personal standpoint that couldn't have been more gratifying. I loved our fans. At heart, I was one of them. As a Brooklyn kid, I played like my life depended on it. I played for the organization, the city, and for those fans.

In true New York fashion, our first-round playoff series had some extra drama. We would be matching up against the New Jersey Nets. The team that drafted me, where I'd made my early mark on the NBA. That, in itself, would have been enough to excite the fans of our respective teams. But it wasn't all.

My younger brother, Albert, was the Nets' starting small forward, the same position I'd played three years earlier. I believe it was the first time in NBA history that brothers would face off in the postseason.

Albert and I were never close. He was three years younger. When you're in twelfth grade, you don't usually hang out with your brother who's in ninth grade. Since I always played on the basketball courts with the older kids, the gap between us felt even wider.

When Albert was in high school—he attended Fort Hamilton, where he'd followed in my footsteps and become a Tiger—I'd already gone off to Tennessee. I doubt he ever saw me on the court; I only got to see him play once, when I was home from college for a visit. By then, he was considered a basketball phenomenon, the best high school player in the country.

Albert always had great talent, great skills. But it was difficult for him living in my shadow. When he was drafted into the NBA, I tried to prepare him for what to expect. I helped him with the game's strategic aspects and shared how to mentally approach it as a sport and business. I don't know how much of it resonated with him. I was his brother, and I loved him, and did what I could do.

The first time we went up against each other on the basketball court was during my second year with the Warriors—Albert's rookie season in New Jersey. It wasn't something I'd looked forward to, but I didn't dread it either. I scouted him like any other opponent, guarded him like any other scorer, and treated him like any defender I had to beat.

On the court, he was just another player.

I don't remember who did what statistically that night. It didn't matter. I do remember that my team won. That *did* matter.

Albert and I got together after the game. He came over to my apartment for dinner. When the season ended, I stayed on the West Coast, so we didn't have any social interaction at all. No phone calls, even. But in the fall, I signed with the Knicks, and that changed our whole dynamic.

After essentially playing in different worlds our whole lives, we were both on the East Coast, just across the Hudson River from each other, and playing for bitter rivals. And now we would be meeting in the playoffs.

This was very different from the regular season. When you are in the playoffs, everything is at stake for your franchise, for your teammates, and for you individually. That's the way I approached every post-season series. That was how I approached the series against the Nets.

As excitement over the series reached a crescendo in the Tri-State Area, I prepared to win.

GAME 1 OF OUR BEST-OF-THREE was on a beautiful Wednesday night in April. The Nets had seeded higher than us, giving them home-court advantage. That meant the series opener would be at Meadowlands Arena, their new home in East Rutherford across the road from the Giants stadium and the racetrack. It made them the presumed favorite.

There was no shoot-around that afternoon. We'd practiced and prepared the day before, keying our defensive schemes on New Jersey's All-Star big forward, Buck Williams.

Buck had been my brother's teammate at Maryland University, and they'd been drafted by the Nets the same year. Our defense also had to make sure we were ready for their crafty, ultra-talented point guard, Michael Ray Richardson—the same player Golden State had received from the Knicks in a trade for me. I'll say it again: The NBA is a small brotherhood.

During this time, I'd bought a home in Franklin Lakes, New Jersey, about a half hour's drive from the Meadowlands Sports Complex. The morning of the game, I got a fresh haircut, making sure I looked and felt my best. As I pulled out of my driveway, I began focusing my concentration on what lay ahead between the lines.

I knew winning Game 1 in a short series was imperative. Ironically, I'd learned it through hard experience when I was a Net and we were swept from the postseason by the Sixers.

Now I was a Knick and would dominate anyone wearing a Nets uniform. Dominate *Albert*. I had to. I had no choice. It was what I was supposed to do. My team had signed me, brought me back home to New York, for moments like this. It was time to deliver when it counted, in the playoffs, like the Knick greats of the past.

As I exited my vehicle in the arena's parking area, I allowed myself a few final thoughts: I was the captain and leader of the team. I would take my emotions deep.

The Nets couldn't stop the unstoppable.

OUR MIND-SET GOING IN was to jump on them from the starting tip-off—and we succeeded, hitting five of our first six field goal attempts. That took the Jersey crowd right out of it.

Everyone on the team did his job. Cartwright was effective under the basket. Our shooting guard, Rory Sparrow, a former Net, got into a quick rhythm nailing outside shots. Hubie assigned Truck Robinson to one-on-one defend against Buck Williams, and he was all over him.

I was also rolling. I went 7–7 to score 14 points in the first quarter, hitting mid-range shots, posting up, and moving off screens without the ball.

I think our full-throttle charge rocked the Nets back on their heels. They seemed to rush their early shots, failing to make any of them.

Albert picked up a couple of personals against me in the first two minutes. With the first one, I knew I had him. I was making good on my commitment to myself. All I saw was his Nets uniform. He couldn't guard me.

In the second quarter, our reserve unit went to work. On defense, they trapped and pressed at the half court to hold the Nets down. Ernie led the offensive attack. He scored at will from everywhere on the floor. An eighteen-foot jumper. A layup. A dunk. That put us up by 11 or 12. It was his best game of the season.

The Nets made a run late in the quarter, inching to within 4, and Hubie put our starters back on the floor. I missed my first shot, but then went 4–4 to end the half with 25 points.

By then, we'd doubled our lead and there was no looking back. Albert had gotten into foul trouble, and the Nets' head coach, Bill Blair, tried mixing up his defense to shut me down. I think he tried four different defenders against me.

Blair had only coached the team for a few weeks after taking over from Larry Brown. Larry had coached the team for a couple of years after Kevin Loughery's departure, but left six games before the end of the season to accept a job at the University of Kansas. I can't think of another instance of a coach doing that near the conclusion of a playoff run.

Blair was a first-year assistant coach, and being handed the team at that stage couldn't have been easy. He was no match for a master tactician like Hubie.

He pulled Albert off me and tried Buck Williams. It didn't work. He double-teamed me. It didn't work. I made my moves to beat the second guy, not the first guy.

One third-quarter play stands out above the rest.

Rory Sparrow was driving the lane, running a fast break on the left side of the floor. But Darwin Cook, a Nets guard, got a hand on the ball, deflecting it off Rory's foot. Close behind Rory, I saw it carom toward the left sideline, rolling out of bounds, and dove to the hardwood to save the possession.

I managed to get my hands on it even as the breath woofed from my lungs. Down on my belly, I saw Ernie out the corner of my eye and fired the ball into his hands. He caught it chest high, took two dribbles, and nailed a jumper, forcing the Nets to call a time-out.

As we walked off the court, Ernie and I exchanged glances and the slightest of nods. We both knew what that meant. We were back doing it. *Ernie and Bernie.* Two New York kids doing it for our home-town team.

The Nets tried to marshal a rally after that, but we put the game out of reach in the fourth quarter, controlling the tempo, making sure we kept up the pressure.

The defining moment of the period came on another fast break. Rory and I were in sync all night, running the floor in transition. This time, when he passed the ball, I received it with my brother defending me again. I went right at him, driving toward the basket as if he wasn't there, making strong contact to draw the foul. I made the basket and sank the free throw.

That was the backbreaker for New Jersey. You could feel the air leave the arena.

We beat them 118–107. It was a complete team victory. I scored 40 points on 21 shots in my first playoff win as a Knick. As captain, as team leader, I'd delivered, and that was very satisfying.

But it was too soon for anyone in our locker room to celebrate.

Game 2 was coming up the next night.

THAT ONE WAS AT OUR HOUSE, and it was packed with Knicks fans. After seeing the team miss the playoffs the year before, they were fired up.

The Nets took the court like they'd been rocked by the previous night's loss. We sensed it and went for the knockout.

This is one time when the box score says it all. We took a 9-point lead in the first quarter, but overpowered them in the second. The score at halftime was 62–39, and Louis Orr, our power forward off the bench, added to it to start the third.

Albert had a good game for the Nets. Truck was even better for us. They made a push in the third quarter but never had a lead. It felt almost like a replay of the first game, with two major differences.

That night, we knew we'd swept the series and advanced.

And we celebrated.

OUR SECOND-ROUND POSTSEASON OPPONENT was the Philadelphia 76ers. In name, it was the same team I'd met back when I was a Net. But this was an even higher-octane version, one of the greatest squads ever assembled. Julius Irving, Maurice Cheeks, Bobby Jones, and Andrew Toney had been joined by Moses Malone, who came over in a blockbuster trade with Houston to give them an All-Star at every position. No one was surprised when they plowed through the league like a battering ram and went 65–17 in the regular season.

When Moses was named league MVP, a member of the press asked him to predict how the Sixers would do in the playoffs.

"Fo', Fo', Fo'," he replied, meaning his team would sweep all its opponents in four games.

They almost did just that.

We were the first team to fall to the battering ram, but if there was any consolation, it was that we were in good company. After defeating us in Moses's predicted four games, the Sixers needed five games to beat the Milwaukee Bucks in the Eastern Conference finals. Then they crushed the Lakers in four in the NBA finals.

Losing always hurts. But we reminded ourselves we'd opened the postseason beating the Nets on their home floor. Our final two games against the Sixers were decided by 2 and 3 points, respectively. We didn't feel so bad. In fact, we felt pretty good about what could happen the following year.

Typically, my second season with a team was better than the preceding one. I would be more comfortable with the system, my teammates, the coaching staff, and even my housing arrangements. I was anxious to see how we'd grow after our second-round loss to the eventual champs.

I definitely used it as a learning experience. For instance, I recalled a play where I received a lob pass that wasn't high enough to dunk, so I snared the ball in midair, landed, and went up with a shot that was immediately blocked by Dr. J and Moses. But it didn't end there. Before anyone else could pull in the basketball, I retrieved it, went up on the *other* side of the rim, and dunked.

I had never executed a move like that before. We lost the game, but I mentally recorded that play.

I always tell young players, "If you successfully perform a new move in a game, go into the gym the next day and practice it. Make it part of your repertoire."

In that first playoff series with the Knicks, I realized there was more to my game than I'd realized. I would carry that forward into the 1983–1984 season.

I knew what kind of player I was. I knew we had a tremendous team, guys who were willing to put aside their egos, accept their roles, and put in their best effort every night.

I went into training camp with a fire, believing we'd have a special year.

I couldn't have foreseen the heights to which I'd rise or realized how magical that year would be for all of us.

17 | Season of Ascension

The magic began with the All-Star Game.

The first half of the New York Knicks' 1983–1984 season was good but not great.

Our team had essentially the same personnel as the year before, though we'd picked up Ray Williams, a big, strong player with a smooth mid-range jump shot. He improved us on both sides of the court, and we were playing hard every night. But our 24–18 record reflected inconsistency.

Hubie always broke the season down into increments. He didn't want us to look at having to win the majority of eighty-two games over half a season.

"Win three out of four," he preached. "Do that and we'll be okay."

We bought into his philosophy, taking small bites out of the schedule. I know Rory Sparrow and Darrell Walker felt it helped them handle the pressure of a basketball season.

Three out of four. That was our aim. Even so, we had a couple of losing streaks we couldn't afford, not with the Sixers and Boston Celtics in our division. They were two of the best teams in basketball, and we needed to stick close to them.

I'd had a solid start, my play during those first months of the season earning me a second All-Star selection as a reserve for the Eastern Conference team. The game was at McNichols Sports Arena in Denver, and almost every great player in an *era* of greats was there.

During my career, I played against fifty-one Hall of Famers. Many would be in the game. The starters for the East were Julius Erving, Larry Bird, Robert Parish, Sidney Moncrief, and Isiah Thomas. The West's starters were Alex English, Adrian Dantley, George Gervin, Magic Johnson, and Kareem Abdul-Jabbar.

My team's coach was K. C. Jones of the Boston Celtics, who had the best record in the conference. He'd seen me play often enough to know what I could do.

In the All-Star Game, players share minutes to showcase everyone's talents. A lot of mine came in overtime, when K. C. inserted me with the game on the line. I remember getting into a scoring duel with Mark Aguirre, the small forward representing the Dallas Mavericks. That was fun, but I didn't take the challenge lightly.

I played to win.

In my twenty-two minutes on the court, I scored 18 points.

Mark hit 13 for the West after giving me plenty of competition.

The East won 154–145.

But something else happened. Something much more important than my performance in that game.

I'd always known I was good. You have to believe in yourself between the lines. I'm not talking about ego off the basketball court. I'm talking about belief and confidence on the court. You need to have it.

In Denver, I felt a switch turn on. That's the only way to describe it. I looked around at some of the best players in basketball—the very best players—and it dawned on me that I was one of them. I had played in an All-Star game as a Warrior, but I hadn't experienced anything close to these thoughts and feelings.

All my hard work had finally paid off. It was magical!

I was one of them.

THE KNICKS WEREN'T GOING TO HAVE an easy ride after the break. We opened the second half against the Spurs, one of the top teams in the West. George "The Iceman" Gervin, one of the league's top players—and an all-time favorite of mine—was their small forward. And there would be no letup as we swung across Texas to face the Dallas Mavericks and Houston Rockets.

I met the team in San Antonio. Aboard the flight from Denver, I sat next to Rick Pitino, our assistant coach, who'd been at the All-Star Game with me.

"It's imperative we get off to a great start in the second half," I told him.

Rick understood. Ray Williams and Louis Orr, my backup forward, were unavailable to us. Louis had the flu; and Ray, an ankle injury. He was one of our best shooters and defenders, and might be sidelined for a long stretch.

I knew that meant we'd have to alter our usual game. San Antonio had a wide-open offense. They played fast-break basketball with very few structured plays. Shorthanded as we were, we couldn't use our usual half-court press to wreak havoc with their transitions. We'd be chasing them up and down the court all night.

I was okay with that. More than okay. I loved running the open floor. That was my game with the Warriors. If my teammates' absence meant scoring more points, I would score more points.

My mind-set for the remainder of the season began on that plane.

I would do whatever was required to win.

I DIDN'T GO OUT FOR WARM-UPS before the game in San Antonio.

Instead, I had a turkey sandwich and vanilla milkshake, and stayed in the locker room. A minute before the team meeting, I stepped out onto the floor, took a single shot, and then returned to the locker room.

After just playing in Denver, and then the flight to Texas, I wanted to conserve my energy. I would need every iota to cover Iceman.

George Gervin was playing phenomenally well at that point in his career, and he got off to a quick start against us in San Antonio.

As I'd promised myself, I did everything possible to keep us in the game. I finished strong in transition, and I hit my mid-range jumpers. George and I went point-for-point all night.

By the fourth quarter, I was getting tired. Then I glanced up at the scoreboard and saw the Spurs were ahead. Iceman had scored 41 points. He could put us away at any time.

We cannot lose this game, I thought.

I picked it up offensively. It's a great feeling to know you can do that at will.

I was in that space.

I hit double-digit points in the final frame. I actually didn't think I was scoring that many. It's that way when you're fixed on executing rather than on a number.

We defeated the Spurs117–113. I'd hit 20 of 30 shots from the field and scored the rest in free throws. Walking into the locker room, I still had no idea about my point total for the night. I hadn't checked the stat sheet at halftime and tended to score in bunches, so it was hard to keep track. No one on my team had mentioned it during the game; they didn't want to jinx me.

Only when the beat reporters asked me about scoring 50 points did I know. I realized I'd had an exceptional night, but the number surprised me. It was more than double my season average.

The bottom line, though, was that we'd won. I didn't even think about scoring 50 after the beats drifted away from my locker.

We were flying straight to Dallas in the morning for our next game.

THROUGHOUT MY CAREER, I challenged myself to perform better in the second of consecutive-night games. It was a personal achievement that helped my team's success. Many players had a falloff in performance. On the Knicks, I especially couldn't allow it. The guys relied on me to be a prolific scorer. It was never truer than on that road trip.

Without Louis and Ray, I would need another big night against the Mavericks. I'd be matched against Mark Aguirre, the forward who'd dueled me at the All-Star Game.

Mark was always difficult for me to guard. A big, wide-bodied post-up player, he outweighed me by twenty-five pounds despite being an inch shorter. He used his lower body like a bulldozer, moving guys like me out of position as though we weren't even there. A DePaul alumnus, he'd been selected by Dallas in the first round of the 1981 draft and, in his mind, was the greatest player in basketball. He would know about my hot night in San Antonio and be determined to cool me down.

That night, I followed the same pregame routine as in San Antonio. A turkey sandwich, vanilla shake. No warm-ups. Then, a single shot before the team meeting and back to my locker.

Never mess around with what works.

It's odd how some things will stick in your memory. As we took the floor, Hubie tore into Bill Cartwright for no reason I could fathom.

"Your man's Pat Cummings tonight. Are you going to goddam play him hard, dammit?"

Cummings was a six-foot-nine big forward who was several inches shorter than most opposing centers, Bill among them.

Hubie tended to berate Bill a lot, and Bill, with his quiet good nature, would tolerate it. But he didn't require that type of motivation. Bill could handle Cummings just fine. I knew I was still in a groove from the tip-off and moved on the floor with utmost confidence.

At one juncture, I rebounded the ball on the defensive end and power-dribbled up the floor. As Mark attempted a steal, I put the ball behind my back without losing the flow of my dribble, and pulled up for a jump shot just above the foul line.

Swish. Nothing but net. Aguirre looked at his hand like a kid who's been caught reaching into the cookie jar . . . and then had the cookie snatched away from him.

Like my move against Dr. J and Moses in the playoffs, that one was new to my repertoire.

At that instant, I knew I wasn't just on a hot streak. I wasn't on a roll. I wasn't even in the Zone, at least not as I'd known it before.

I was at my peak. I could feel it in my mind and body.

My *peak*.

I remember that we had a five-point lead in the game's final seconds. Aguirre had fouled out. As we set up for what was going to be the last play of the night, I heard my teammates yelling to Rory Sparrow.

Their voices seemed to come from far away, somewhere on the other side of a long, long tunnel.

"Give B the ball! Give B the ball! Give B the ball!"

With my peripheral vision, I saw that our entire second unit and coaching staff were on their feet.

Later I found out that the media behind the bench had told Hubie I'd scored 48 points. At that moment, I didn't have a clue. I'd hit 19 of 27 shots and didn't know that either. I only knew I had been on fire again.

"GIVE B THE BALL . . . !"

I received the pass on the left side of the floor. Oh, how I loved the left side of the floor. My defender was Jay Vincent, a six-foot-seven second-year forward who became my future teammate—briefly—on the Washington Bullets.

I drove left toward the baseline, but Jay cut me off.

Uh-uh.

Reaching into my bag of tricks, I spun back, squared up toward the rim, and rose from the floor. A split second before I released the ball, I thought, *No way I'm missing this shot.*

The basketball flicked softly through the net as the buzzer sounded. We won. 105–98.

Spent, I began walking back to my bench. But before I got there, the whole team mobbed me. Bad ankle and all, Ray Williams had me in a chokehold. Guys were patting me on the back and teasing me. It was a truly unforgettable moment, not only because I'd scored 50, but because my teammates were so happy for me. I relished the feeling but knew I could still improve upon my game.

Then I was in the locker room, surrounded by reporters. One told me I was the first player to score at least 50 points on back-to-back nights since the legendary Wilt Chamberlain two decades earlier. A couple of others, Elgin Baylor and Rick Barry, had scored 50 or more in consecutive games. But Chamberlain and I stood alone with our record.

Though I never would have compared myself to the Big Dipper, I was honored to stand in his company for a night.

THE NEXT MORNING, we had an early flight to Houston for the third leg of our Texas trip. It must have been six o'clock, or one of those gritty hours when it's still half dark out, and I was bleary eyed boarding our bus.

As I turned toward my seat, Darrell Walker rose and gave me an exaggerated bow. I laughed out loud. Meanwhile, the guys were all applauding. I was as stunned and moved as I had been when they mobbed me in the arena. It was fantastic to be appreciated, but we won each of the 50-point games as a team. I always emphasized that.

I arrived at my hotel room in Houston to a ton of messages (remember, this was before cellphones). The Knicks' public relations team coordinated all interview requests, and there must have been dozens. Ladies I'd dated in the past were also calling the PR department with their phone numbers. *Sports Illustrated* was sending someone to Houston to interview me for a story—and see whether I could score 50 three games in a row. I was even invited on the *David Letterman Show*.

We had a couple of days off before our game with the Rockets, and I attended the one they played the night before ours. I was astonished when the announcer introduced me, and the crowd rose in a standing ovation.

Oh my, I thought. *What have I done? This is huge.*

The truth is, I felt a little uncomfortable about the *SI* piece. I never tried to manufacture points unless the outcome of the game was on the line. The idea of padding stats was contrary to everything I believed. I was simply a very consistent player with a high basketball IQ.

I wondered if the *SI* reporter had considered the quality of the opponent we were about to play. Houston was one of the elite teams in the Western Conference. They were led by the heralded rookie center Ralph Sampson, who had been the number-one pick in the 1983 draft. He was supported by a solid group of teammates, including long-forgotten guys like Allen Leavell and Lewis Lloyd. There was also Caldwell Jones, and the magnificent Elvin Hayes playing his fifteenth and final season in what would be a Hall of Fame NBA career. I would face Robert Reid, someone I thought was the best defender in the league among forwards.

Three 50-point games in a row?

Even as I took in the applause at the Summit, I knew we'd have our hands full trying to get out of there with a win.

I DON'T THINK ENOUGH IS SAID about Robert Reid's career. He'd been a second-round pick from St. Mary's University, a school not known for producing high-caliber basketball talent. But Robert played in the league thirteen years, mostly with the Rockets. He twice helped them reach the NBA finals, in 1981 as a teammate of Moses Malone, and in 1986 on a squad anchored by Hakeem Olajuwon and Sampson. Robert's presence is sometimes overshadowed by those incredible players, but he was instrumental to the team's success.

Robert brought his defensive A-plus to the Summit after my consecutive 50 pointers. The day before, he'd told the press he was about to face the Moses Malone of small forwards. It was high praise. Malone's relentless physicality exhausted his defenders. I would play in a similar mode, beating you up even when I had the ball. Guys around the league came to expect it.

Robert knew the spotlight was on our matchup. He didn't want to become a footnote in the first 50-point scoring trifecta in NBA history and forced me into my secondary moves all night long. He was six feet eight and had great defensive anticipation.

My own focus wasn't on meeting the hype. Dallas was probably the best game I ever played. I'd done some things on the court that I'd never done before. In that game, I had a certain mindset, a feel, a *rhythm*, that allowed me to see through everything around me. The seams in the defense appeared much larger than they were.

I wasn't going to try and duplicate that performance. It was a trap to think I could. I wasn't about that. I was about doing whatever I could to help my team win. Only the amazing Wilt Chamberlain could score 50 points a game!

I expected Robert to give me fits defensively. But there was another thing that limited my points that night—and it was *un*expected.

I've mentioned the Knicks under Hubie Brown were a set offense team. Each play had a number, and Hubie would shout them from the sidelines as the action on the floor developed. Some were designed specifically for me. Say an opposing player scored from the free-throw line. As we walked the ball back up the court, Hubie would shout out the play.

"Forty-two!"

That was my number. I'd run down the left-hand side of the floor and cut across the lane as my teammates set a screen. When I arrived at the low block on the right-hand side, there would be an entry pass, and I'd take my shot.

Forty-two, thirty-three . . . they were numbers I'd hear every night. But I rarely heard them in Houston.

I was baffled when Hubie didn't ride my hot hand. He used a highly structured offense that didn't give me many scoring opportunities.

I've since wondered if he was sending a message that I wasn't bigger than the team. I didn't need it. But he was the coach, and we were young men. He probably worried I'd be susceptible to all the attention I'd gotten after the back-to-backs.

As it turned out, we won the game 103–95. That was what really counted. I scored 25 points, and Ray Williams, coming off his injury sooner than anticipated, hit 19 points off the bench in as many minutes. Ray was one of our team's unsung contributors that season.

That ended our road trip. We'd gone 3–0 against the stiffest competition out west, exactly what I had in mind when I told Rick Pitino we needed a great second-half start.

But it was only back in New York that I truly realized how much had changed for me.

Our first home game was against my old team, the Golden State Warriors. The Garden crowd buzzed when I stepped out onto the floor for warm-ups, and I got a roaring welcome during John Condon's introduction. It was like the ovation I'd received in Houston times a hundred.

I was no stranger to recognition, but this was different. I knew the fans looked forward to me scoring another 50. It was like a lid had been blown off the box in which I'd spent my entire career. Listening to the cheers, I knew there was no climbing back inside.

I moved the ball around that night, going out of my way to incorporate my teammates into the offense. I wanted to be sure they understood all the attention would not turn me into a ball hog.

The box score reflects how evenly the points were distributed. I scored 19 points. Sparrow scored 12. Truck Robinson and Bill Cartwright each scored 22. The remaining points were spread out among our second unit.

But I couldn't ignore the fact that things were different. I was a superstar. *An NBA superstar.* A new level of expectation had been put on me.

I would do whatever it took to live up to it.

18 | "Who Cares? We Won!"

The NBA's 1983–1984 postseason had two major format changes that are still in place today. First, the number of teams that qualified for the playoffs was expanded from to twelve to sixteen teams. Second, the first-round series went from three to five games.

By late April, the Knicks had clinched a postseason berth. But seeding was important to us.

There was no doubt the Boston Celtics would be the Eastern Conference champions. Red Auerbach was no longer head coach, but he still pulled the strings behind the scenes. As general manager, he'd collected some of the grittiest players in the game with some wily trades and acquisitions. Boston's roster included four future Hall of Famers: Larry Bird, Kevin McHale, Robert Parish, and Dennis Johnson.

We didn't want to see them in the first round.

Philly was the second best team in our division, and the third best in our conference behind the Milwaukee Bucks. They weren't the wrecking crew they were the year before, primarily because they hadn't played well on the road. But Doc and Moses were Doc and Moses.

We didn't want a first-round matchup with them, either.

We were a confident group, but we had a pragmatic outlook. We were in a close race with the Nets for the fifth and sixth slots. The way things were shaping up, our opponent in the five-game opening round would be Philly or Detroit.

Neither would be an easy opponent. But we wanted the Pistons. We felt we could compete with anyone, but knew they weren't equal to Boston or Philly. This was three years before the Bad Boy era, when

Isiah Thomas was joined by Dennis Rodman. The team's two best players in 1984 were Isiah and Bill Laimbeer. Laimbeer was also probably
the league's dirtiest player, but I'll come back to that later.

As we entered our final month of regular season play, I knew we
needed to keep pushing to stay ahead of the Nets. Three things stand
out when I recall that short string of games. They would all have ramifications for the postseason.

The first happened in a late March home game against the Celtics.
Eight minutes into the first quarter, I was driving hard toward the basket
with my defender, Cedric Maxwell, riding my hip when I tripped over
his foot and fell to the hardwood. I severely dislocated my right middle
finger and was sent to the hospital to have it reset and splinted.

I probably should have stayed out. Hubie and Mike Saunders, our
trainer, were concerned I might aggravate the injury. But they left the
call to me.

I told them I couldn't be sidelined more than a few days to get
treatment. We were in a scramble for a playoff position. I was needed
on the court.

Ten days later, we were in Atlanta, my first game back, and I dislocated my *left* middle finger. At the time, it seemed a total fluke. How
do you injure the exact same finger on the opposite hand? Nothing like
it had ever occurred to me before.

This time, Mike strongly argued that I sit. I refused again. I knew that
if I gave in to my injuries, I would be ineffective for the rest of the year.

My teammates needed me.

I remember the disbelief on his face, but he didn't try to change my
mind. Instead, he taped my fingers together, and I went out and played.

It was really kind of comical for the next few games. I would run the
court with my hands up in the air like a surgeon in a scrub room, trying
to avoid contact. Finally, Mike and our team doctor, Norman Scott,
fashioned special casts for my two middle fingers. They helped, but
only by degrees. Dribbling, rebounding, scoring . . . it hurt all the time.

My fingers took a whole year to heal. I couldn't even shake anyone's
hand for six months. But what is pain? You can't allow it to affect what
you do. You go within, mentally.

I remember deciding that someone upstairs had sent me a message. *Go deep, Bernard. Go deep.* Meaning I had to deepen my level of concentration to overcome the constant pain.

The third thing that happened is a memory of a different sort. I was up against Dr. J in the last game before the playoffs—a home game, at Madison Square Garden. With our fifth-place berth guaranteed, my goal was to get in my work without further injuring my fingers. But once the game action started, I didn't think about the pain. I was wired to compete.

Doc played me straight up—his feet spread wide, never yielding the right or left side to give me an edge. There was a moment in the game when I gained possession of the ball between the top of the key and the foul line. Doc was defending me in his usual stance.

I remember thinking, *Are you ready? Come along for the ride.*

I raised the ball over my head to freeze him. Then in one sweeping motion, I brought it down from right to left, went around his right leg, and drove left, with a left-hand dribble, into the lane toward the basket.

I was a half step quicker than Dr. J, and that was enough. He stood frozen at the foul line. Moses Malone stepped into the lane and fouled me, but I made the basket and the free throw for a 3-point play.

It felt good to execute and score. It always felt good. But the play held a greater significance for me.

That was the moment I finally knew I had caught Dr. J.

Caught him.

The amazing Julius Irving. *Little Spal, you did it!*

Let me tell you, it wasn't a bad way to head into the playoffs. Throbbing fingers and all.

WE FINISHED THE SEASON 47–35, two games ahead of the Nets. That gave us a matchup with Detroit in Round 1 of the Finals. Although the Pistons' record was only two games better than ours, they'd beaten us four games out of six that season and held home-court advantage. That was all they needed to be considered odds-on favorites.

Although we had the second best record in the league after the All-Star break, the press called us underdogs. That wasn't how we felt about ourselves. We were a confident group. We understood that the regular season and postseason were different. You could take lessons from regular season results, but there was no connecting thread.

We believed the New York Knicks could compete—and win—against anybody.

GAME 1 WAS APRIL 17 at the Silverdome in Detroit. The Pistons hadn't made the playoffs since 1976–1977, when they suffered a first-round loss to the Warriors. Their city was jumping.

I liked playing at the Silverdome. It had a live floor. Some arena floors are dead. You don't get much lift on them. But I could elevate very well there. The wood had bounce.

Still, we knew it would be difficult capturing that game on the road. But Games 2 and 5 were also in Detroit, and we needed to return to the Garden with no worse than a split. If we took Game 1, the remaining four games would be evenly divided between New York and Motown. While the Pistons would still host a possible fifth elimination game in their arena, we could partially neutralize their home-court advantage.

Detroit came out gunning that night. Rory Sparrow did a great job of keeping Isiah's scoring in check, but he made up for it with his court awareness, directing his team offense with assists, steals, and rebounds.

Meanwhile, we were cold offensively. Only Bill Cartwright and I were making our shots. Before we knew it, the first quarter was over and we were down by 14.

Hubie decided I'd need to carry the offense and began calling my number on play after play. The frequency of his calls surprised me. But he understood we couldn't afford to fall any further behind. I would receive the basketball until the other guys found their rhythm.

Kelly Tripucka, Detroit's small forward, was my primary guard. He was a prolific scorer and had a good night shooting the ball. But he was a flat-footed defender and couldn't stop me from getting my points. I'd go right up over him time after time.

Now, about Bill Laimbeer.

Early in the game, I went up for a layup, and he smashed my hand against the backboard. I knew he did it on purpose. And he knew I knew. It caused me serious pain, but I couldn't retaliate. If I were tossed, he'd get exactly what he wanted.

He was a dirty player. No other Piston deliberately tried to take advantage of my injuries.

I got my points despite his illegal hits. But we couldn't catch up to Detroit. They played tight defense, and Isiah had a sixth sense for finding the open man. By halftime, they'd built up a 13-point lead.

The third quarter was a repeat of the first two. I scored 10 points to put us within 12, but we couldn't get any closer. Meanwhile, Hubie had gotten tossed for arguing with the officials.

Goddam, I thought. *We can steal this game*. But we had to get stops.

That was when Rick Pitino called a full-court press on defense. We'd done it throughout the season, and it all seemed preparation for that moment.

We went into lockdown mode.

The Pistons couldn't run their plays, couldn't pass, couldn't do anything offensively.

We'd forced them into a holding pattern. Now we needed to make our push.

At 1:17, the score was 93–87. I drew a foul from Tripucka with the ball in my hands, dropped two free throws, and trimmed the deficit to 4.

Enter Darrell Walker.

Isiah was moving the basketball up court when Darrell cut toward him, stole the ball, and fired it over to me. A perfect pass. I shot from ten feet and made the basket.

I would have known the ball went in without seeing it. I was there and not there. On some other plane.

The score was 93–91.

We had forty-three seconds.

Darrell slipped behind a double team, stole on a bounce pass, and got fouled.

He made one out of two. The score was 93–92. A point separated us.

We had twenty seconds.

It was Rory Sparrow's turn. Though he had trouble scoring all night, he'd been left in for his defense.

Laimbeer had his hands up to catch a pass. Rory tipped it. And was fouled.

Standing at the key as Rory prepared for his free throws, I was like a high-voltage wire. We all were.

He went two for two.

The score was 94–93. *Our* favor.

Nine seconds. The ball in Isiah Thomas's hands. Darrell on defense. He didn't give Isiah an inch.

Trapped, Isiah got the ball to Laimbeer. With the game's final seconds evaporating, he hurled it toward our basket from midcourt.

You could see right off that it wasn't going in.

We won the game.

Oh my goodness! I thought, and leaped toward the pileup of Knicks on the court.

I SCORED 36 POINTS IN GAME 1, but couldn't have cared less about my total. We'd topped the Pistons in their house. That was my only concern.

Two nights later at the Silverdome, Detroit's head coach, Chuck Daly, rotated my defenders to throw me off my game. Tripucka. Earl Cureton. Kent Benson. Cliff Levingston. They came at me one after another and really beat up on me, trying to bang me out of my sweet spots.

I concentrated on their vulnerabilities. They were weaknesses I'd been filing into my mental database all season long. I could jump right over Tripucka. Cureton always bit at my fakes, and Benson couldn't match my speed. Levingston could jump and had a slight edge in height, presenting the most difficulty. But most players jumped away from a taller defender. I jumped right into Levingston. It's hard to block a shot at close range.

I hit 46 points that night. Twenty-three came in consecutive baskets, all during a five-and-a half-minute span in the first quarter. I found out afterward that the 23-in-a-row broke a record set by Wilt Chamberlain. Again, our names were linked.

But we lost despite all that. 113–104. The Pistons' defense held the rest of our team down, and we couldn't stop Isiah.

On the plane home, I told our coaching staff we had to get Bill Cartwright more involved in the offense. We needed a second scorer, and he was one of our best. To me, the handwriting was on the wall. If we didn't get Bill some shots, we were going to lose the series.

I didn't care about my numbers. I didn't care about broken records. Someday I'd have time to look back at things of that nature, but none of it really mattered to me.

What mattered, *all* that mattered, was that we needed to win Game 3 back home in New York.

MY TEAM WAS HUNGRY FOR A WIN, and our fans shared that hunger. When Madison Square Garden got loud, your bones would shake. We felt it stepping on the court for the tip-off, and so did the Pistons.

We played our best first half of the season in Game 3. Defensively and offensively, it was a complete team effort.

Hubie wanted to avoid falling into predictable defensive patterns and used a switching defense that kept Isiah Thomas off balance. Thanks to Rory Sparrow and Darrell Walker, he didn't score a single point before the break. Neither of them gave Isiah any breathing room as they rotated their assignment guarding him.

On the offensive side, Hubie called Bill Cartwright's number all night.

"Thirty-five!"

That was Bill's play. We'd set a three-man screen on the right, have one of our guards pass him the ball on the left side of the key, and then cut through the key to draw off the defense. The idea was to force Detroit into a one-on-one against him.

It worked. Bill had unusual quickness for a seven-foot-one center and could outmaneuver anybody guarding him.

We were up 54–36 at halftime. Isiah finally figured things out in the third and fourth quarters, scoring 29 points in one of his whirlwind offensive tears. But we were playoff tested. It was one of our advantages over the Pistons. We knew they would make a run at some point and didn't panic when it happened.

Bill dropped 22 points that night. I scored 46 for a second game in a row.

We beat the Pistons 130–113, taking a 2–1 series lead that had them on the brink of elimination.

Nobody on the Knicks felt like heading back to Detroit for a Game 5.

We had our foot on the Pistons' throat and wanted to put them away on our home court.

DETROIT HAD DIFFERENT INTENTIONS, though you couldn't tell from the way they started out.

We hit 8 unanswered points in the opening three minutes. When Detroit had the ball, they rushed their shots. When we had possession, we either put it in the hoop or drew fouls that sent us to the free-throw line. Ray Williams started out looking like he'd have his best game of the series. Truck Robinson scored on a snap pass from Ray in the paint, and the Garden crowd went wild.

Chuck Daly smelled a rout and called a twenty-second time-out. I don't know what he told his guys. Maybe he was just giving them a chance to exhale. But they came out sharper and more determined and put themselves right back in the game.

Kelly Tripucka had an excellent night from the floor. He made 21 points, only 1 less than Isiah Thomas. If you study that basketball game, though, it had Isiah's handprint all over it. The story isn't in his point total but in his 16 assists and control of the tempo. He was mercurial running through traffic and feeding Tripucka and Laimbeer the ball. He played forty-two minutes and got the most out of his second unit. Four out of five men on their bench were in double digits. Earl Cureton, a backup power forward, hit some key baskets.

I scored 41 that night for my third 40-plus point game in a row. Bill hit 24. Between us, that came to over half our team's total points. And that was the problem.

For most of the night, we were nip and tuck with the Pistons. But we didn't match their collective offensive production, and in the third quarter, they finally pulled ahead of us.

Still, we kept things close. Near the end of the third, the score was 87–83, their favor. Then 87–86. In the fourth quarter, we were still neck and neck. The score was 92–90, theirs. Then 101–97.

But we couldn't overtake them again. The Pistons made 6 out of their last 8 shots, and Isiah managed the clock well in the final minutes. I could tell he'd grown over the course of four playoff games and learned how to protect the lead.

Detroit won the game 119–112. As we walked off the court, the loudest thing in the Garden was the sound of the Pistons high-fiving each other.

We were headed for a Game 5 showdown in Motown.

IT WOULDN'T BE AT THE SILVERDOME. The arena had booked a tractor pull and was unavailable for the game. I know how crazy that must sound. It sounded crazy to the Knicks. We were in the NBA playoffs. How do you schedule a tractor pull? But I guess somebody or other didn't think the Pistons would be successful enough to reach Game 5.

Anyway, the game moved downtown to a place called the Joe Louis Arena. It was home to the Detroit Red Wings hockey club.

We didn't like it. They didn't like it. The Pistons' fans didn't like it, either.

I don't think there could have been a worse time to come down with the flu. But it hit me like a freight train the day before the game. When we got to our hotel, I had a sore throat and high fever. My dislocated fingers weren't making me feel any better.

I was in rotten shape.

I didn't attend shoot-around on game day. When our team left the hotel for the arena, I went down to get on the bus and then realized I needed to stay back and conserve my strength.

"I have to go back upstairs," I told Hubie. "But I'll be ready tonight."

He and Mike Saunders were skeptical. But I knew I'd take the court.

When I was a kid, my father always said, "You have to work even when you're sick." It was one thing I learned from him that stuck with me my whole life.

My teammates had fought all season long for the opportunity to make the finals. I was their captain. I wasn't going to let them down.

Rick Pitino had also caught it; the day before, he'd checked into Lenox Hill Hospital in New York with a 104-degree fever. Somehow, he made it to Detroit for the game.

Meanwhile, I was still suffering from the flu, my throat so sore I could hardly swallow. I refused to look at a thermometer. I didn't need one to tell me I was burning up.

The Joe Louis Arena looked like a gigantic airplane hangar. But that wasn't the worst part. The worst was that the air-conditioning system was broken. I've read it was 95 degrees in there. That's wrong. It was closer to 125 degrees. Ask Hubie Brown; I think he checked.

Hubie was dripping sweat all night. Later on, he'd say that he would slosh around in his shoes whenever he walked the baseline. They were filled with perspiration.

Chuck Daly didn't enjoy the sweltering heat any more than Hubie. He was a clotheshorse, the kind of guy who wore a silk shirt and diamond cuff links. His light-blue Brioni sports jacket must have cost plenty. Before the game was over, it darkened to navy blue from sweat. He grumbled later that the dry cleaners could never restore it.

That game was the most intense I ever played. I concentrated so deeply that I hardly remembered anything about it afterward. All I know was that every time we seemed to have victory in our hands, Detroit came back at us. They wouldn't give up. They just kept coming back.

Hubie insisted we stay on our feet during time-outs. He'd never done anything like that before. I think he was afraid the heat would overcome us if we took our seats. We were going on pure adrenaline. Meanwhile, I was still burning up with the flu. So sapped of strength I could hardly stand, I sat on the floor.

We started the fourth quarter up 85–79, then added some points and went ahead by 8. That was a big lead down the stretch. Or it should have been. But Isiah was relentless. He would score. I would score. *He* would score. Then I would come back and score . . .

We were carrying our teams, and we knew it. All we *didn't* know was which of us would outlast the other.

Then Isiah exploded. With ninety seconds of regulation left in the game, he went off, scoring 16 consecutive points.

Think about it. 16 points in 90 seconds. You can't even do that in the playground. It was unheard of.

Isiah was six foot one and weighed 185 pounds. The smallest guy on the court. He was stealing the ball and hitting 3-point outside jumpers. He was burying 2-point field goals and getting fouled for the extra point. Bank shots, layups. Time and time again. Rory couldn't stop him. Darrell couldn't stop him. He just went to another place. That's the only way to put it. I've been to that place myself.

With about forty seconds on the game clock, we led 112–106. Then Isiah was fouled on a layup to make the score 112–109. After his free throw, Bill Cartwright inbounded to Louis Orr, but Detroit forced Louis out over the baseline, and Isiah once again had the ball on our side of the court. He dribbled into the paint, took a short jumper, and put it in for two.

Detroit was within a point of us. The game clock down to thirty-six seconds.

Hubie called a time-out. He wanted to talk about our next possession, knowing it could be the last of the game.

He got onto one knee and put his board on the floor. As I sat there in the huddle, I saw he was diagramming a play for Cartwright.

I couldn't believe it. I was the best player on the team. I was averaging over 40 points a game. It was my responsibility to take the final shot. Win or lose, I had to own it.

I'd never in my basketball life questioned a coach. No one had to teach me that. The coach is the coach. You're a player, you play, and allow yourself to be coached.

But our season was on the line. Not just the game. Our *season*.

"Hubie," I said.

He kept drawing something up for Bill. His head down.

"Hubie," I repeated. "Do I have the right to take it myself?"

He didn't respond. It was very noisy in the arena. So I said it louder to get his attention. Much louder.

"Do I have the RIGHT to take it myself, Hubie?"

He looked up at me. I was telling him I was going to break his play.

You hear about players feeling pressure in big moments. Hubie must have felt some kind of pressure in that huddle. But he never showed it.

Finally he said, "Yeah."

The time-out ended. We inbounded the ball, and I waved Bill off.

Earl Cureton was my defender. He'd had a big game in Game 4 and was feeling it.

"Come on," he growled. "Bring it."

I heard him. But his challenge didn't faze me. I wasn't going to change what I wanted to do. Namely, make a play for us to win.

I dribbled and then did something I ordinarily *didn't* do. I put the ball between my legs.

I wasn't being flashy. I did that for one reason alone.

I had nine half-court King spots on that side of the lane. They were numbered in my mind, and I wanted Spot Number Five. But sometimes the defense was good enough so I couldn't just go my spot. I had to set up my move. Disguise what I wanted.

Earl was six foot ten and a solid defender.

I set him up, the ball between my legs to throw off his rhythm. Then I drove left to slow his lateral movement, took one, two dribbles . . .

Spot Number Five.

I faded and shot and the ball went in.

The score was 114–111 with twenty-six seconds left in the game.

With twenty-three seconds to go, Isiah drained a three to tie the game at 114–114 and send us into overtime.

LAIMBEER SCORED THE FIRST SHOT coming out of overtime. That can take the wind out of the opposition.

We didn't let it. One of our second-unit guards, Trent Tucker, answered with a jumper to tie the score again. Then I followed up on a missed shooting attempt by Louis Orr and slam-dunked to put us up by two.

As I started toward the opposite end of the court, my injured hands sang out in agony.

What is pain? Go within.

That set us on a roll. I think we scored 7 straight after the dunk.

But Isiah wouldn't quit. He bucketed another 3 from twenty-six feet. I answered with a turnaround jumper from sixteen feet. Then he drove to the net and dropped 2.

It was a relief to everyone in a Knicks uniform when Isiah fouled out of the game with about a half minute on the clock. The Pistons came back at us one more time, but we knew we had them the instant he left the court.

Bill Cartwright scored the last two points on free throws and then it was over. We beat them 127–124. I'd scored 44 of our points.

I might have dropped from fever and exhaustion if my teammates hadn't held me up with their hugs.

IN THE LOCKER ROOM, a beat reporter told me I'd scored 213 points in the five-game series. It broke a playoff record set a quarter century before by Hall of Famer Elgin Baylor.

I remember grinning at the reporter. Baylor was an incomparable player. But at that moment . . .

"Who cares?" I said. "We won!"

Of course, we couldn't bask.

The Celtics had eliminated their first-round competition, the Washington Bullets, in four games. They would be our opponent in the semifinals.

We were flying up to Boston that very night.

19 | Battling Boston

The Boston Celtics were considered the beasts of the East. Their roster was impressive. I've spoken of their four stars—Bird, McHale, Parish, and Johnson. But Cedric Maxwell was a playoff-tough small forward, and players like M. L. Carr, Danny Ainge, and others gave them a highly effective second unit.

My team didn't fear them.

As Hubie might say, if you want to know why, think of the number three.

We'd faced them six times in the regular season and split 3–3 in wins and losses. Six times the previous year we wound up with the same 3–3 record.

That would suggest we matched up well against them, and we did at every starting position. We also felt our second unit was the best in the NBA. Their press-and-trap defense gave opponents conniptions. They held and built on leads and were fundamental to our success.

Still, we knew we'd have our work cut out for us. We were tired after the grueling Detroit series. Physically, mentally, and emotionally wiped out. Our overtime game with them was on Friday night, and Game 1 against Boston was Sunday—an afternoon game. While Isiah and company were pushing us to the limit in steamy Joe Louis Arena, the Celtics were home watching us on television. They'd had four days to rest up after defeating the Bullets. It would be tough going up against their front line with less than twenty-four-hours rest.

We arrived in Boston late Friday night. Before going up to my hotel room, I bought the next morning's paper. I liked getting a feel for whatever NBA city I visited, and always read the newspapers when I was on the road.

It would have been impossible to miss the boldface sports headline: "WE'RE GOING TO STOP THE B–TCH!"

The source of the quote was Cedric Maxwell. He was obviously referring to me. His full, unedited comment was, *"He ain't gettin' forty on us. We're going to stop the bitch!"*

The paper's sports editor had cleaned up his language.

That quote was all anyone wanted to ask me about in our pregame press conferences at the Boston Garden. But I didn't have anything for them.

Cedric's comment wasn't motivating to me. It didn't bother me. What he said didn't matter. It just made him look silly, and I wasn't going to react.

But Cedric kept trying. Later, when the series moved to New York, he walked up to me before the opening tip. I had my Game Face on.

"Why do you *look* like that?" he said. "Are you crazy?"

I didn't say a word to him. I knew what he was doing. Teams will always try to provoke the opposition's best player. But nothing anyone ever said would throw me off my game.

In the series opener, however, I quickly saw what Boston had devised to stop me on the court.

The first time somebody fouled me, I got hit by two other guys after the call. That was the strategy. One guy took the foul, two guys hit me. In the head. Since only one foul can be assessed on a play, they got in those other hits without penalty. The refs couldn't call it.

Unlike Detroit, Boston was playoff tested. They knew what they had to do.

That kind of thing wasn't new to me. Don't forget where I grew up. In Brooklyn, if somebody did that to you in the playground, you did the same thing to him.

The Celtics were tough. But I could be as physical as they were. And as the series went on, I would be. The question was whether the rest of my team could match that necessary level of physicality.

There isn't much to say about Game 1. The Celtics knew we'd be fatigued after Detroit and dominated us with their passing and fast breaks. We had too many early turnovers, and that helped put them up by 9 at the end of the first quarter. At halftime, they led by 20.

When a team of the Celtics' ability and experience builds up that kind of lead in a playoff game, they don't relinquish it.

We lost 110–92. After the way we'd played against the Pistons, it was an awful letdown. We weren't happy with ourselves. But nothing was decided. We'd dropped one game in the series. There were six left to play.

GAME 2 TAUGHT ME SOMETHING NEW. Or at least set me up to learn it.

I had a bad performance and only scored 13 points. The Celtics did everything they could to keep the ball out of my hands. That was their strategy, and they executed it well. Rory Sparrow put it best when he said they fronted me and played me from the back, but never the same way two times down the court.

The hits on me after foul calls escalated. I liked and respected Kevin McHale, but once, after he slammed me, I told him I'd kick his ass the next time it happened. I hoped my teammates would back me up, but if they didn't, I would take care of it myself. I couldn't let our opponents keep banging me around.

But I won't blame my poor play on the hits.

What hampered me most was Boston's circle defense. Someone on their scouting or coaching staff had figured out it was the best way to guard me on the low block, where I made the majority of my points. It was the one defense I hated to see.

Cedric Maxwell applied it very effectively in that second game. Whenever I moved to receive the ball, he circled me. From the front, to the side, to the back, and then around front again. Once I locked a defender into position, I could receive a pass and make any shot I wanted. As long as he circled, I couldn't make contact and couldn't pin him down.

Rory was our point guard. His job was to feed me the ball from the left or right wing. But as Maxwell continued circling me, staying constantly in motion, it would appear I wasn't open to receive his pass. He didn't know *when* to pass, and I wasn't sure what to do about it.

The Celtics won Game 2, 116–102. For the second night in a row, we never took a lead.

When you start a seven-game series down 0–2, you're written off in the press. But we weren't writing ourselves off. Game 3 was back home, at Madison Square Garden. We'd have our fans behind us.

I had some things to figure out, though. And there was no time to sit around doing it.

I DIDN'T GO TO HUBIE WITH MY PREDICAMENT. I was his superstar player. His team captain. He needed to feel confident in me. If I rattled his confidence, the guys would pick up on it. We were in too tight a spot to let that happen.

We returned home on April 29, hours after our defeat in Boston. The next game wasn't until Friday night. It gave me a chance to rest up, shake off my lingering flu symptoms, and get treatment on my hands before Tuesday's team practice.

After a good night's sleep in my own bed—I hadn't been home since before Game 5 in Detroit—I called my old friend and mentor Pete Newell, who ran the Big Man Camp in California and had recommended me to the Warriors when my life and career were at a crossroads.

Now I'd turn to him at another decisive moment.

"Pete," I said over the phone. "I don't know if you watched any of the Boston games—"

"Bernard?"

"Yeah?"

"We go back," he said. "I've watched."

I thought about what he'd done for me years ago. My gratitude still felt fresh.

"I need your help, Pete," I said, and explained Boston's defensive strategy. "I can't pin them. I can't make contact. And my guard thinks I'm not open and goes away." I paused. "What can I do?"

He was only quiet for a minute.

"Okay, listen," he said. "Here's my advice . . ."

I PULLED RORY SPARROW ASIDE at Tuesday's practice, explained the problem Maxwell was giving me, and then spelled out Pete's solution.

"Wow," he said.

"Yeah," I said.

We smiled at each other and worked on getting it down.

IN THE OPENING MINUTES OF GAME 3, our crowd gave us everything we could ask for, cheering us on at the top of their lungs and razzing the Celtics with "Boston Sucks" chants. They'd shown up for us.

We showed up too. Rested, refreshed, and ready. We showed up.

Boston scored first, but Hubie started out by routing our offense through Bill Cartwright, and Bill was on his game. He dropped in 14 or 15 points before the quarter ended.

I got my chance to test Pete's solution in that same period. I was on the block, Maxwell circling me. Out the sides of my vision, I saw Rory out on the left wing, looking for his chance.

When Maxwell circles you, there's going to be a break in that circle, Pete had explained. *If he starts out in front of you, goes around to the bottom toward the baseline, then comes around behind you . . . that's the break point. Tell your guard that's when to make the pass. Whether or not you look open to him. Just make the pass.*

We executed to perfection. Rory snapped the ball to me. Maxwell saw it and moved around to my left. But by the time he reacted, the pass was already made, and I was expecting it.

The basketball was in my hands. I scored.

What Rory and I did was so effective, Maxwell stopped circling me. I totaled 24 points.

Hubie's adjustments also worked. We moved the ball around the court and got everyone in an offensive flow. Bill finished with 25 points; and Rory, 15. Ray Williams had one of his best nights of the postseason and added 22 of his own.

As we grew our lead, the fans' war cry got louder. We could hear it reverberating through the Garden:"*Boston sucks! Boston SUCKS! BOSTON SUCKS!*"

Boston's players had come into the game saying the Knicks were in the grave.

If so, we jumped out of it and got a 100–92 win. Our crowd was so raucous you'd have thought an earthquake tremor was rumbling through the arena.

We were right back in the series, with another home game coming up.

I FELT GAME 4 WAS ANOTHER MUST-WIN. We were heading back to Boston for Game 5 and needed to make sure it wasn't an elimination game. A Game 4 victory to tie the series in New York guaranteed that, no matter the outcome on the road, we could look forward to one more at home.

I'd never thought in terms of scoring a certain number of points. But I told myself I would go out and be aggressive.

The crowd was on its feet from the start. People stood in the aisles waving homemade signs. I can't really convey how I felt hearing my name announced that Sunday afternoon. You know how it feels when you pull off a sweater full of static electricity? It was like that for me. Like sparks were snapping off my skin.

As our teams gathered outside the jump circle before tip-off, the noise around us built, and built, and built.

Then the ball was in the air.

My first basket came off a double team. I was on the block guarded by Maxwell. Rory passed me the ball from the wing after getting clear of the Celtics' point guard, Gerald Henderson. Henderson broke away from Rory to double-team me, but I bounced the ball once as I feinted to my left, and then went through both defenders for a short turn-around jumper.

I scored 12 points by the end of the quarter to help give us a 10-point lead. It was the best I felt during that series. I'd beaten the circle defense, and Maxwell looked lost.

The Celtics threw everything they had at me. Switches. Double and triple teams. The hits got harder and more frequent. But it didn't slow me. I had everything working.

All games have one or two tone-setting plays. Game 4's came in the second quarter.

Maxwell was behind me after I received a pass from Ray Williams. Bird was on me. Kevin McHale was a step away defensively. Danny Ainge was a step away.

A triple team. Four defenders counting Maxwell.

I wasn't concerned with the first two guys in front of me. I had moves to beat the third guy.

I quickly saw the break point to the middle, drawing contact. I wasn't passing off the ball that close to the basket. Worst-case scenario, I'd go to the line. But I sank a short fadeaway jumper and came away with a 3-point play.

Minutes later, I had another play that might have tilted the game in either direction.

We were up by five. 42–37. As Ray Williams moved the ball up court, Hubie called out a number:

"Forty-two!"

Power right. My play.

This time, Hubie was being the chess master, thinking several moves ahead.

With Ray Williams moving the ball up court toward the Celtics' basket, I took position on the left block, Maxwell guarding me. Marvin Webster trailed above the three-point line to screen off McHale in the back court. As our play developed, Darrell Walker cut to the basket from the left baseline.

Maxwell cheated toward him, anticipating a quick pass from Ray to Darrell.

On the left side of the lane, Danny Ainge, who had great court awareness, picked up on the play. He raised his arm and gestured toward the left, signaling Maxwell to protect against a backdoor lob from Ray to me.

Ray and I exchanged glances. Play on. As Ray made his throw, Maxwell tried to recover and get back on me. But he was already dead.

I stepped into the paint to receive the pass. Maxwell backed toward me, raising his arm, trying to put his body between me and the basket.

Too late.

I went up into the air, caught the ball at the high point of its arc, and dunked, drawing contact from him to earn a free throw. As our bodies collided, he fell back onto the hardwood.

The Garden erupted. Maxwell's comment about me to the Boston press had been picked up by the New York news media. The fans knew about it and had it in for Cedric.

He sat up to their gleeful cheers, shaking the cobwebs out of his head.

In the playground, we'd have called that sweet revenge. I could've added insult to injury and stared down at him, hand on my hips. Some guys brought that kind of thing to the NBA, but I never even did it when I was a kid. Why start now and get the Celtics fired up? I knew who I was.

Go take a seat, I thought, and went straight to the free-throw line as he got up and walked to the sidelines.

Parish replaced him on the court.

That play defined how my team performed night. Physical offense and lockdown defense. The Celtics liked the fast break, but our half-court press threw off their rhythm and kept them from running the ball to the hoop.

I didn't know how many points I was scoring but could tell I was scoring a lot. No single Boston player was close. Yet when I glanced up at the scoreboard, I never saw much separation between us. Larry Bird was going to get his share of points. You knew that. But four or five other Celtics put up numbers in the solid double digits. It kept us from pulling away that afternoon.

That would stir up concerns for me. I could be dominant, but I couldn't dominate the Celtics as I'd done with Detroit. With four future Hall of Famers on their squad, they had too many guys.

But all that was for later on. There was no celebration. We had what we needed. A 118–113 win. I'd scored 43 points, a good afternoon.

Now the Knicks were heading back to Boston with the series tied 2–2 and the opportunity to close out the series at home.

GAME 5 AT THE BOSTON GARDEN followed the series trend—each team holding its home court. That meant a rough night for the Knicks.

The Celtics ran on us. Our defense didn't do a good enough job of slowing them down. Once again, they had a balanced attack, with all five starters and Kevin McHale putting up strong double-digit totals. Like Bird, I was going to get my points. But we didn't come close as a team.

A lot of basketball fans remember the brawl at the end of the third quarter. We were down 85–74 after rallying from a 20-point deficit, and Darrell Walker was driving toward the basket to try and bring us within 8 or 9.

Danny Ainge deliberately fouled him. Nothing wrong with that. Our teams had gone at it all series long. But Ainge went too far. As Darrell was barreling up the lane, Ainge raised both arms and hit him openhanded in the throat and chin.

Darrell's head snapped back. It's the kind of move that can put someone in the hospital, or worse.

Darrell went at Ainge and hit him in exactly the same way. It was kind of a *how do you like it?* shot. Then Ainge's fists came up, and Darrell's fists came up, and their arms were swinging, and Ainge tackled Darrell, and they landed on the floor. A second later, three or four Celtics were on top of Darrell.

I ran over to break up the fight, but it was only Darrell and me in a mountain of green-and-white uniforms. I was trying to pull Darrell out from underneath the pileup when somebody shoved me from behind and I spilled over a couple of Celtics.

When I recovered, I saw M. L. Carr come off Boston's bench and punch Darrell as he lay on the floor. I went after him in spite of my dislocated fingers. It was a cheap shot.

Five minutes later, Darrell and Ainge were ejected from the game, and our teams were back at it with the basketball. It was a playoff game. Things happen in the heat of competition.

I just wish we'd won. But the Celtics took it 121–99.

We would be getting back on the Boston–New York shuttle facing elimination.

GAME 6 WAS ON A FRIDAY NIGHT in May. As I drove from my Jersey home, I was deep in concentration. I paid careful attention to the highway traffic and the closeness of the cars around me as I passed through the Lincoln Tunnel's narrow lanes into Manhattan. But I had already entered an inner tunnel, a space that wasn't physical. It was the same space I'd inhabited as Little Spal on the courts at Whitman, practicing, practicing, shooting a basketball in the pitch darkness, feeling it leave my fingers and visualizing its spin and trajectory, even with my eyes shut, even without seeing or hearing, not needing my outer senses to tell me when it found the center of the hoop.

The game was about what was inside, not outside. Many things had changed in my life, but that was always the same. It was about what was inside.

I was determined to carry our team to victory that night. I'd told myself the series would be decided in Game 7. We wouldn't lose to Boston, our archrival, at Madison Square Garden. We would not fall at home.

We didn't fall.

We played one of our best games ever. It had to be one of our best against a team like the Celtics. That night, they didn't run. We trapped them in the half court. We didn't let them find their rhythm.

They fought hard. Every rebound was contested. We couldn't get second-chance shots.

All night, I was in that inner space. The space where I was most comfortable, where I most belonged. Where I could express myself with a touch, a leap, and a quick release, putting the basketball exactly where I wanted it.

Hubie knew. My teammates knew. I scored 44, but we were all in it together, unselfish, embracing our roles, doing whatever it took to win.

Fourth quarter. They roared back at us late in the fourth. But we kept fighting them off. With three minutes left and my team up by 11 points, I put in 2 to make the lead 100–87.

Then Rory Sparrow was ejected on a flagrant foul against Bird. Rory got his forearm on him as he drove toward the basket, and Bird went down. Referee Earl Strom called the flagrant.

Bird just went to the free-throw line. He knew there was no intent. Every player on the floor knew it. Rory took a harder hit earlier and it wasn't called. He was our point guard, our playmaker. But Bird was the Celtics' best player, and the officials remembered the scuffle in Boston. They were calling it tight.

That hurt us.

Two-and-a-half minutes later, the Celtics had come back within a basket. We were at 106–104, and they had the final possession.

Hubie put Marvin Webster into the game for Bill Cartwright. Bill was the better scorer, but Marvin gave us tougher defense. Hubie had decided our 2-point margin would have to be enough. He didn't want overtime. He wanted that game to end in regulation.

Everybody on the court knew the Celtics would inbound to Bird. Everybody in the stands knew they were going to Bird. Some of the fans started the Madison Square Garden *"De-fense, de-fense"* chant. Some were clapping. But mostly people were quiet and holding their collective breath.

I looked around at my teammates and clapped my bandaged hands. "Let's go," I said. "Let's go."

Then Bird got the ball, and Marvin was all over him, but Bird willed himself free and pushed toward the basket and took a short jumper from the right block, last shot.

He was off balance. The ball bounced high off the glass, rolled off the rim.

Buzzer.

The Knicks and Celtics were tied at 3–3 in the series. Just as we'd been tied at 3–3 in the regular season for the past two years. It felt as if this was the way things were meant to be.

Game 7 would be uncharted territory for both teams.

MY CONCERN ABOUT THE GAME was pretty simple. In the Boston Celtics, we were going up against a very seasoned and experienced team.

Their starting point guard, Dennis Johnson, had won a championship with the Seattle Supersonics and been Finals MVP. Kevin McHale possessed the quickness, strength, and intelligence to escape double teams; we had nobody at his position to contain him, and that made him key to their success against us. Robert Parish, their seven-foot-tall center and power player, was an unyielding post defender and offensive threat.

In one play early in Game 7, I was cutting through the lane when Parish hit me with a forearm shiver to the face in front of my bench. It was an unmistakable message. I'd scored 44 against his team a couple of nights before. Parish was letting me know they meant to keep that from happening at the Boston Garden.

I wanted to go after him because no foul was called. But I didn't take the bait. The Celtics would have liked nothing better. If I got tossed for fighting, it was game over for my team. Parish would have cut the head off a dangerous snake.

There are times when you have to take the hit.

Johnson, McHale, and Parish—a formidable combination on the floor.

But there's a reason I haven't yet mentioned the fourth man. The Celtics' *key* man.

In my years in the NBA, I'd faced the brilliance of Julius Erving and the electrifying dominance of Dominique Wilkins. Whenever I played against Wilkins, I hoped he wouldn't embarrass me. They were two of the best forwards ever to take the court.

But Larry Bird was unlike any forward I ever played against.

At six foot ten, he had the height to shoot over me. He was the best passing forward in the league, and had lightning accuracy with no-look passes. An outstanding rebounder, he also possessed exceptional ball handling skills on the open floor.

Bird could beat you in many different ways. Earlier in the series at Madison Square Garden, with seconds left in the game, I was inbounding to Truck Robinson, when, just as I released the ball, I peripherally caught Bird moving toward it for a steal.

Oh shucks, I thought.

Fortunately, Truck retrieved the rock. We were lucky.

I'd thought Bird and I might offset each other in that final game. But he had other plans. Just as I'd refused to lose the series in New York, he was determined not to go down in Boston and brought the full aggregate of his basketball prowess to the court. He rained three-pointers that hit nothing but net. He passed the ball off the dribble like Pistol Pete Maravich in his prime. He controlled the game's tempo and would not be denied.

There are some things you never forget as a player. The highs and the lows. The lows always sting.

The Celtics were very effective at keeping the ball out of my hands. They doubled up on our guards so they couldn't pass it, and they doubled up on me whenever I caught it. They were determined not to give me any shots.

But the bottom line is Bird outplayed me that day. He did whatever he wanted, scoring 39 points. Most of them were from the perimeter, opening up the paint for his teammates.

I held our home court, and Bird held his, and the Celtics had one more at home than we did. Game 7, winner-take-all. They won 121–104.

After the game, I went into Boston's locker room, shook Bird's hand, and wished him well. Emotions were still high; our teams had had a hard-fought series, and it was like walking into a hornet's nest. But as leader of the Knicks, I felt I should congratulate them.

The Celtics advanced to become the eventual NBA Champions, defeating the LA Lakers in seven games.

Our season was over. We went home.

20 | The Injury

Tomorrow isn't guaranteed. We act like it is, we make our plans and promises, but you never know what can happen to throw them off the rails. Nothing shows us this better than sports.

I had played the finest basketball of my life in the 1983–1984 post-season and become everything I always intended to be on the court. At the end of the season, I was voted league MVP by my peers. While the Knicks' loss to the Celtics was hard to stomach, we nursed our wounds and, with time, set our sights on the future. We thought we'd be competing for NBA titles for years to come.

It didn't work out, though. Our title dreams were crushed before the 1984–1985 season began. Bill Cartwright fractured his foot in the preseason and was lost to us for the entire year. Marvin Webster, his backup, was battling a serious illness that ended his Knicks career. Then, two games into the season, Truck Robinson also suffered a foot injury.

We never recovered from those losses. Almost from the start, Hubie was forced to pull players from the developmental leagues to fill our vacancies. They came and went.

By the time we arrived in Kansas City on March 23, we were dead last in the Atlantic Division. We knew we weren't going to make the playoffs. Neither were the Kings. The arena was nearly empty.

My own performance hadn't been affected by our team's misfortunes. I was averaging over 30 points a game for the season. I came ready to play every night.

At that exact point in the season, I was negotiating with the Knicks to sign a contract extension. I had two years left on the five-year, $5 million deal I signed with the team upon being traded from Golden State. We were able to keep the talks quiet, amazingly so, given the media attention in New York.

Interestingly, Hubie had told me before the start of the season that the Knicks had been pursuing John Paxson, a Portland Trailblazers shooting guard who'd become a free agent. They'd offered him $1.2 million a season, more than I was making as the highest-paid player on the team.

"Are you still on your original contract?" he'd asked.

"Yeah," I said. Then half playfully added, "And I was only voted MVP over Magic, Bird, and Dr. J."

Hubie kind of smiled. But I'd always believed that if you sign a contract, you should live with it unless the club comes to you and says it wants to do a new deal. The Knicks had approached me about the extension. I never asked them or any team I played for to renegotiate. I didn't believe in that. But I wanted to remain a Knick, so I was happy to think it might happen.

When Hubie finally asked if I had a problem with the Knicks signing Paxson, I said, "No. I don't. Just let *him* take the last shot when it counts."

I don't remember if he laughed or not. They never signed Paxson. I have no idea why.

Anyway, the Knicks had been talking about an extension for a while. But there was something else going on. Something I didn't mention to anyone except Bill Pollak. For about a week before the trip to Kansas City, I'd been having a premonition that I would be injured. The feeling wouldn't go away.

The day before the game, I called Bill to find out the status of our discussions. He informed me there was a five-year, $8 million offer on the table, but said he thought I could get more if we continued to negotiate. It was a very open, friendly dialogue, and Bill felt confident it would reach a positive conclusion.

"Let's give it a little longer," he said.

I wasn't convinced and told him about my premonition. The last time I had anything like it was years before, when my drinking was out of control and I'd gotten a sense I was going to die. This feeling was even stronger.

"I can't shake it, Bill," I said. "It's the reason I contacted you. I really think you should wrap things up."

He didn't know what to make of my request. But I was very serious and asked if we should take out an insurance policy.

Bill replied that he didn't think so. "We're almost there," he explained. "Insurance is very expensive."

We left it at that and hung up.

The day of the game, I'd spent part of the afternoon with my buddy Doug, a former teammate at Fort Hamilton High School. After college, he'd received a job in Missouri and now lived in a town called Marshall, about ninety minutes from the arena.

Doug was a gregarious guy, a pleasure to be around. We'd talked for hours, reminiscing, joking, and catching up. For a little while, I was able to forget the Knicks were in the middle of a terrible season.

After lunch, Dougie and I drove to the arena together. I'd arranged for him to have game tickets, and he went to his seat as I prepared in my usual way. I got into my uniform, sat in front of my locker, put on my left sock and shoe, my right, and put a towel over my head. Then I lowered my head and closed my eyes.

I started playing out the game in my mind. I positioned the Kings' defensive players where I knew they'd be on the court, then saw myself successfully performing every one of my moves against them. I shot my jumper from all my favorite spots; the baseline, the elbow, just inside the lane. I spun right, then dribbled, drove to the rim and delivered the ball with my left hand. Then I did the same move to the opposite side. I sprinted down the left side of the floor—*my* side of the floor—and exploded toward the rim.

I did the visualization for several minutes. Even the kids from the development leagues knew not to talk to me. It was intense. Some nights, I was already sweating when I lifted my head.

Right before game time, I went out for my warm-ups. I took a first shot close to the basket. I increased the distance until I was shooting twenty-footers as if they were layups. I worked on my low-post moves on my own, talking to no one.

I was doing everything I always did to get ready. It didn't matter if I was in Kansas City and we were going nowhere, or the Boston Garden with the playoffs and pride on the line. My routine never changed.

Then the ball went up and we jumped.

Though the Knicks weren't very good, we were in every game, thanks to Hubie's high-pressure style of defense. Teams didn't want to deal with it, so it enabled us to play above our heads most nights.

Just not that one. The game got away from us and was pretty much out of hand early in the fourth quarter. When you don't have depth or strong talent, you either get blown out early or hang close until your opponent finally pulls away.

That's what happened in Kansas City. The Kings distanced themselves from us near the end.

Coming out of a time-out, Hubie called one of his plays for me. It seemed certain we'd lose, but he hadn't pulled me from the game. I wouldn't have wanted to sit. In that way, we were the same. We gave our all every night, no matter the odds.

The play didn't happen. We had a breakdown. Reggie Theus retrieved the ball on a turnover and headed up court toward our basket.

I did not give up on the play. The game was minutes from being over, we had no real chance of winning, and were in the middle of a long, hard road trip. But it was all about the moment. I'd been in that situation a thousand times. I was healthy as I'd ever been. If I caught Theus, I might get a steal or deflect his shot.

He jumped for his layup. I planted and went up for the block, trying to catch him.

I've already told you what happened next. The rifle-shot crack of my knee exploding while I was in midair. The pain that was like nothing I'd ever felt in my life. I curled into a ball and pounded the floor.

Then Mike Saunders was kneeling beside me. He was joined by the Kings' team doctor. The fans in the arena were silent. The only sound was my screams.

I'd dealt with sprains, pulled hamstrings, the dislocated fingers, you name it. I never dreamed a single play could end my career. But I knew this injury was different. As I lay on the floor of that arena, I was sure my premonition had come true. I was done.

I remember several of my teammates lifting me up and carrying me to the locker room, where my knee was examined and tested. This was long before every sports arena had a sophisticated MRI machine. When someone checked for knee damage, he would put his hand behind the knee, fingers interlocked, and pull forward. If all the ligaments were attached, nothing moved, indicating the joint was stable and tight.

My knee moved too far forward. It felt mushy.

I sat on the table and again thought, *This is it*. My spirit sank.

When a player goes down, other players feel it. No one on either team cared about the game's final score. But while guys came to console me, they didn't stay long. No one wants to be around a player who's suffered such a catastrophic injury. It reminds every athlete of his own vulnerability. Of how suddenly things can end for him. You feel almost as if you have a contagious disease.

We ultimately left the locker room and boarded the team bus. I was brought out to it in a wheelchair, my knee swollen beyond belief and wrapped in ice. I sat in the front seat, staring out into nowhere as everyone boarded.

The bus was hushed en route to our hotel. Mike wheeled me to my room and left. I'll never forget hearing him break down in tears outside the door.

Dougie was there with me. He'd met me in the lobby. We stayed up all night in my room without talking. I just sat in the wheelchair and cried. I couldn't handle the prospect of my career being over.

The next morning, I left for the airport with the team. Just as when we left the arena, no one spoke. Hubie never said anything to me. I never expected he would. His philosophy was very basic. In the game, there is no weakness. If someone gets hurt, you replace him and go on. That's how it goes in professional sports.

Mike helped me off the bus in the wheelchair. The Knicks were continuing on the road, with games to be played. I was headed back to New York.

As the team bus pulled out of sight, I sat thinking I'd never ride on one again.

I was taken to a gate to wait for my flight. Something happens to a highly trained athlete when he's injured. Mentally, I was still running and soaring in the air. Even as I sat in my wheelchair, my knee torn apart, I felt myself soar. But in reality, I needed someone to help put me on the plane.

As I ascended, heading east, I was swamped with self-pity. *Why? Why?* I thought of everything I'd accomplished, not just in basketball, but in life, and felt it had all been taken away from me. I was twenty-eight-years-old and my career was over.

But halfway through the flight something reignited in me. I knew what I was facing, knew my knee was no longer sound. This wasn't the torn cartilage I'd experienced in college. Later, I would find out I'd ruptured my anterior cruciate ligament, broken a bone, and torn my lateral meniscus cartilage. ACL injuries are very rare in basketball, and no one had ever returned from one to play at a high level.

I didn't need a diagnosis to have every reason to believe I couldn't come back. I knew what had occurred challenged the very core of who I was. But my heart was made in Brooklyn.

I can do this, I thought. *Yes, yes, I can.* However long it took, I'd be back.

21 | The Journey Back

On March 24, 1984, I was admitted to Lenox Hill Hospital on Manhattan's Upper East Side, where tests and an exploratory surgery soon confirmed what doctors immediately suspected. I had a full ACL tear, torn cartilage, and a broken bone in my right knee.

It couldn't have been any worse.

I remember calling Bill Pollak from my bed to ask that he locate the nation's top orthopedic surgeons and see whether they could fly to New York to examine my knee. Meanwhile, I spoke to members of the hospital staff and requested medical journals relating to my injury. I had frankly never heard of an ACL tear before. But I wanted to learn everything about it and use the same analytical approach I'd taken overcoming every other obstacle in my life.

I didn't know any other way.

One at a time, the doctors arrived from around the country. I recall seeing three prominent surgeons within a matter of days. I was also examined by Dr. Norman Scott, the Knicks' team surgeon. I asked each of them the same question: "Do you believe your technique will allow me to become an All-Star again?"

The three doctors Bill had contacted all said no. I would never play again. Surgery would be required for me to even walk normally again.

Only Dr. Scott answered, "Yes," emphatically.

His open knee procedure, he explained, was radically different from the others. Called modified iliotibial band surgery, it was also fairly untested. But Dr. Scott had confidence it could give me the outcome I desired *if* I was willing to follow his instructions to the letter and undertake rigorous physical therapy. The iliotibial band was a muscle and could be strengthened over time.

It wouldn't be easy, he warned.

I told Scott that was okay. I'd made my decision. I was going with him.

My surgery was scheduled for April 1, 1984, April Fool's Day.

The date probably should have made me a bit nervous. It didn't.

I was eager to get things underway.

DANIA SWEITZER WAS A FORMER ALL-AMERICAN swimmer and one of the best physical therapists in the country. At the time, she was working at a private physical therapy center in New York. They received a lot of patients from Lenox Hill Hospital doctors, including Norman Scott.

During the 1984 basketball season, I had gone to the center to rehab a sprained ankle and worked with Dania for several weeks. I'd thought she was skillful and committed, and truly cared about her patients.

A few days before my operation, I asked Dr. Scott to contact her. When she came to see me at the hospital, I asked if she would be my therapist moving forward. She agreed. But I needed to make sure of something and asked her a version of the question I'd presented to Dr. Scott.

"Dania, do you know what you're getting yourself into?" I said. "I don't want to *just* play basketball. I want to be the best. So I'll ask again. Do you *know* what you're getting yourself into?"

She looked me in the eye.

"Yes," she said.

It was same answer I'd gotten from Norman Scott. My team was assembled.

I never questioned Dania again.

MY LAST WORDS TO DR. SCOTT after being wheeled into the OR were, "God Bless."

His eyes met mine, and he nodded, and the anesthesia mask went over my face.

My surgery went without complication, but the pain after I woke up was awful. I was shocked to find forty-one metal staples holding my knee together. On the first night post-op, the nurses gave me morphine and I hallucinated that Bengal tigers were coming out of the wall. I was just about to climb out of bed to escape them, when someone grabbed me and pushed me back down on the sheets. It was a good thing. If I'd stood up, I would have destroyed my reconstructed knee, probably beyond repair.

After that close call, I asked to never again be given morphine. I was not going home with a drug problem. I'd coped with pain before and knew I could manage it.

WITHIN DAYS OF THE OPERATION, Dania began visiting me at Lenox Hill. She wasn't allowed to officially start as my therapist, because the hospital had its own PT staff. But she was able to oversee what they were doing there.

They started moving my scar tissue a little, moving the knee. It was excruciating. They also strapped on a huge device called a continuous passive motion, or CPM, machine to flex my tendons. Again, it was very painful—I remember breaking out in sweats—so they discontinued it for a while.

Another machine my body didn't tolerate was the TENS unit. The TENS would send electrical pulses into my leg and strengthen the muscles by making them expand and contract. It also broke up scar tissue.

The TENS gave me a full body spasm. Every muscle in my body felt like it was clenching. I screamed in pain. My mother, who was at the hospital every day, was down the hall and heard me.

As we went along, Dania told me that some of her female patients compared the pain of breaking down scar tissue to giving birth, and some thought it was even more painful. But Dr. Scott had explained that I would not gain mobility without breaking the adhesions. So the TENS was incorporated into the routine.

I would never recover full mobility in my leg. Scott was very concerned about hyperextension of the knee, so he buttressed it with sutures. But as a result, I'd be unable to completely bend it.

I returned home at the end of April. The Knicks had provided a customized hospital bed that would fit me, but I was unable to leave it. I couldn't even lift my leg off the bed.

As I lay on the bed each night, I thought about the uncertainty ahead. No NBA player with my injury had ever successfully returned to the game. The few who did were only shadows of their former selves. The odds were against me.

But I refused to be denied.

MY FIRST HOME SESSION WITH DANIA was on May 1, exactly a month after my operation.

She did a complete evaluation, with Mike Saunders, my Knicks trainer, standing by as she examined me.

"Let's see." Dania gently touched my wounds wearing sterile gloves. "We have moderate to severe effusion of your right knee . . . the suture line's healing well, with two open areas at mid-patella. One's half an inch, the other an eighth of an inch, seeping sanguineously . . ."

"Dania?"

"Yes?"

"English, please."

"Some of your wounds are still open, and you have a little bit of blood and fluid draining from them," she said. "But everything looks clean."

I nodded. "What's next?"

"We're going to set goals for every day," she said. "To improve your range of motion, increase your strength, improve your gait pattern—"

"Specifically meaning . . . ?"

"I'd like to get you to stand up over time, and then bend down enough to sit on the toilet."

I looked at her. "That would be nice," I said.

THAT FIRST DAY, we had a CPM machine delivered to my house.

With the CPM, you strap your leg in from the ankle to the knee, and then set the device to bend your knee at five degrees more motion than you can do on your own. The machine very slowly bends and straightens, bends and straightens, for between four and six hours a day. I would need to stay in bed the entire time the CPM was attached.

Initially I couldn't lift my leg up off the mattress without Dania's assistance. But after a few days, I was able to lift it, and we went from five- to sixty-degrees range of motion on the CPM.

Six days after I returned home, Dania arrived with a pair of crutches.

"Are you ready for these?" she asked.

"If you say I am," I replied, "I am."

DANIA AND I WORKED TOGETHER six days a week, a minimum of five hours a day, for the next two years.

She guided me every moment, and no day was ever the same. I saw rehab as climbing Mount Everest—an inch up, an inch up—and no one ever climbed it in a day.

Dania refused to put limitations on me. She came to understand me as a person and changed her professional acumen based on what was needed for the type of injury, individual, and athlete my case represented. When so many counted me out or said I was finished, she did not; her therapies and encouragement would get me through every challenge.

But she had help. Or I should say, *we* did. A couple of winged guardian angels.

Aldo and Florence were a mated pair of ducks that came around every day for weeks, landing in my backyard, waddling up to my terrace door, and pecking at the glass as if to say, "Come out, Bernard!"

When I saw them pecking, I'd pull myself into my wheelchair and feed them. They would stay on the brick terrace all day and then finally fly off at dusk.

"One of these times," I would tell them, tossing handfuls of bird food, "you two are going to see me get out of this chair by myself."

Of course, they couldn't possibly have understood me.

But I often imagined they did.

I AWOKE WITH A TERRIBLE THIRST.

I'm not sure how late it was, but it was night time and my first wife was asleep upstairs. I'd fallen asleep in my wheelchair after a long, wearying day of therapy.

Now I desperately craved a drink of water. There was a small adjoining room with a water cooler in it, but getting to the cooler would be a problem. My home's previous owners had owned a dog, and they'd attached a pet gate to the door frame. Though we always kept the gate open, my chair was too wide to clear it, and I was not yet comfortable enough on crutches to do more than get from my custom bed to the wheelchair.

I stared at the gate for a long minute. The thought that I could not get a glass of water upset me. I'd never felt so helpless in my life.

Suddenly I wheeled myself across the room to the stairs. There was a kitchen on the second level of the house, and one of the sink cabinets had a toolbox in it.

I'd had an idea.

Climbing out of the chair onto the stairs, I sat down on a bottom step and pulled myself up the rest of them backward, one by one, on my butt. When I got to the top, I shimmied across the kitchen floor, took a pair of pliers out of the toolbox, then slid back across the kitchen to the stairs and worked my way downstairs again.

Back in the workout area, I slid across the floor to the gate and grinned at it like a wolf.

"You know what I'm going to do now," I muttered, holding up the pliers.

That gate would no longer block me. I tore it out of the wall and got my drink of water.

The next morning, my wife couldn't understand why I did it.

"Why didn't you *call* me?" she said.

I just told her it was something I needed to do myself.

But the truth was, I needed to *prove* something to myself. And I'd done it.

If I could go to those lengths for a drink of water, I knew nothing in the world would keep me from playing basketball again.

SOMETIME IN MAY I was fitted for a leg brace and started getting around a bit more on my crutches. One morning toward the end of the month, I took my first steps without them.

The day before, Aldo and Florence had made their regular appearance on my patio, pecking at the glass, sticking around till sundown, and then taking wing.

They didn't show up that day. Or ever again. It made me a little sad, but I thought I understood what had happened.

I could walk. I'd be okay without them. I felt they knew it.

They knew.

And they'd gone wherever guardian angels go when they are no longer needed.

"BERNARD," DANIA SAID, "YOU'RE SWEATING."

"Am I?"

"Yes," Dania said. "Like crazy. Is something wrong?"

"No . . . no . . . nothing."

It was May 31, my fifth week of rehab. I could now walk haltingly with a brace on my right leg. Major motion in the knee now went from 20 to 105 degrees. It wasn't totally straight, and it didn't totally bend.

Dr. Scott had wanted me to begin a swimming routine to advance my progress, and one of my neighbors, a few houses down, offered the use of his outdoor pool. Since I lived in an area where the homes had spacious grounds, it was a long walk. But walking was part of my gait training, and Dania and I went there together in our bathing suits.

"Be honest, Bernard," she said. "It isn't even that warm out. Is walking still that difficult for you?"

I shook my head. "No," I said, and hesitated. "I'm just really scared."

She looked confused. I didn't blame her. I needed to explain.

"I'm petrified of water," I said. "When I was a kid, my mother always told me, 'Boy, you stay away from that water.' And now they're telling me to go *into* the water."

Dania seemed dumbstruck. But I was telling the truth. I would not go to the beach or public pools when I was young. My mother forbade it. For some reason, water scared her to death, and she passed that fear on to me. I never learned how to swim.

When we finally got to the pool, Dania's eyes opened wide. She could not stop laughing. A few days earlier, I'd phoned a local swim shop to have various items delivered there. A life preserver, a kickboard, a snorkel, scuba goggles and fins, nose plugs, ear plugs . . . whatever I thought would keep me afloat. It was enough equipment for a team of navy frogmen.

After a few minutes, Dania persuaded me to wade into the shallow end. It was maybe two-and-a-half, three-feet deep, but that was as far as I would go. I must have looked ridiculous standing there in water barely up to my knees.

Eventually, Dania convinced me to lie flat on my belly on the water while she held me up with her hands. Then she got me to bend my legs and stand from that position. I realized that at six foot seven, I wasn't going to sink.

Once I felt safe in the water, she taught me to kick. Then stroke. Then kick and stroke rhythmically. Then kick, stroke, and lift my face out of the water to breathe.

It was a long process. But thanks to Dania, I overcame my fear of water and learned to swim. It was indispensable to my gradual healing.

These days, when Dania and I get together and reminisce, we laugh when one of us tells the story. But I'm as proud of that accomplishment as my consecutive 50-point games. And more grateful to Dania than I can ever hope to express.

IT WAS THE END OF JULY. Week thirteen of my rehab.

I swam in the pool for an hour, doing what Dania called kick-pull-swim drills.

They were difficult. One lap you did nothing but kicking. The next lap you only pulled using your arms, no legs. And the third lap, you did a full swim. I'd become a good enough swimmer to pull through the water without using my legs at all.

When I was finished with the hour of swimming, Dania looked thoughtful. We were still in the pool.

"I feel we can start jumping drills today," she said.

"Right here?"

She nodded. "We're gonna start mimicking what you'd do at the basketball court," she said. "In the water, it won't have as much force."

"PUSH! PUSH! HARDER!"

It was August and hot. I was on the Cybex machine, a high-tech isokinetic cross-trainer that could adjust the resistance at every point in the range of movement. It gave a computer readout of how many pounds of force I was able to impart with my right leg relative to my left. We were looking for parity on both sides, but it would be some time before we achieved that.

Dania drove me relentlessly.

"Harder! Push!"

I went deep and pushed down with my legs. The Knicks had installed the $35,000 Cybex in my house. Per my request, the team had given Dania whatever she wanted at their expense—a leg press, a treadmill, a stationary bike, electrical stimulation devices, other things. But the Cybex was the most important piece of equipment in my rehabilitation.

"Push!"

I grunted, my Game Face on, sweat dripping down my forehead.

And I pushed.

I TROTTED SLOWLY up the right side of the court, dribbling the basketball, a relaxed tempo. I loved the sound of the dribble.

It was week twenty-three, early October, and I was about to take my first layup since the injury.

A month earlier, we'd gotten permission to use the pool and gymnasium at Ramapo College in New Jersey, not far from where I lived. Dania would get to my house between 3:15 and 3:30 in the afternoon, and we would do about ninety minutes on the machines. Afterward, we'd go to Ramapo, where I would swim in an Olympic-sized pool and then go on the court.

I started out in the gym with a little trotting, sidesteps, and walking figure-eights. Within two weeks, I was doing some uncontested shooting drills called walk-throughs. I would follow them with two laps around the gym, and later three. Next we added very basic slide drills and taking foul shots.

Dania had been a phys. ed. major before she became a therapist. She'd spent a year coaching basketball for high school girls, so she had a sense of the skill sets involved in the game.

We would sit and plan what we were going to do. I'd give her elements of my regular practice routine, and we would tone them down or change them. Whatever worked for us.

Now I dribbled, dribbled, reached the hoop, and put the ball up against the board with one hand.

It fell in. I looked at Dania as she recovered the basketball.

"Progress," I said.

She nodded and snapped the ball back to me.

STANDING UNDER THE NET, off to one side, I went up and tapped the ball off the backboard with two hands. Tapped the ball, tapped the ball, tapped the ball. Each time I went up to tap, I was jumping up. Then tapping, coming down, going right back up, tapping, tapping, like that, back and forth.

It was a drill I'd done my whole life so I could be quick on rebounds. I needed to regain my explosiveness under the hoop.

We were deep into October.

Progress.

"RIGHT! LEFT! LEFT!"

I faced Dania with the basketball. She was slight, five foot four or five. A foot and change shorter than I was. We must have been a sight as she shouted her orders.

We'd added slide drills on command, the very same court drills Gil Reynolds had made me do on the court. I would slide and run sideways to the left, right, at an angle forward, an angle backward. My body was either erect or bent for the low post, my hands out to defend.

"Left, right!"

It was almost seven months into our work together.

We were coming up on a big test.

NOVEMBER 8, 1985, week twenty-eight.

I had difficulty jumping off my bent right leg on a hard left-side layup drill. I couldn't get the lift. But that was okay. I had no problems jumping off both legs. I did something else that day. We were always prepared to make adjustments.

Sprinting hard to the basket, accelerating on the dribble, I sprang up off the floor, high off my left foot, the ball coming up in two hands . . .

Airborne.

I dunked. My first dunk since the injury. A rim rattler.

I turned to Dania.

"Not bad," I said.

She smiled. "Pretty good, *I'd* say."

We kept it secret. We were concerned that if people heard about it, they would think I was ready to come back. And I wasn't. There was a great deal of speculation among the press about my return, but I didn't speak to them. I didn't want any wrong or inaccurate information getting out. It was too soon to raise expectations.

Three weeks later, I was fitted for new orthotics for my running shoes. My right foot was bothering me a little, and that was holding me back. I also had some soreness in the back of that knee. But I was jogging full court, and doing outside shooting and layups at a decent speed. I was seeing improvement in my right leg jumps. I was getting more height.

Throughout the month of December, I increased the frequency of my full-court drills. Toward the end of the month, week thirty-three, I was able to start a running program.

I decided to have a Christmas Eve press conference. The Knicks organized it to be held at Madison Square Garden.

Dave DeBusschere and Dr. Scott were present, along with a gaggle of print, TV, and radio reporters. Seated at a podium in front of the Knicks banner, I told them things were going well, but still I couldn't give them a time frame for my return.

What I didn't say was that, for the first time, I knew would be able to resume my career.

IN MARCH 1986, week forty-four, we took my basketball work over to the Knicks training facility at Upsala College. The move had great significance. I wouldn't have made it unless I knew, at last and without a doubt, that I was coming back.

Giddy as a little kid, I asked Dr. Scott to come with us and challenged him to a full-court footrace. We raced from one side of the court to the other. He won—I couldn't keep up! I was twenty-eight and he must have been in his forties. I couldn't keep up.

That was okay. I'd built up my skills from the time I was in third grade. *Little Spal*. I could do it again. I was reassembling the puzzle. It had to be done step-by-step.

I'd come home every day, pat myself on the back, and then put my rehab out of my mind. Otherwise, it would have consumed me.

I opened up to other things. I started listening to live jazz, going out to jazz clubs at night. I came to know the musicians and understand the similarities between their approach to playing music and mine to playing basketball. Both involved passion, discipline, study, and self-expression. Both were rhythmic and musical.

Working out at Upsala, I got to the point where I wanted to simulate game action. Dania was fine with playing the role of an opposing player. I would have her stand in front of me, like a defensive guard, when I was coming up court for a layup. At first, she was stationary and I'd just run around her. But after a while, she'd move from one side to the other, or feint toward me, like a player.

I wore my Game Face every day during those sessions. It didn't intimidate her. It had intimidated other players, but not Dania. She understood me.

I sometimes wondered if she realized the difference it made when she'd agreed to come to my home in the early days. I needed isolation at that time. I needed to push the world away and operate in a zone without anyone else around but her. If I'd had to go to a physical therapy center, I wouldn't have made it back.

A few weeks into our workouts at Upsala, Dania arrived looking peaked. When I asked what was wrong, she said she'd been nauseous and vomiting. She thought she might have a stomach bug.

As it turned out, she and her husband Ron were having their first child. When I learned about it, I told Dania I no longer wanted her to do basketball drills with me. I didn't want us taking any risks with her pregnancy. She didn't want to stop. She insisted she was okay doing the work. But I finally won the battle.

Ron was also a trained therapist, an excellent one, and he took over all the basketball work. Dania and I would do weekends in the pool at Ramapo, and Ron would work with me at Upsala. Sometimes she'd come to observe, but she no longer did on-court stuff.

It would take me another full year to prepare for my return to basketball. Besides working out with Ron Sweitzer, I had Mike Dummett, a six-foot-seven, 235-pound Upsala player, come in to rebound and play some one-on-one. I added a jump shot to my game, which I didn't have before the injury. Not a mid-range. A long shot. Deep in the corners, deep on the wings. I knew I was going to need it, because I'd lost some of the explosiveness that had always let me get by players.

In late March 1987, I felt ready to step back on an NBA court. But I hadn't yet made the announcement or even informed the Knicks. With only two weeks or so left in the season, I didn't have much time.

I needed to choose a date . . . and not just any date.

In my mind, it had to be the right one.

22 | Back to the NBA

There's really no such thing as a quiet Friday night in New York. But as far as they went, April 10, 1987, didn't have a whole lot going on besides the Knicks-Milwaukee game.

A quick check of the sports pages told me the Yankees would be on the road in Kansas City. Coming off a frantic World Series championship run that captivated the city, the Mets were at home playing the Atlanta Braves. But it was just a few days into baseball season, and the weather out in Flushing, Queens, was chilly. People would not yet flock to Shea Stadium for an evening game.

Out in the Meadowlands, meanwhile, the Nets were hosting the Boston Celtics with nothing at stake for the home team. After a woeful losing season, they would struggle to bring fans into the arena.

What else?

I flipped through the concert listings. Nothing stupendous. Paul Simon's run of shows at Radio City Music Hall wasn't starting for another couple of weeks.

So far, so good, I thought.

I considered the date in terms of the Knicks' remaining schedule. I noticed they only had one other Friday home game, and that was on the next-to-last night of the season. On the other hand, an April 10 return would give me a full week of games to get the feel of NBA hardwood back under my sneakers.

Unfortunately, the Knicks weren't exactly big news at that time. They'd done as poorly as their Jersey rivals that year, sharing the Atlantic Division's cellar.

But the Knicks weren't just about basketball. They were Broadway, show business, and bright city lights. As a player, you had to understand that.

I was a New Yorker. I had always understood. I'd *embraced* it.

I set the date in my mind and phoned the Knicks.

With no one to share the stage on April 10, the spotlight would be turned squarely on Madison Square Garden for my comeback.

I HAD ANTICIPATED THE FANS' RECEPTION when I took the court; we'd always had a special connection. What I didn't foresee was how it would affect my play. Letting them through my armor threw me out of step. I couldn't control my emotions.

I distinctly recall Bob Hill inserting me into the ball game very quickly—in the first five minutes of play. I got a tremendous roar from the crowd when I walked onto the court. It was even louder than the one I'd heard when I was introduced.

I thought, *"I have to make this happen. The fans are here. My teammates are standing and applauding me . . ."*

I didn't want to let them down. But it wasn't just that. I was a free agent at the end of the season. I'd been gone for two years, with an injury from which no one had ever recovered. I had to prove to the league that I could still perform. My career was on the line.

I took the first shot that came into my hands. It was a jumper on the left-hand side of the floor, angled just away from the foul line. I didn't get a great look. I normally might have passed the ball or driven down the line. But I needed to get the shot out of the way and took it . . . and missed.

It wasn't my only bad shot that night.

I still believe I would've had a good game if I made that first basket. It probably would have settled me down. As it was, I scored 7 points and shot for a low percentage from the floor. Some of it had to do with Don Nelson isolating me, putting Paul Pressey on me man-to-man. Nelson hadn't watched my warm-ups out of idle curiosity; he saw the rust on me and knew I always had trouble with Pressey.

Still, I left the game feeling good about myself. It wasn't my shooting that encouraged me, it was my movement. Running up and down the floor with everyone else. Being able to defend—not very well, because I was isolated—but defending within a team concept.

I did okay and felt I would only get better.

Walking off the court, I did something I'd never done before in my career. I'd always kept my Game Face on until I was back in the locker room. I didn't need to think about it. It was automatic.

That night, I walked straight over to Dania and Ron and hugged them.

I didn't need to think about that, either.

There were thick lines of fans waiting outside as my limo exited the arena's parking area. They applauded, gave me the thumbs-up, held out autograph pads.

"Way to go, Bernard!" one guy shouted.

I broke down crying in the car. It wasn't just the emotions of the game. It was two *years'* worth of emotions surging up in me.

All my hard work had paid off. I knew I could do it. Knew I could play.

At long last, I was back.

MY PLAY IMPROVED WITH EACH GAME. The next night in Boston, I scored 20 points as a reserve in twenty-eight minutes. I was the second-highest scorer on the team after Gerald Wilkins, the starting small forward, and he was on the floor almost ten minutes longer.

I'd been icing all day before that game and would do it for the rest of the season. Before games, after games, during flights, in the hotel, on the bus, in the locker room—I would get a towel and ice pack, put them on my right knee, and then wrap an Ace bandage tightly around them. I didn't want to risk having my knee swell up. If that happened, I would be done.

Rory Sparrow was the only member of our 1984 playoff team still on the roster, and we were pretty close. He sat down beside me on the plane out of Boston and nodded his chin at the huge, freezing bundle on my knee.

"B," he asked, "Is it worth it?"

I didn't need to think about my answer.

"Yeah," I said.

I AVERAGED 22.7 POINTS over my six games back and went into the off-season feeling confident I would continue to improve and eventually put up All-Star numbers again.

The Knicks didn't share my confidence. They had no faith that my knee would hold up and showed only half-hearted interest in a new deal. Ultimately, they passed on signing me.

I was disappointed. At the end of that season, I'd been publicly verbal about wanting to stay in New York. That wasn't like me. I always let my play do the talking. But I wanted to be a Knick until I retired. I'd worn the jersey with unsurpassed pride. I was sure that if I stayed with the team and had a chance to play with Patrick Ewing, we would win a championship together.

However, management had changed. Dave DeBusschere was gone, Hubie was gone, and even Bob Hill was gone after the season concluded. A new regime took over, and they thought what they thought.

I had no problem with that. I'd lived my dream and had been captain of the New York Knicks. They made a business decision, and I was ready to move on.

Did I want to prove their decision wrong? Of course. I was a competitor. And I was determined to show the world it was a mistake to doubt my skills and passion.

As a free agent, I received interest from several teams. Ironically, one was the Celtics. During the offseason, I even traveled to Boston to meet with Red Auerbach.

"You know, we already have a pretty good small forward here," he told me, chomping on a cigar.

"I know." I realized full well Larry Bird was their franchise player, and that I would be a reserve off the bench.

Auerbach eyed me through a cloud of smoke.

"Then why would you want to play with us?"

Easy answer.

"I want to win a championship," I said.

WHEN ALL WAS SAID AND DONE, the Washington Bullets put the best deal on the table. My old coach with the Nets, Kevin Loughery, was now head coach in Washington, and that may have had something to do with their excitement. Our mutual respect had never faltered, and we looked forward to our professional reunion.

My knees held up. I averaged 17.2 points per game in my comeback year *and* played sixty-nine games, starting thirty-eight. The following year, I started eighty-one of the season's eighty-two games.

In my third year with Washington, I started *all* eighty-two games on the schedule. I played with the old chip on my shoulder, wanting to prove I was still the best in the NBA.

From 1988 to 1991, I averaged 20 points per game or higher each season. It culminated in me reaching 28.4 points a game in 1990–1991. At the end of that year, I was the third highest scorer in the league behind Michael Jordan and Karl Malone.

In the middle of the season, I received a phone call that would bring me to tears. It was Abe Pollin, owner of the Washington Bullets. His message was brief but powerful.

"Bernard," he said, "you've been chosen as a starter for the Eastern Conference NBA All-Stars."

The phone shook in my hand. When a reporter asked about my selection, I answered with tears of joy streaming down my face. I would be in the starting five with Michael Jordan, Charles Barkley, Joe Dumars . . . and Patrick Ewing.

It was the only time Ewing and I ever played together as teammates, a taste of what might have been. But it was far more than that.

I'd reached my goal. I was an All-Star again.

That night in Charlotte was one of the most special of my life. At thirty-four, I was, at that time, the oldest player to start an All-Star

Game. I got the loudest cheers after Michael Jordan. Fans understood my accomplishment.

Bob Costas, the famed sportscaster, was at the game. He approached me afterward to congratulate me.

I nearly told him on the air that I wanted to retire after that night. I'd climbed my Mount Everest. I didn't need to pursue a championship. I had nothing more to prove as a player. But I bit my tongue. I didn't want to say anything in a state of high emotion. The next game on the Bullets' schedule was one I'd eyed since my selection—the Bullets were playing the Knicks in New York. Part of me could hardly believe the coincidence. But another part of me wasn't sure it even was coincidence.

It seemed, somehow, meant to be.

The New York media were abuzz about my All-Star appearance. It was all over the sports pages.

The first thing I did when I got to my hotel was call my mother.

"Mom," I said, "I got you tickets to tonight's game." I paused. My parents had attended every game I'd played as a Knick. They'd refused special treatment and taken the subway, not letting me arrange for a car service or taxi. "Don't be late . . . I'm hitting 40 tonight."

She didn't react much. Mom was mom. She'd never been demonstrative. I'm sure she was surprised, though. It wasn't like me to predict point totals. But that night was different. As special in its way as the All-Star Game.

It was a close game, but I was on fire, scoring 23 points in the fourth quarter alone. The fans' support was magical. Whenever I was at the foul line, they rose from their seats and cheered. The ovations got louder as the night went on.

It was a true homecoming and a vindication. I wanted to show my family and the fans why I'd been named an All-Star. I wanted to give back to everyone who'd cheered for me, believed in me, through the years. I pumped my fist in the air every time I scored in the fourth quarter, not to embarrass anyone but to make a statement. Just because nobody had ever returned from the kind of injury I'd suffered did not mean it couldn't be done. People thought I was sending the Knicks a message. But that wasn't on my mind. My performance that night was really a thank-you to the fans of New York.

And I was determined to win.

I scored 49 points and we won.

I SPENT FOUR GREAT YEARS IN WASHINGTON. But in the fall of 1991, before the start of what would be my final season with the Bullets, I returned to New York to have my right knee examined by Dr. Norman Scott. I'd been experiencing a lot of pain and was concerned about its stability.

Dr. Scott found nothing structurally wrong with the knee. His groundbreaking surgery had held up. But what little cartilage remained in my knee after two prior surgeries—I'd had the first in Tennessee—was arthritic and needed to be removed. I would miss training camp and the next two seasons.

I never suited up for the Bullets again, and would eventually sign with the Nets for the last three months of the 1993 season.

All elite athletes experience a moment when they know they are truly finished with the game. This reflection often happens when you're in mid-season and you realize that you, your game, and your level of competitiveness have changed; it happens when players you've always beaten begin to dominate you, or when you notice that your body is winding down.

Mine came as I played for the New Jersey Nets in the final year of my career, when head coach Chuck Daly matched me up against Chucky Brown—who embarrassed me time and time again on my first day of practice.

But I'd already known it was time. The third knee operation had taken its toll on me. I ignored the signs for a while. But that day against Brown—with the media watching our practice—I couldn't run any-more. Not from myself, age, or Father Time. When you're on a team, you're part of a system and can hide behind that. But one-on-one, you can't hide. Everyone, including me, could see I'd soon be done as an NBA player.

I went home after each game that season and realized I was a scrub, something I had not been since the sixth grade. There was nothing I could do about it.

When the 1992–1993 season was over, I kept thinking about the moment in North Carolina, when I'd almost made my announcement to Costas. I could no longer compete to my standard.

It was time.

I retired following the 1993 NBA season with 19,655 career points. Twenty thousand was a nice round number, and I suppose I could have chased it down. But for someone with a reputation as a scorer, I'd never cared about points, though I ultimately did score them in my backyard.

Only the birds and squirrels witnessed it, and that was all right with me.

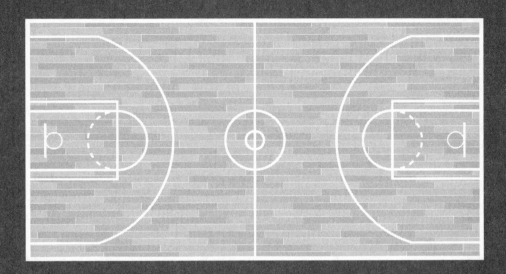

Moving Forward

23 | Life After the NBA

I sat in my backyard in New Jersey, staring at the orange and gold flits of movement beneath the surface of my koi pond and cried.

It was the spring of 1993, several weeks after my retirement from the NBA became official. I'd been crying a lot during that time and didn't know why.

I felt a terrible void inside me. A huge emptiness. I didn't understand it. I only knew it wasn't from missing the game. I'd left it all on the floor and had no regrets.

I needed professional help.

One day, I reached for the phone and called a hospital in New York.

"I can't tell you who I am right now, because I'm a public figure," I said. "But I'm in need of emotional therapy."

Given the name and number of a doctor, I soon started seeing a psychologist. My therapy was slow. It was painful. I cried during most sessions.

Over time, I learned that the core of my pain emanated from my mother's lack of connection. The beatings in the kitchen, the lack of a single hug, had left me with a gaping hole in my heart. Throughout my life, I'd try to blunt my pain with alcohol and sex, but the emotional wounds were still fresh and the void hadn't been filled.

After long weeks of therapy, I decided to call my mother and ask her why she'd beaten me as a child. She took a while to answer me.

"It was just how I was raised," she said.

She didn't expand, but she didn't need to. Mom's parents had done the same thing to her. She simply hadn't known any better.

This problem remains widespread in the black community. It causes pain throughout our lives, and even causes us to hurt others. Studies tell us it is rooted in a time when slaves were savagely beaten by their masters as "corrective" punishment for perceived wrongs and disobedience. First-generation African Americans saw it as the norm and passed down the pattern of beatings from parent to child to grandchild. We have yet to address it and related issues that lead to so much anger among our young people.

I was fortunate. I sought help. Initially, I went to therapy twice a week. Over the course of my treatment, I realized I hadn't done anything to warrant the beatings. I stopped blaming myself, and my feelings of guilt dissipated.

There was still unresolved pain. Mom didn't know how to express her emotions. She'd tried when we spoke about the beatings, but her few words to me were the best she could manage. It was another of those qualities that can be passed down from one generation to the next, and was one I inherited. We kept our feelings bottled up.

I tried to move on. But I felt a lingering emptiness inside. I didn't know exactly why. I didn't know how to fill it, or *what* would fill it.

In time, I found out.

A YEAR OR TWO LATER, I was going through a divorce and feeling miserable. I'd wed my first wife when I was with Golden State, wanting to show signs of stability to league executives after years of personal problems.

It had been a difficult fourteen-year marriage. I was not a good husband. I committed multiple infidelities over the years, hoping to fill the emotional hole inside me with sex. But the sex only seemed to make me more aware of the emptiness at my core. I was still searching for love.

I regret my mistakes to this day, and only came to understand why I made them through therapy. In order to move forward, I'd have to go back.

The divorce proceedings were very tough. Eventually, I moved out of my Jersey home and into an apartment in Manhattan. Right around that time, I was doing a Friday night radio show with broadcaster Ian

Eagle on WFAN-AM, the pioneering sports talk radio station that was then broadcasting out of a studio in Queens. I was proud of my work on the program, but I was lonely and somehow unfulfilled.

One night in 1995, I walked into a restaurant for takeout food and saw the most stunning woman I'd ever set eyes upon. I was not looking to meet anyone new. I didn't expect that I would. I was leading a mostly solitary existence and liked it that way at the time.

But something drew me to the woman. It wasn't only her beauty. It was her elegance and grace.

Fortunately, I saw there was no ring on her finger. Also fortunately, I was nattily attired.

I knew I couldn't leave the restaurant without introducing myself. She was not a basketball fan. Though she grew up in New York, she'd never seen a Knicks game in her life and had no idea who I was until I told her.

Shana and I began dating right away, and saw each other constantly for the next month. But we never spent the night together. I didn't even bring her back to my condo in the city, or my New Jersey home. The divorce was not yet final; although separated from my wife, and only speaking to her through my attorney, I was still a married man and felt it would be disrespectful.

During that first month, Shana never told me that her mother was Susan Taylor, the renowned editor-in-chief of *Essence Magazine*. Because I was in the middle of a divorce, she was afraid I would shy away from any possible publicity that might be attached to dating someone with a famous mom.

When she finally told me, I was shocked. Susan and I had mutual friends. We'd even socialized on a few occasions. And Shana was right. If I'd known about Susan, I might have shied away from her early on. I did not want my divorce to become a public spectacle.

But it was too late. I was in love. We kept seeing each other.

Something unexpected happened when I finally brought Shana to my home after the divorce was finalized. On my wall was a signed poster given to me by the artist Romare Bearden, a depiction of a mother reading to her young child. Shana saw it and gasped.

"Oh, my goodness!" she said. "That's me and my mom!"

It turned out that Bearden, a friend of mine, had seen the two of them at a function and taken a photograph. They'd been the inspirations for his piece.

I was speechless. I'd collected art for years, but had lost many favorite works in the divorce. The print was one of the few left on my wall.

At that instant, I understood the powerful attraction I'd felt for Shana right off. She'd been in my life before we physically met.

She was my soul mate, and would soon become my wife.

IF I HAD NOT STUMBLED UPON THAT RESTAURANT, if I hadn't gained the courage to say hello to the most beautiful woman in the world, I would not have my daughter Amina.

Her birth in 1998 was at once the greatest and the most trying day of my life.

Shana and I had gone to the hospital to prepare for it, knowing she was only hours away. But while the doctor was examining her, the baby's heartbeat started to disappear from the cardiac monitor.

All hell broke loose in the room. The umbilical cord was wrapped around our baby's neck. Shana was rushed to the operating room, a crowd of nurses and orderlies pushing me out of their way.

At that very moment, I saw my in-laws, Susan and Khephra, walking up the corridor. They had no idea what was happening until they saw Shana being wheeled off.

I stopped to reassure them—or tried my best—and then dashed over to the OR, plunging through its swing door without asking permission.

In the few seconds I'd used up speaking with my in-laws, she'd been opened up. There was blood everywhere. The baby had been removed from her abdomen but was blue and motionless on a table, surrounded by doctors trying to revive her. They massaged her chest and feet as she lay there like a limp doll.

I backed out of the room to regroup and then reentered, hoping for a sign of life from our child. There was none.

I'd never before known the kind of fear I experienced in those horrible moments. It had never existed for me until that point. If we lost our baby, how would I find the words to tell Shana?

"Is our baby going to be all right?" I repeated silently. Over and over. "Is our baby going to be all right . . .?"

No one answered. But after what seemed an eternity, I saw the electrical pulses on the ECG screen and heard the relief in the doctors' and nurses' voices.

Our baby would be okay. Our *daughter*.

Maybe life's best gifts aren't meant to come easy. I don't know. But Amina has been the most incredible blessing I can imagine. My only child on planet Earth.

As Amina grew up, I was determined to give her the emotional love I did not receive as a child. I talked to her about the trials and tribulations we all are bound to face, how to be a good person, and how to achieve what you want in life. Shana and I gave her a loving environment and ensured she was in an educational system that developed her academically, unlike the failing schools I'd attended as a child. So much pain in our society can be cured by love, affection, and caring. I know it's been said before, but the truth is that it all starts at home.

When Amina sat on my lap as a toddler, I'd call her "Little One." Now she's a beautiful young woman, a student at Spelman College. At five feet nine, she seems to have inherited her father's height. I *know* her looks and good sense come from her mom.

I still call her Little One when she visits from school. She won't let me stop, even though she towers over Shana. And by the way, she has her own nickname for me. Dadum. Not Dad, not Daddy. *Dadum.* It's the first word she ever spoke.

Little One and Dadum. That's just how it is with her.

I kid her about it all the time, but wouldn't want things any other way.

24 | A New Life

In 2003, I was contacted by Bruce Ratner, chief operating officer of the real estate development company, the Ratner Group. He wanted to acquire the New Jersey Nets and move the team to Atlantic Avenue in Brooklyn, an area bordering on the neighborhood where I grew up. Ratner had some ideas about getting me involved in his plans and asked to discuss them over steaks in New York.

Shana and I lived in Georgia, just north of Atlanta. We'd moved there when Amina was two years old; it was a nice, quiet place to raise her. So I had to fly up for our meeting.

Ratner offered me the job of executive vice president of the Nets. The Ratner organization would enroll my daughter in private school and arrange for a driver to bring her there and back. And provide other generous perks.

For all my professional success, I'm a kid from Brooklyn at heart. It was a stunning offer.

I seriously contemplated it. The deal was obviously lucrative, but it appealed to me for deeper reasons. I hadn't achieved all my success without help, and I believed in giving back. Over the years I'd worked with the Boys & Girls Clubs of America, the National Cancer Society, and National Cares Mentoring. I spoke on Capitol Hill for the NBA Stay-in-School program and for world hunger relief efforts. I'd established an endowment scholarship fund at the University of Tennessee to assist disadvantaged youths seeking a higher education. I was also bestowed an Honorary Doctorate from Long Island University in downtown Brooklyn.

The thought that I might contribute to the revitalization of my old neighborhood was a strong enticement. The Coca-Cola, Mattel, and other factories I remembered from childhood had once offered people steady—if low-wage—work, but those businesses had all closed their doors or relocated. No decent job opportunities were left, and the unemployment rate was over 50 percent. I felt that a new basketball arena would be a powerful economic stimulus for the community.

I entered into discussions with the Ratner Group and remained in New York as they slowly progressed.

I typically never traveled with Shana on business trips. My talks with Ratner wore on, keeping me away from home longer than I'd expected. That put strains on our marriage, and I eventually brought my wife north, hoping to smooth them over.

I'd been so focused on the project, Shana felt shut out of things. After ten years together, we weren't communicating the way we should have been. She knew how much I loved her—how truly she completed me—but she was adamantly opposed to moving to New York.

We wound up arguing in our hotel room. When I look back at that awful night, it's clear to me that the tensions associated with the Ratner negotiations brought issues we'd never faced to the surface. Issues of trust and openness. Emotions welled up in a way neither of us could have imagined. Things got physical, and the police arrived. I explained what happened to them, but they said they would have to take one of us in. Though they did not file charges, they arrested me.

Shana and I would attend marital counseling and grow closer and more trusting as a result of the incident. Together, we made the decision to stay in Georgia, raising our daughter in the place we called home. We've been married for two decades, love each other madly, and look back at that night at the hotel as a learning experience.

But it still pains me to think of it, and I wish it had never occurred.

AS THE YEARS PASSED, and I drew further away from my basketball playing career, I continued to keep my hand in the game through broadcasting. The show I cohosted with Ian Eagle on WFAN led to other on-air opportunities. After NBA TV launched in 2003, I was hired as a part-time announcer for the network. I also occasionally handled some color analyst work on local Knicks game broadcasts in New York, including in-studio work for MSG. I earned two Emmy awards for my broadcast work, something I never would have envisioned when I'd dropped my communications major in college.

It was somehow perfect, however, that Amina was my only audience for one of the more personally interesting basketball moments of recent years. In February 2008, Kobe Bryant broke a Madison Square Garden record I'd set a little over twenty-three years earlier, on Christmas Day 1984, when I became the first player to score 60 points in a game at Madison Square Garden. That happened in a loss to the New Jersey Nets, and as someone who cared only about winning, I'd felt the record was something for others to appreciate more than I could.

Still, I started watching the Kobe game on television with my fellow basketball fan, Amina. Kobe was visiting with the Lakers in what would be a 126–117 win over the Knicks.

About five minutes into the game, I turned to her and said, "Little One, your Dadum's record is going to be broken tonight."

Kobe was a unique player, and I saw it in his eyes. I remember when he went to the free-throw line with 59 under his belt. "Come on, let a Brooklyn kid keep the record," I said to the TV screen.

But I knew it was history, and that was okay. If I could have traded some of my own 60 for a victory over the Nets that long-ago Christmas, I'd have done it in a second.

Six years later, Carmelo Anthony would break the Garden record as a member of the home team. I was on a flight to Houston and missed the game, but found out when my phone started lighting up with texts and voice messages.

In all honesty, that was a delight. Carmelo has told me he patterns certain aspects of his game after mine, so I felt connected to his performance. He's one of the best offensive players we've ever seen. If anything has changed about the NBA game since my era, it's that many players choose creativity over the sort of consistency that can only be achieved and refined through constant practice.

Carmelo practices. And he's from Brooklyn.

In my eyes, it's a winning combination.

ON SEPTEMBER 8, 2013, I was inducted into the Naismith Memorial Basketball Hall of Fame in Springfield, Massachusetts. I couldn't have imagined a greater honor.

When I think of that day, I always remember how it felt standing in front of an auditorium filled with the greatest legends of the game, and looking out at the proud faces of Shana, Amina, my mother-in-law Susan L. Taylor, and my father-in-law, Khephra Burns.

But that's not even the first thing that comes to mind.

The first thing is waking up that morning in my hotel room. It was early morning, the sun barely risen. As Shana and Amina slept, I went to the window with my phone and opened the YouTube app. Keeping the volume low so as not to disturb them, I listened to a gospel song by the great Marvin Sapp, "Never Would Have Made It Without You."

I quietly sang along, my face wet with tears. I wept for those who came before me, who'd shouldered greater burdens than I ever did, made sacrifices beyond anything I could imagine, so that someone like me could reach the heights of achievement.

I thought of Nat Sweetwater Clifton, who was among the first three black NBA players and was the first black member of the Knicks. Muhammad Ali, the Greatest. I thought of people who had nothing to do with sports—Rosa Parks refusing to give up her seat on the bus. Martin Luther King. The poet Langston Hughes. My aunt Perline and grandmother, Evelyn Brown. My parents, Thomas and Thelma King.

I wished my parents could have been there for the celebration. I thought of them as I ascended the steps to make my induction speech before a crowd of basketball luminaries that included Larry Bird, my old rival on the court. But Mom was far too ill.

In 2009, she was diagnosed with bone cancer. The disease quickly took its toll. I hurt for Mom as her health deteriorated. She'd always been a strong woman. Seeing her ravaged by cancer, reduced to a shell of herself, was terrible.

My father was not a young man, and he was unable to care for her on his own, so we placed her in a nursing home where she could receive the proper attention. Dad visited her there every day and would not leave her side to join us in Springfield.

That afternoon at the Hall of Fame, my presenter was the indomitable basketball great Dominique Wilkins. They called him the Human Highlight Film. I referred to him as the Unguardable One. It was a nickname based on my personal experience with Dominique on the court.

As I prepared myself to address the audience, I thought of my long journey from the blacktop courts of Brooklyn. I thought of countless playgrounds, half-moon backboards, the sharp hit of elbows, and the music of the dribble. Game Face hardened, intensity knowing no bounds, I had traveled a long road to the doors of the Hall of Fame, made my mistakes, and learned my lessons.

I'd placed only one call that weekend. It was to my friend Ernie Grunfeld, the other half of the Ernie and Bernie Show. He'd been recovering from surgery and was unable to travel, but I knew he was there in spirit.

I will never forget how it felt to face the podium, then finally hear the words, "And now, welcoming Bernard King into the Hall of Fame, Dominique Wilkins . . ."

I was there. I had made it. I stood beside the basketball heroes of my youth, Willis Reed, Walt "Clyde" Frazier, Earl "The Pearl" Monroe, and Dave DeBusschere.

I stood beside them.

The captain of the New York Knicks, Bernard King.

Conclusion: I Love You, Son

It was just over a year after my enshrinement into the Hall of Fame. An early autumn day in New York City.

Brooklyn Hospital is located off Flatbush Avenue on the west side of Fort Greene Park. A large bay window in Mom's room overlooked the park, the very place she'd once brought me and my brothers on summer outings. Turning toward it, I could see the Prison Ship Martyrs' Monument, where I'd fallen and broken my arm when I was a kid.

I remembered Mom trying to straighten it when it became stuck at dinner, the fork near my mouth. A faint, sad smile touched my lips.

I stared outside for several minutes and then looked back at Mom, lying in her bed, breathing shallowly, the blanket and bed sheet pulled up over her shrunken body. She'd been in and out of hospitals for years, stoic as ever, as she fought the ravages of bone cancer. In and out, undergoing treatments, surgeries, never a word of complaint.

I'd brought a CD player to the care center where she'd been living before her fragile condition took a downturn. When I visited her there, I would put on Mahalia Jackson, James Cleveland, all her favorites. I wanted Mom to enjoy her gospel music.

But here, the ICU was quiet.

I sat there looking at her. I'd spent many hours visiting her after her surgeries and treatments. But I felt this time was different. I felt it would be the last time I would ever see her. She was too frail to sit up, to eat, and almost too weak to open her eyes. She could barely even talk. Her ordeal, her suffering, had taken a toll.

I visited the New York area fairly often from my home in Georgia. There were special functions and charitable events, some associated with the Knicks or Hall of Fame, others sponsored by athletes or celebrities. When possible, I was glad to help out.

This time I'd come in for a fund-raiser in Westchester, a golf tournament, and I had taken an early flight so I could spend some time with my mother.

I arrived at the hospital before visiting hours. At first, they wouldn't let me up to see her. But when I'd explained I was only in town for a short while, the staff made an exception.

I talked to her a lot that day. I don't recall much of what I said. I was just trying cheer her up with stories about Amina, childhood reminiscences . . . whatever filled the sterile hospital room silence. She was too weak to respond or contribute stories of her own. At times, I wasn't even sure she heard me. But I kept talking to her. I truly believed I would not have another opportunity.

After a while, I had to leave for the tournament. Mom had been drifting off, and I thought it might be best to let her sleep.

I rose off my chair and was about to kiss her goodbye, when I saw her lips moving slightly . . . almost too slightly to notice. She was trying to talk, but couldn't muster a voice.

I leaned forward, put my ear to her lips, waited.

"I love you, son," she whispered.

Then she settled into sleep.

I stood up, looking at her, holding on to the back of my chair. The walls of my throat were thick. But I felt something inside me. In my chest. If someone had asked me to describe it, I couldn't have. Not right at that moment.

I kissed Mom's cheek, told her I loved her, and turned toward the door.

I had to go.

When I reached the golf course, I found a quiet knoll and sat in the shade of a tree for a while, away from everyone else. And I cried.

"Lord, take your arms to our mother," I said. "It's time for her to go home."

Mom died about a week later.

But I need to mention something.

As I went to join the tournament's golfers, walking across the neatly manicured green, I finally understood the feeling I'd had at her bedside.

I was filling up. My *heart* was filling up. The emptiness within was gone. It had been replaced with love.

Only Mom could have done that for me. And she knew it.

I love you, son.

I'd waited to hear those words my entire life. And wrapped within those words was a hug.

The greatest gifts in life don't come easy. I really *do* think they aren't meant to. But we need to be ready for them. We need to recognize them when they appear to us. Like an eight-year-old kid standing under a basketball hoop in an elementary school cafeteria, the ball too large for his hands, the rim high above his head, we need to look up, always up, and realize that when the great gifts come, you need to be ready for them, because they can sweep you into a lofty realm you never thought existed.

A world where paths merge in an unexpected journey, and you are made anew.

Bernard King
April 12, 2017

APPENDIXES

○ ○ ○ ○

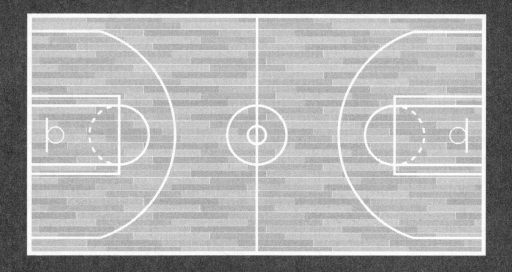

King Spots: Scoring To Win

I never thought I was a gifted player. I saw myself as an analytical player. I treated the basketball court—and the game—as if it was a puzzle. That's the reason I had a 51 percent career shooting percentage.

My goal was to perform at the same level every night. But if you rely on creativity alone, you will never be consistent. Preparation was always the key to my success.

I cannot overemphasize basketball's mental aspects. Reading psychology books taught me to be analytical at a very young age, and that thought process enhanced my life and my game.

Most people see a basketball court in terms of its painted markers: baseline, sideline, free-throw line, three-point line, block markers, and shooting lane. When I look at the floor, I see something totally different—a grid so precise it can be computer-modeled. As a four-time All-Star, I had set places to shoot on the low post, the wing, and even in the open floor, where I was all but unstoppable. Understanding this concept can make any player more confident, and any coach a better coach.

I diagram the basketball court using standard NBA/collegiate dimensions: 94 feet long, 50 feet wide, with a distance of 15 feet from backboard to foul line.

My half-court scoring grid includes 9 spots on the left-hand side of the floor, 9 spots on the right-hand side of the floor, and 4 spots from the front of the rim to the top of the key. The 3-point line offers 3 added spots on the left, 3 spots on the right, and 1 in the middle above the top of the key. This totals 29 spots to work from, depending on your skill sets.

Now let's break it down further. I'm going to divide the 9 left-hand spots (oh, how I loved the left side of the court!) into groups of three. *Note that they are replicated on the right-hand side of the floor.*

SPOT 1: First block on the left lane.
SPOT 2: Horizontal to Spot 1
SPOT 3: Horizontal to Spot 2

SPOT 4: Up the lane, midway between the foul line and block
SPOT 5: Horizontal to Spot 4
SPOT 6: Horizontal to Spot 5

SPOT 7: Side of the foul line (called foul line extended)
SPOT 8: Horizontal to Spot 7
SPOT 9: Horizontal to Spot 8

Next, I'll break down the 4 spots on the left-hand side of the 3-point line. Visualize yourself standing at the line, and again note *these spots are replicated on the right-hand side of the floor.*

3-POINT SPOT A: Horizontal to Spot 3 (above)
3-POINT SPOT B: Horizontal to 3-point Spot A
3-POINT SPOT C: Horizontal to 3-point Spot B
3-POINT SPOT D:: Above the top of the key in the middle of the line

Beating The Defense

Scoring requires understanding defense, not simply being a proficient shooter. Once you understand your opponent's defensive strategy, tactics, and skills, then your success comes down to how well you execute your shots on any given night.

In the NBA, the defensive strategy is based on scouting reports. For school or playground players, I recommend keeping your own mental notes as the game is played. Additionally, I suggest keeping a database of your opponents' tendencies. In other words, be your own scout.

The key to understanding defense is to know there are only five ways a single player can defend against a shot from the wing.

Left side or right side, a defender can:

1. Force the offensive player to the left after the catch because he has a weak dribble going left.
2. Force the offensive player to the right after the catch because he has a weak dribble going right.
3. Allow an offensive player the outside jump shot, because the jumper's proficiency at it is questionable.

   Note: When you watch NBA, collegiate, high school, or youth league games, and you see a player shy from an open jump shot, it is because he's been taken out of his comfort zone.

4. Play an offensive player "tight" or close, because he shows an inability to break down a pressure defense. This often leads to a turnover because the offensive player will pass under pressure as the shot clock runs down.
5. Deny an offensive player the entry pass. We see this defense when the offensive player shows an inability to catch the ball where he would like to receive it—a fundamental skill that is often neglected, even at the professional level.

   Note: Never allow a defender to force you away from the ball beyond your spots. If a defender has his left foot above your right leg, or right foot above your left leg in a deny position, go back door on the wing.

Again, there are only five possible defenses, or ways to guard someone from the forward position in the half court. This means every offensive player needs five moves to offset the defense and free himself to shoot from one of his sweet spots.

I would practice shooting from one of the 22 primary sweet spots, and 7 additional 3-point shots, each and every day. That is how you become efficient and unstoppable.

Using this method, I shot over 50 percent and averaged 22.5 shots a game over the course of my 16-year NBA career, once with a league-leading 32.9 points per game.

Key Statistics and Honors

NBA

Teams

1977–1978: New Jersey Nets
1979–1980: Utah Jazz
1981–1982: Golden State Warriors
1983–1987: New York Knicks
1988–1991: Washington Bullets
1992–1993: New Jersey Nets

Career Statistics

	Games	Rebounds	Assists	Steals	Blocks	Points
Season	874	5,060	3.3	1.0	0.3	19,655
Playoffs	28	121	2.3	0.9	0.2	687

Honors

Hall of Fame

Enshrined in the Naismith Memorial Basketball Hall of Fame on September 8, 2013

- NBA All-Rookie Team 1977–1978 with the New Jersey Nets
- NBA 1980–1981 Comeback Player of the Year Award as a member of the Golden State Warriors in 1980–1981
- Second-team All-NBA honors in 1981–1982
- First-team All-NBA selection 1983–1984 and 1984–1985 with the New York Knicks

- Third-team All-NBA selection 1992–1993 with the Washington Bullets
- Led the NBA in scoring in the 1984–1985 season, averaging 32.9 points for the Knicks
- Four-time NBA All-Star (1982, 1984, 1985, 1991)
- Tied for 25th on the NBA's all-time list for career regular-season scoring average with 22.5 points per game
- Totaled 19,655 points in 874 NBA games
- Set the New York Knicks single-game scoring record of 60 points on Christmas Day 1984 against the New Jersey Nets
- Scored 50 points in consecutive road games on back-to-back nights against the San Antonio Spurs and Dallas Mavericks
- During a 1984 NBA Playoff series against the Detroit Pistons, King averaged 42.6 points while leading the Knicks to a series win

University of Tennessee Honors

- No. 53 officially retired on Feb. 13, 2007 (first Tennessee men's player to receive that honor)
- Tennessee Basketball All-Century Team
- 2008 SEC Basketball Legend
- 1986 *Lakeland Ledger* 25-Year All-SEC Team
- 1977 Consensus All-American
- 1977 co-SEC Player of the Year (AP)
- 1977 All-SEC first team (AP, UPI, Coaches)
- 1976 All-American first team (USBWA, Helms Athletic Foundation)
- 1976 All-American second team (UPI, Converse)
- 1976 All-American (AP, NABC)
- 1976 SEC Player of the Year (AP, UPI)
- 1976 All-SEC first team (AP, UPI, Coaches)
- 1975 All-American first team (Helms Athletic Foundation)
- 1975 All-American second team (UPI, Converse, *Basketball Weekly*)
- 1975 All-American third team (NABC)
- 1975 SEC Player of the Year (UPI)
- 1975 All-SEC first team (AP, UPI, Coaches)

Acknowledgments

The endeavor of writing a book requires an immersion of mind and spirit. I am indebted to each individual who has contributed to my life's journey and this book, directly and, in some cases, indirectly.

Thank you to my wife, Shana, for your loving support and your understanding of the process of writing this book, which often kept me at work into the wee hours of the morning.

Thank you to my wonderful daughter, Amina, who in many ways served as the catalyst for *Game Face*. As a student at Spelman College, your learning will soar to greater heights than mine.

Special thanks to:

My parents, Thelma and Thomas King Sr., who toiled for decades doing their very best on behalf of the family. I am sure your prayers were helpful.

My mother-in-law, Susan L. Taylor, who I call Mums. I appreciate your unconditional love and support. You inspire and lovingly change the lives of our youth through your mentoring organization, caresmentoring.org.

My father-in-law, Khephra Burns, who writes for a living. Now I know the difficulty of that job firsthand. We have to go hear some more jazz music.

Dr. Norman Scott. You successfully gave me the foundation to save my NBA career. What we accomplished was unprecedented.

Dania Sweitzer, my physical therapist. There are no words to express my gratitude to you. I asked you in my hospital room, with forty-one metal staples running down my knee, "Do you know what you are getting yourself into?" Three doctors said I'd never play again. You told me I could. My goal became your reality, and your commitment never wavered. You are the best.

Ron Sweitzer, Dania's husband and my physical therapist. A team can't win without backup. In basketball it's the sixth man; in baseball, a relief pitcher. On our team, you were that and more. You and Dania will always be in my heart as part of our incredible winning team.

My friend Hank Carter of Henry J. Carter Hospital.

Vinnie, Theresa, and Travis Viola.

Bruce Bender.

Tom Konchalski. My path may have traveled in a different direction if not for you.

Jerome Preisler, fellow Brooklyn kid. There are times in life, and moments in time, that transcend everything and give you pause. You are an individual who provokes thought. I couldn't have collaborated with anyone but you on *Game Face*. Chemistry is important in a team relationship, and we had that in abundance. I enjoyed revealing my life's journey to you. Your ability to write is exceptional, and you are capable of seeing the story within the story. Thank you for your contribution and friendship.

Coaches' Corner
NBA: Al Attles, Chuck Daly, Hubie Brown, Kevin Loughery, Rick Pitino, Wes Unseld.

Tennessee: Coaches Ray Mears and Stu Aberdeen, Rick Barnes.

Junior High School: Coach O'Rourke.

Fort Hamilton High School: Coach Ken Kern.

Brooklyn Coaches: Gil Reynolds, Lester Roberts.

To the legendary Pete Newell, I appreciate all you did.

Naismith Memorial Basketball Hall of Fame: Jerry Colangelo, John Doleva, Scott Zuffelato, George Raveling, Mannie Jackson, Fran Judkins.

New York City Basketball Hall of Fame.

Tennessee Sports Hall of Fame.

Tennessee

University of Tennessee Athletic Department, University of Tennessee College of Communication.

For your friendship: Condrege Holloway, Mike Chase, Gerald Oliver, Ed Balloff, Ken Rice, Dr. Overholt, Harry Bettis, and Floyd Raley.

NBA

Commissioners: David Stern, Adam Silver.

Charlie Rosenzweig, Senior Vice President Entertainment & Player Marketing.

Paul Hirschheimer, Senior Vice President of Multimedia Production.

Trainers

Simply the best—Mike Saunders.

Fritz Massmann.

Naismith Memorial Basketball Hall of Famers

Standard bearer: Julius "Dr. J" Erving

Special thanks: Earl "The Pearl" Monroe, Dominique Wilkins, Charles Barkley, and Nancy Lieberman

Players' Court (NBA players from whom I stole a move)

Alex English, Larry Bird, James Worthy, Mark Aguirre, Gus Williams, Kiki VanDeWeghe, Billy Knight, and Rudy Hackett.

Brooklyn B'Ballers

Mel Davis, Ken Charles, and Armond Hill

B'Ball Crew

John Rushmore, Fred Mobley, Harvey Edwards, Doug Ritter, Fred Screen, Wilburn Hill and Gordon McCrae

Broadcast Pool

Marv Albert, John Ward, John Sterling, Craig Carton, Ian Eagle. John Condon, the irrepressible voice of Madison Square Garden.

Owners' Office
New York Knicks: James Dolan; New Jersey Nets: Joe Taub; Brooklyn Nets: Brooklyn Nets Ownership Group; Golden State Warriors: Joe Lacob, Franklin Mieuli; Washington Wizards: Ted Leonis.

My NBA teammates: Darrell Walker, we teamed together with the Knicks and Bullets. You always had my back; you are family. I have always enjoyed our conversations. John Williamson, Marvin Webster, Pat Cummings, Ray Williams, Manute Bol, and Moses Malone. Moses, you will always be in my memory. Rest in peace.

Tremendous appreciation goes to my friend for life, Ernie Grunfeld. The Ernie and Bernie Show lives on in *Game Face*. Our chemistry on court at the University of Tennessee was amazing.

Sidney Poitier, my idol growing up. I tried to emulate him in my youth. The only time in my life I was ever speechless upon meeting someone was when I met Poitier.

The Knicks organization allowed me to live out a dream of my youth suiting up for the franchise. Every day I paid homage to the great Knicks legacy of Willis Reed, Earl Monroe, Walt Frazier, Dave DeBusschere, and others by playing at the top of my game.

Thank you to everyone at Da Capo Press for making this book possible: Dan Ambrosio, Senior Editor, for his patience and enthusiasm; Miriam Reid, Editorial Assistant; Michael Giarratano and Kevin Hanover, PR and Marketing; Mark Corsey at Eclipse Publishing for his beautiful book design.

Thanks to my outstanding representation for this project: Doug Grad of the Doug Grad Literary Agency, Inc.; Lawrence Davis.

And for their assistance with photographic materials: New York Knicks: George Kalinsky, Rebecca Taylor; Golden State Warriors: Raymond Ridder; Washington Wizards: Rebecca Winn; University of Tennessee Athletic Department: Thomas Satkowiak; Valerie Hodgson, President, Fort Hamilton High School Alumni Association.

Index